Alive & Kicking

Alive & Kicking

The True Life Story of an NFL Star's Battle with Ulcerative Colitis, Ostomy Surgery and Hepatitis C

BY ROLF BENIRSCHKE
WITH MIKE YORKEY

Rolf Benirschke Enterprises, Inc. San Diego

CONTENTS

Dedication

To my parents, Kurt and Marion Benirschke. You were always there, especially during the darkest hours.

And to my wife, Mary, whose love for me and our children, and so many others, is a joy and inspiration.

Acknowledgements

One thing I've learned playing team sports is that every player is critically important if the team is to be successful. As I reflect on the players involved in producing this book, I feel compelled to share my appreciation as best I can. I am deeply indebted to them all.

This book started with an idea and the support of my attorney, Leigh Steinberg, and John Wiebusch of NFL Properties, but it couldn't have happened without input from Arn Shein, Mike Plant, and the constant encouragement of my assistant Debra Marshall. It was a chance meeting with an old high school acquaintance, Mike Yorkey, however, that allowed us to put together the story the way I felt called to write it. Without Mike's talent and commitment to the project, I am not sure it would ever have been accomplished.

Although *Alive & Kicking* was written to encourage people facing difficult times, particularly those struggling with inflammatory bowel disease or ostomy surgery, it was also a chance for me to tell Mom and Dad, my brother, Steve, and sister, Ingrid, how much they've meant to me. They were an unmatched support during my toughest times, and I will never forget that. I love them more than I can ever express.

In addition, I believe every son needs to reconcile his relationship with his father at some point in his life. One of the many blessings that came out of my illness was that it allowed my father and me to do just that and move our relationship to a new level. For that I am grateful.

The framework for this story is my football career as a San Diego Charger. I have wonderful memories of the coaches I played under and the guys I played with, as well as the front office that gave me a chance to earn back my job when they could have discarded me. Their names are too numerous to mention, but their humanity will never be forgotten.

I can't think of my football career without remembering the people of San Diego who encouraged me during the dark days in the hospital and who inspired me in the uncertain times of my comeback. They accepted my vulnerability and played a huge part in my recovery. I am fortunate to still reside in San Diego, and I continue to this day to be treated with an affection that is unbelievable to me.

Also, I can honestly say I owe my life to the exceptional medical staff at UCSD Hospital in San Diego and Mt. Sinai Hospital in New York City. To the doctors and nurses who gave me my second chance, I extend my thanks.

When I was searching for information on coping with my disease, the Crohn's and Colitis Foundation of America came forward. Terry Jennings, Suzanne and Irwin Rosenthal, Bill and Shelby Modell, Dr. Irwin Gelernt, Jane and Dan Present and many others were a great help. I will appreciate them always.

In addition, I owe a lot to my special friends at ConvaTec, a division of Bristol-Myers Squibb. Liz Doyle, Joe Solari, Scott Gilles, Geoff Morris, Linda Pruitt, and others gave me the opportunity to fulfill a dream of providing hope to those who find themselves sick and desperate.

I have been impacted by some very special people in my life, but none more than my business partner, Earl Eastman. We all need mentors, and I found one of mine in Earl. His remarkable wisdom, integrity, and genuine faith came at a critical time, and he has been a wonderful encouragement and a standard that I aspire to live up to.

Finally, my life would be very empty without my wife, Mary. God has placed me with the kindest person I have ever met, and a partner that I fall deeper in love with every year. We have been blessed with four wonderful children—a special little girl, Kari, and three fabulous boys: Timmy, Erik, and Ryan. God has been so good to us. Enjoy the book!

Introduction

There's a good chance you're holding this book because you're looking for some encouragement. Or, perhaps you or someone you love is suffering from Inflammatory Bowel Disease (IBD), such as ulcerative colitis or Crohn's disease.

Currently, more than two million Americans are living with these debilitating intestinal ailments, with about 70,000 men, women and children undergoing ostomy surgery each year. If you are among this latter group, you are adjusting to a whole new way of life with an ostomy appliance.

Ostomy surgery is a traumatic event. I know. I've been there. But I'm here to tell you that life is definitely still worth fighting for. When I was hospitalized in 1979, my life hung in the balance, and at one point, doctors braced my parents to expect the worse. Yet, by the grace of God, I survived through two life-threatening operations, and during my long rehabilitation, devoured every inspirational book I could put my weakened hands around.

I read and reread *Gifford on Courage* by Frank Gifford, in which the "Monday Night Football" announcer and former New York Giant star singled out ten inspirational athletes who overcame tremendous odds. I enjoyed *Life on the Run*, the autobiography of New York Knicks star Bill Bradley. Another book that meant a great deal to me was *Joni*, the compelling story of Joni Eareckson Tada, who was left a paraplegic following a swimming accident as a teenager.

Those bright, inspiring books—as well as my Christian faith—gave me hope during my darkest hours. But none of those books was written from the perspective of an ostomy patient. I vowed one day to commit my story into a book to encourage others if I recovered.

As for my background, I was the placekicker for the San Diego Chargers in the late 1970s through the mid-1980s.

During the 1979 season, I suddenly became very ill, collapsing on a team flight from the East Coast back to San Diego. In a matter of hours, I was a scared, 24-year-old football player fighting to stay alive.

But I'm getting ahead of myself here. You'll learn more about my illness and recovery in the coming pages, as well as how to live with ostomy surgery. Yes, you have a bright future, and you'll discover why in *Alive & Kicking!*

Thanks for joining me.

CHAPTER 1

Redemption

Sunday, January 2, 1982
Miami, Florida
The Chargers vs. the Dolphins

Even before I heard Coach Don Coryell call for the field-goal team, I was jogging onto the moist turf of the Orange Bowl. The score was tied 38-38 in a game that *Sports Illustrated* would later say was the second greatest in NFL history (*Sports Illustrated's Special NFL Classic Edition*, Fall 1995).

The Chargers and Dolphins had battled in oppressive 77-percent humidity and 79-degree heat for more than four hours, and it had finally come down to this—a chance for me to ice the game with a 29-yard field goal 14 minutes into overtime.

I didn't hear the capacity crowd of 75,000 rise to their feet and scream at the top of their lungs. I was in my own little world, oblivious to everything around me. The Dolphin fans were exhorting their team to block my field-goal attempt or pressure me into missing. The fans knew that if my kick was good, the Dolphin season was over.

For nearly five quarters, the capacity crowd had witnessed San Diego and Miami playing a game of "Can You Top This?" with two offenses that couldn't be stopped. The two clubs had generated more than 1,000 yards in total offense and produced more great plays than most fans see in an entire season.

But the game didn't start out that way. We had jumped out to a 24-0 lead in the first quarter, as Charger quarterback Dan Fouts riddled the Dolphin secondary. Every play we called seemed to work. We were so far ahead that the guys on our bench were already talking about playing the Cincinnati Bengals in the AFC Championship game the following week. As far as we were concerned, the fat lady was singing. This game was history.

That kind of thinking was nearly fatal. You should never underestimate a Don Shula-coached team. In a gutsy move, Shula benched his struggling young quarterback David Woodley in favor of Don Strock, a veteran backup. Strock brought a hot hand to the Dolphin offense, throwing a quick touchdown strike and getting the team close enough for a field goal.

The Dolphin comeback had begun. Just before halftime, Shula caught everyone by surprise. He called for a "hook and ladder"—the kind of school-yard play that kids diagram in the dirt.

Trailing 24-10, Strock threw fifteen yards downfield to a well-covered Duriel Harris. As our secondary closed to make the tackle, Harris lateraled to a trailing Tony Nathan. The play worked perfectly, and our defense was completely fooled. Nathan pranced down the sideline untouched, and ten yards before the end zone, he raised the ball high into the air, taunting the nearest Charger pursuer.

The Miami crowd went absolutely nuts! The roar was so deafening that I couldn't hear a teammate swear in disgust three feet away. Even though we were still ahead 24-17, we had clearly lost the momentum. Stunned and angry, we limped into the locker room with our heads down. I wondered how we were going to regain our composure and preserve our fragile lead.

My question was answered when Dan Fouts, the last

player off the field, stormed into the locker room. We were all sitting there, staring at the carpet with our eyes glassed over.

Fouts, the most competitive player I've ever met, was absolutely livid. He reared back and fired his best pass of the day, hurling his helmet the length of the dressing room. The helmet caromed off a locker, nearly hitting receiver Wes Chandler.

"What the @#$% is going on?" screamed Fouts. "Get your @#$% heads out of your @#$% butts. We're still leading this thing. They haven't stopped us yet! We're not going to let this bunch of @#$% take this @#$% game away from us. No @#$% way!"

Dan's words woke us up, but he had a point. The Dolphin defense hadn't stopped us at all, and if we could just get a little help from our defense, we could still win this game.

"C'mon guys, Dan's right," yelled Big Russ Washington, our 300-pound offensive tackle. "We've come too far this season to let these @#$% stop us."

The mood in the locker room changed, and I could feel the team's resolve return. We were ready to battle again.

Backs to the Wall

The second half, many experts say, was one of the best in NFL history. The Dolphins caught us at 24-24, then we went ahead 31-24. But they answered with two touchdowns to claim the lead, 38-31. Then Miami threatened to put the game out of reach in the last five minutes, driving down to the Charger 21 yard line. But our defense finally came through when Gary "Big Hands" Johnson stripped Dolphin fullback Andra Franklin of the ball and we recovered.

Fouts, taking advantage of the reprieve, marched us 82 yards for the tying score with just 40 seconds to go. With everyone celebrating on the sideline, I still had to kick the PAT, or point-after-touchdown. It seemed like I was the only one on the field who knew this extra point wasn't a gimme.

Although I was very nervous, I got it through.

On the ensuing kickoff, the coaches instructed me to squib-kick the ball to keep it out of the deep receivers' hands. That strategy backfired when the Dolphins recovered on their 40-yard line. Our defense had hardly slowed Miami all game, and it didn't take them long to get into field-goal range. With four seconds to go, Shula waved in Uwe von Schamann to kick a game-winning 43-yarder.

But our special teams coach, Wayne Sevier, had a brilliant idea: Insert 6'6" tight end Kellen Winslow at the center of the field-goal block team. Kellen had already played his heart out all afternoon, even having to be carried off the field several times because of exhaustion. Now he was being called upon one more time.

With the fans on their feet, anticipating a last-second victory, Kellen somehow willed his tired body high into the air and blocked von Schamann's kick.

Overtime!

Going for the Win

As the captains went out for the coin toss, I was keenly aware that overtime games were generally decided by a field goal. I knew I had to be ready.

We got the ball first, and before anyone could catch their breath, Fouts had us on the Miami nine-yard line. On second down, the Charger coaching staff — not wanting to risk a fumble — decided to go for the game-winning kick.

"Field-goal unit!" barked head coach Don Coryell.

I ran onto the field with my holder, Ed Luther, but only half of the kicking team followed me. They hadn't heard Coryell over the roar of the crowd. For several chaotic moments, confusion reigned as a dozen Chargers ran on—and off—the field. Meanwhile, I tried to count helmets as the play clock ticked toward zero.

Should I call time-out?

"Eddie, we're not set!" I yelled.

"We'll be okay," he said hurriedly. "We're close enough. Just kick it."

Ed looked toward the center and called for the snap. The ball was hiked, he set it down, and I started toward the ball like I had done ten thousand times before.

But something went wrong. I watched in disbelief as my 26-yard kick sailed wide left.

I had missed. I had failed. I had let my teammates down. The Miami fans cheered wildly while I headed back to the bench—the loneliest walk of my life. All I could think of was how hard my teammates had fought for this game and how I had blown it.

A couple of the guys came up to me. "Hang in there, Rolf, we're going to get you another chance," but they say that all the time. I knew I wouldn't get a second chance.

I stood stunned while a renewed Dolphins team took over and quickly marched the ball into Charger territory. Behind the Miami bench, I could see von Schamann kicking into the practice net. Surely he wouldn't miss a second time.

When our defense finally stiffened, Shula sent in von Schamann to boot a 34-yarder for the win.

Once again, it was our turn to wonder if our season was over. Would I have to live with my miss the rest of my life? I wanted to turn away and not look, but I couldn't.

The crowd seemed to quiet and hold its breath as the field-goal unit lined up. All eyes were fixed on the Dolphin kicker, believing he would finally end this marathon. The pressure was almost unbearable. I watched the snap and the ball as it was placed in a perfect hold. Uwe started his approach, but he appeared to rush the kick. He didn't hit it well, kicking it low and into the outstretched arms of defensive end Leroy Jones. The ball bounced harmlessly away.

It couldn't be! We were still alive, and now I had to get my head back into the game.

I immediately began stretching and jogging up and down the sidelines. Was this game ever going to end? Now it was Fouts' turn to go to work. Key catches by Winslow, Chandler, and Charlie Joiner quickly moved us down to the 12-yard line. Once more Coach Coryell yelled "Field-goal unit!" Ironically, it was second down again.

Well, it's nice he still has faith in me, I thought as I jogged back onto the field. *I've got to make this. I can't let my buddies down again.*

As we huddled for the last time, I searched the torn-up field for a good spot to kick the ball from. No one said anything to me. My teammates had learned long ago that I preferred to be left alone, to focus and concentrate on the task at hand.

Surprisingly, the butterflies were gone. I couldn't hear the crowd or the taunts the Dolphins were yelling at me. I couldn't see the Miami defensive line jumping up and down trying to distract me. I was totally prepared for this moment.

Twenty-nine yards. Pretty straightforward for an NFL kicker. This time, everyone was ready. The snap was perfect, Ed's placement was where it should be, and I knew right after I hit it that the kick was good.

As I watched the ball fly high over the crossbar, a deep feeling of satisfaction came over me. The game was over, finally. The Miami fans had been treated to a wild ride, but as I looked around, I noticed that the Orange Bowl had become eerily quiet. In fact, the only noise was coming from our bench and a little band of supporters that had made the long trip from San Diego.

As I turned toward our sideline, I could see several players jumping for joy and hugging one other, while others simply fell to the ground, overcome with exhaustion and emotion. It really was over this time, and we had won.

Upstairs in the broadcast booth, NBC's Don Criqui and John Brodie told a nationwide audience that they had just been treated to something very special.

"If you don't like this football game, then you don't like football," Criqui gushed. "This was one of the most exciting NFL games ever played."

Postgame Pandemonium

Our dressing room was a madhouse. The pendulum of emotions we had experienced—opening up a huge lead, seeing it disappear, and then having to fight with all we had to finally win—left everyone physically and emotionally spent.

Louie Kelcher, our 330-pound defensive tackle, wrapped Dan Fouts in a bear hug that threatened to squeeze the life out of him. Running back Chuck Muncie stood on a bench and alternately swirled a towel and exchanged high fives. Most of the sweat-drenched players were too tired to celebrate.

Suddenly, the lights were extinguished. The laughter and other sounds of jubilation slowly quieted.

"Men . . . the Lord's Prayer," commanded Coach Coryell. Reciting those few lines of Scripture was a Charger tradition after every game—win or lose. This time, however, God's Word never seemed so fitting or so special. I joined four dozen weary but grateful men as we got on our knees in the darkened room. The familiar words flowed: Our Father, who art in heaven, hallowed be thy name. . . .

When we came to the kingdom, the power, and the glory, I stopped reciting. I took a moment to thank God in my own heart, for giving me a second chance to kick the game-winning field goal. Then my thoughts turned back more than two years. We had just lost to the New England Patriots. I had boarded the team plane weak, dizzy and fighting to stay in control. . . .

I slumped in my seat and tried to sleep, but several times I awoke with terrible cramps. I walked like a zombie back to the lavatories, shut the door and looked at my pale face in the mirror.

I was spaced out, and I knew it. I sat on the tiny toilet and let it go. I felt the usual liquid exit my rectum, and then I stood up to see what it looked like. It was all blood!

This was not the first time blood had passed my bowels; I had been hemorrhaging rectally off and on for a year. But this time the bloody mess in the stainless steel toilet frightened me.

I limped back to my seat and collapsed. My world went black, and the next thing I knew Jeff West, our punter, was shaking me.

"Are you all right, Rolf?" he asked urgently. Jeff put his hand to my forehead. "My God, Rolf, you're burning up."

Jeff turned around and yelled, "Someone hurry and get the doctor. He's hot as hell."

It was only a minute before one of the Charger's team physicians got to my seat. He saw my flushed face, sized up the situation and stuck a thermometer under my tongue.

"He's 103 degrees!"

The team doc quickly ordered several of my stunned teammates to carefully lay me across three seats, and then wrap me in several blankets. Although my body may have been burning up, I was freezing. My teeth started chattering.

A Charger official asked the pilot if a message could be relayed to my parents in La Jolla: Rolf is very sick, and he may have to be hospitalized. Please meet the plane when we land at 9:30 p.m.

The ending of the Lord's Prayer brought me back to the present. The lights came back on, and the celebration resumed.

Our equipment manager, Sid "Doc" Brooks, began picking up sweaty jerseys and mud-stained yellow pants with our distinctive lightning-bolts down the side. Doc knew we were about to be mobbed by reporters, but he also knew an NFL locker room was an open invitation for hangers-on to walk off with some "souvenirs."

After a few minutes, Rick Smith, our public relations director, made his way to the heavy orange door and placed his hand on the lock. "This is it, guys," he announced. "Ready for the media?"

"Hold it, Rick," yelled Louie Kelcher. "Give us some more @#$% time. They can wait."

Finally, the pounding on the door forced Rick to open up, and a herd of sports journalists, TV reporters, cameramen, and sound people stampeded their way in. They immediately surrounded Fouts, Winslow, Joiner, and the other stars of the game. Before long, a small army of media types also found me in front of my locker. They formed a semicircle seven-deep.

The energy and assaultive noise level was like nothing I'd ever been a part of. Bright lights shone in my face, making it hard for me to see. Guys with pencils and pads started yelling questions.

"Did you know it was good when you hit it?"

"Did anyone say anything to you after you missed the first kick in overtime?"

"What would you have done if you had missed the second one?"

"Did anyone say anything to you before you went out for the last kick?"

"Was that the most pressure you've ever faced?"

"Is this your biggest thrill?"

I answered each question patiently and thoroughly, knowing that it was the media's job to replay each morsel of information to a world anxious to see, read, and hear every little detail.

Since there were far too many members of the media to interview any one player at a time, the journalists would move from one player to another in packs. That meant every few minutes a new group of reporters and cameramen would appear. Once in place, they peppered me with the same questions.

"Did you know it was good when you hit it?"

"Did anyone say anything to you before you went out for the last kick?"

"Was that the most pressure you've ever felt?"

"Is this your biggest thrill?"

I repeated the same answers, and then the reporters slipped away to the next player while a new group took their place.

"Did you know it was good when you hit it?"

"Did anyone say anything to you before you went out for the last kick?"

"Was that the most pressure you've ever felt?"

"Is this your biggest thrill?"

I couldn't help but smile as I answered the last question for the umpteenth time.

"Yes, it was the biggest thrill I've ever felt . . . in a football game."

In a football game.

None of the reporters caught the significance of those last four words, but I didn't expect them to. You see, I was thrilled just to be alive and kicking.

CHAPTER 2

The Early Years

Growing up, I always enjoyed athletics, but I certainly never expected to play professionally. My brother, Steve, and I always participated in whatever sport was in season: tennis, baseball, skiing, ice hockey, or soccer.

To our father, Dr. Kurt Benirschke, sports were recreation. Athletics were meant to keep us physically fit and teach us lessons about discipline and hard work, but beyond that, sports were only for fun. To make sure we never got too engrossed in athletics, we never owned a TV, which meant Sunday afternoons in the Benirschke home were not spent watching NFL doubleheaders.

Dad was always doing something productive, and when you learn about his background, you'll understand why. He grew up in Adolph Hitler's Germany during the 1930s and 1940s, and when the war broke out, he was a medical student at the University of Hamburg. Dad was forced to interrupt his studies to serve in the medical corps.

While stationed in the Battle of the Bulge region in Belgium, Dad contracted hepatitis. He almost died in the hospital, but, ironically, the hepatitis may have saved his life as it kept him away from the front lines.

When the war finally ended, Dad resumed his medical studies, and he looked forward to becoming a doctor. Unfortunately, his father had passed away, and being the only son, his mother expected him to forget medicine and return home to run the family laundry business.

But Dad was not cut out for that line of work, and he knew it. He realized that the only way he would be able to pursue his dreams in medicine would be to strike out on his own. So in 1949, he dropped a bombshell and announced to the family that he would be leaving the Fatherland and immigrating to the United States. Although he didn't know a word of English, he was determined to become a doctor despite the disapproval he was sure to feel.

His family didn't take him seriously at first, telling him he'd be back in six months. With their criticism ringing in his ears, he arrived on a freighter in New York City with a few dollars in his pocket and a fierce desire to succeed in his adopted country. He knew just one person in New York City, a German named J.J., who helped arrange a job as a delivery boy for a Manhattan publishing house.

Kurt spent three months running errands. When he felt confident his English was good enough, he applied and was accepted to an internship program in Teaneck, New Jersey. It was there Kurt met a pretty nurse named Marion Waldhausen. They soon discovered they had much in common.

Born in the U.S. to German parents, Marion was raised in Berlin. Unfortunately, their family's home was bombed early in the war, and she and her mother fled the country for the U.S. When Marion began her nursing career, she quickly became a popular young lady at the hospital. Marion Waldhausen didn't lack for suitors.

But the young nurse found herself drawn to the solid young doctor from Germany with boundless energy and genuine concern for his patients. They went out a few times, but because they were both so busy at work, most of their interaction was professional.

Then Kurt was accepted to the Harvard Medical School,

where he would complete his residency. He moved to Boston, and although he and Marion tried to maintain their friendship, the distance made it difficult.

As fate would have it, Marion developed a serious kidney infection that needed major surgery. When Kurt learned she planned to be operated on in Teaneck, he was horrified. He immediately arranged for her to be transferred to Boston, where she could receive what he considered the best treatment. Of course, Kurt could also keep a close eye on her, as well.

The extensive surgery required that Marion be hospitalized for a month in Boston. Kurt, ever the attentive doctor, managed to "drop in" several times a day to make sure things were going as planned.

One afternoon shortly before she was to be released, Marion had some news for Dr. Benirschke.

"When I'm better, Kurt, I've decided to move to Montana," she admitted. "Mom moved out West a little while ago, and she wants me to join her."

"Montana is a long, long way, isn't it?" asked Kurt, still unsure of his U.S. geography.

"Yes, it is," said Marion sadly.

Later that day, Kurt bumped into the chairman of the pathology department. His supervisor immediately recognized the long look on Kurt's face.

"What's wrong?" he asked.

"Marion just told me she'll be leaving for Montana soon," replied the young resident.

"What are you going to do about it?"

"I'm not sure. I love her very much, but I can't ask her to marry me. I don't have any money."

"I know," said the chairman, shuffling his feet. He had visited Kurt's apartment and seen the orange-crate chairs and threadbare furnishings. "If she really loves you, money won't matter," he offered. "Besides, you're one of the best residents we've ever had, and you have a bright future in medicine. You know that if you don't ask this girl to marry you, you'll never see her again."

Buoyed by this encouragement, Dad proposed before she left, and Mom answered in the affirmative. Mom did travel to Montana, but instead of living there, she informed her mother of the good news. Dad followed a short time later in his $50 car, driving more than 2,000 miles to formally ask for her hand.

Kids Arrive

Mom and Dad married in 1952, excited to start a family. That didn't take long. Steve was born a year after the wedding, and I arrived on the scene two years later on February 7, 1955. We were joined by our sister, Ingrid, in 1956.

We lived for four more years in Boston until Dad was offered the chairmanship of the pathology department at the Dartmouth Medical School. He was just thirty-seven at the time—the youngest chairman the department had ever had.

Growing up in the college town of Hanover, New Hampshire, was very special for our family. Hanover was a small community where everyone knew everybody and where crime was nonexistent. Walking or riding our bicycles home from grade school was always an adventure. We often stopped off at Dartmouth's huge athletic practice fields to watch whatever team was in season. I loved shagging balls for the soccer team, and I'd kick missed shots back to the players. I had plenty of fun doing that, and also discovered I had a pretty good leg.

In winter, the snow and cold temperatures didn't keep us indoors. Instead, we learned to ski on the local hills, and as we got bigger and better, we graduated to the steeper slopes of Stowe and Killington, where we began to race.

When I was in fourth grade, I discovered another winter sport that I *really* liked—ice hockey. The first cold snap of the season was exciting, because it meant the neighborhood gang could head over to the frozen lakes on the golf course or Occum Pond to play hockey. Occum Pond was the best since it was almost a mile long with fast, clear ice. For me, there was nothing more exhilarating than passing a puck back and forth with a couple of buddies while skating the entire length of the pond.

As we got older, we were always trying to find time to skate and, every now and then would sneak into the rink on the Dartmouth campus. I can remember climbing through an open window at 9 p.m., and turning on the lights for an hour of pick-up hockey. We'd do anything for "ice time," and I loved every minute of it!

To get in shape for hockey, most of us played soccer in the fall. The two sports are similar in tactics and strategy, and I soon developed a passion for the game. In ninth grade, I made the high school varsity soccer team, although I was still quite small for my age. I was looking forward to three more years on the team when suddenly, my life turned upside down.

Coast to Coast

In the middle of my freshmen year, Dad caught us all off guard by announcing that he had been offered a teaching job in San Diego. Dad and Mom flew out west to visit the area, decided it was a wonderful opportunity, and made the decision . . . to move the family!

Dad, who had been the chairman of the pathology department for ten years, was instrumental in developing the program into one of the best in the country. But he was a restless man, always looking for new challenges. The idea of a new teaching position at the University of California at San Diego intrigued him.

The campus was located in La Jolla, a seaside town about fifteen miles north of San Diego. Mom had grown weary of long winters, and the thought of never having to shovel another walkway in her life brought a smile to her face. Sunshine always seemed to put her in a good mood, so when school ended in June, we packed up the car for the trip west. Mom may have been the happiest member of the family.

My older brother Steve wasn't so happy, however. He had just finished his junior year, becoming one of New England's top ski racers. In addition, he would be leaving his good friends and having to finish his senior year in an unfamiliar school.

The move was difficult for me, too. Junior hockey in San Diego didn't exist, and I learned that La Jolla High didn't even have a soccer team! Ingrid, who was going into ninth grade, had the easiest transition, but I can assure you the long drive to the West Coast was not the most enjoyable car trip the Benirschke family ever made.

That first winter without hockey skates and downhill skis was a real adjustment. San Diegans see snowflakes once a century, and I stifled a laugh when I heard locals complain about the mercury dipping into the forties. But we made the best of it and quickly got used to going to the beach in January!

Besides not offering the sports we were used to playing, I had another problem. I was little. I mean really little! I was a skinny 5'4" and weighed just 112 pounds when I started my sophomore year.

Despite my size, I was still fairly coordinated. My gym teacher, Gene Edwards, saw some potential in me. The potential he saw, however, was not so much my athletic ability—it was my weight. You see, Edwards was the wrestling coach (and the football coach), and he didn't have anyone to wrestle at the 112-pound weight class.

I had barely heard of the sport, and I certainly had never seen a wrestling match in my life. But for some reason, I allowed myself to be talked into joining the team.

What a mistake! In my first match, the referee had barely uttered "Wrestle!" when I was on my back, pinned in just seventeen seconds. It was a humiliating loss, but I vowed to finish what I had started, so I completed the season.

I was ecstatic, however, when a bunch of transplanted East Coasters and a few foreign-exchange students who loved to play soccer formed the school's first team during my junior year. Besides allowing me to play a sport I truly loved, soccer also gave me a chance to gracefully end my wrestling career. Thank goodness!

One afternoon after soccer practice, a couple of my friends who played on the football team talked me into seeing if I could kick footballs the way I could kick a soccer ball. I found out later that they had arranged for Coach Edwards to be watching from a distance.

After kicking ten field goals with relative ease, they moved me back to 50 yards. I drilled it. That's when I noticed Coach Edwards strolling my direction. "How would you like to kick for us next year?" he asked, with a smile on his face.

Not again! The memories of my embarrassing wrestling career were fresh in my mind, and I wasn't certain I was ready to try something new like high school football. I knew Coach Edwards was from the old school, which meant he thought placekickers should play another position as well as participate in *all* practice drills. Although I had grown some since my sophomore year, I was still skinny at 5'11" and 140 pounds. The idea of getting crunched by 200-pound linemen in tackling exercises was not the way I wanted to spend my senior year at La Jolla High.

"Ah . . . I don't know," I told Coach Edwards. "I'm kind of little. If I could just kick, I'd be glad to give it a try. Otherwise, I'm not sure it's for me."

He agreed, and the next season I became La Jolla High's first kicking specialist. Our season-opener was a night game, and late in the first half, our offense stalled at the 20-yard line.

Before I knew what was happening, I heard Coach Edwards yelling, "Field-goal unit!" As if in a dream, I headed onto the field for my first-ever field-goal attempt. My shoulder pads felt funny as they bounced around, and my head swam in the football helmet. Poor lighting made the goal-posts look far, far away.

"C'mon, Rolf, you can do it," said my holder, Don

Gravette, in the huddle. He gave me a smile and slapped me on the helmet. "Pretend it's practice."

The team broke the huddle and lined up on the ball. I counted off seven yards from the line of scrimmage; it would be a 37-yard kick. Suddenly everything seemed to slow down, just like in the movies. It seemed to take forever for the hike to reach Don and for him to place it on the ground. I moved toward the ball, planted my left leg and swung my right. I met the ball with my instep and followed through, lifting my head to watch the ball clear the line and lazily climb into the dark night toward the goalposts. The ball hung for what seemed the longest time as it sailed easily over the crossbar. A feeling of deep satisfaction shivered through my body.

I jogged off the field like I had been kicking field goals all my life. I couldn't stop grinning. Teammates rushed out, slapping my loose helmet and pounding my shoulder pads.

My kicking career had begun!

Recruitment

I kicked a record number of field goals that first season, mostly because La Jolla High had never really had a kicker in its history. I went 12-for-14, including a 45-yarder that got me named "Prep Athlete of the Week" by the *San Diego Union* newspaper. Remember, this was the early 1970s, and soccer-style kicking was a new thing at the high school level. In fact, Garo Yepremium, Jan Stenerud, and a handful of other NFL soccer-style kickers were just beginning to replace the traditional toe kickers in the pros.

When the season was over, I was surprised to be named to the "All-League" first team. Suddenly, football coaches from Stanford, UCLA, Cal Berkeley, San Diego State, and other schools began calling about me. I wouldn't exactly say I was heavily recruited, but there was some interest.

One of the calls came from Coach Don Coryell, already a local legend at San Diego State. Coryell invited me to

52,000-seat San Diego Stadium (as it was known back then) to watch the Aztecs play their final game of the season. For a high school kid, this was Big Time.

As I was escorted into the locker room before the game to shake hands with several San Diego State players, I felt like a wide-eyed little kid. From there, I was ushered upstairs to the press box, where I got my first chance to watch sportswriters in action—at the buffet table. Stories of their appetites are renown, but so is the deadline pressure they must work under. Everything was so new and exciting that I took in as much as I could, never imagining that this would all play a significant part in my life down the road.

The calls from major college football coaches amused my family. We never thought they were *serious*. The real world, Dad reminded me, wasn't kicking a football around on Saturday afternoons. Science—not sports—was part of our everyday dinnertime conversations.

As for my major, I really wasn't sure what I wanted to study. My brother was pre-med at UCSD, and he seemed intent on following Dad into the worthy profession of medicine. Dad, however, never put pressure on me to become a doctor; he just wanted me to study hard in college. I knew early on, however, that my future was not in medicine. At the same time, I was still unsure what career to choose. I sometimes envied those who seemed to know exactly what they wanted to do and where their future was headed. That wasn't me, though. I found I did okay just living one day at a time.

When I discussed my options with my parents, we talked about my passion for animals, which had developed from our early days in Boston. Dad had built out our cellar with thirty-six cages to study the breeding behavior of several different species of monkeys and I was allowed to go down and feed them. I treasured those times.

We became a family that collected butterflies and moths. Whenever we traveled on vacation, Dad packed several butterfly nets in the trunk. When we arrived back home, we would spread the wings of the butterflies and frame the various species on the basement walls.

On weekends, I often accompanied Dad to his lab on campus, where he would explain the various projects he was working on. They ranged from his study on human twins to trying to understand why armadillos have identical quadruplets every time they have offspring.

Dad had become a world authority on twins and the placenta, but he was increasingly curious about how the animal world might benefit from his work. When we moved to San Diego, Dad convinced the San Diego Zoo to set up a research center dedicated to understanding and preserving endangered species.

When my high school graduation arrived in June 1973, Dad surprised me with an unusual gift. That summer, he gave me the opportunity to attend the Wilderness Leadership School outside Durban, South Africa. I would join five other students from around the world to learn and experience man's relationship with the environment by spending twenty days living in game reserves.

The school's founder, Ian Player (brother of professional golfer Gary Player) believed that if he could bring young adults into the bush and expose them to nature like they've never experienced before, then they could have a tremendous impact on wildlife conversation when they became older. He was right. The Wilderness Leadership School would have a profound effect on my life.

Part of my time was spent at the Umfolozi Game Reserve, where I helped with a white rhino project. The rhinos were in danger of becoming extinct, and they needed to be tranquilized and moved to less-crowded game preserves elsewhere in Africa or readied for shipment to zoos around the world.

We were a small party of six when we camped for the night taking turns standing watch. Since only one of the game guards had a rifle, it was spooky being the only one awake at 2 a.m., silently stoking embers and wondering what man-eating animals were lurking just beyond the light of the fire. The game preserve was home to lions, cheetahs, wild buffaloes, and elephants, and the entire time it was very clear to me that we were the visitors.

Plans Are Made

When I returned from South Africa, I knew what I wanted to study—zoology. The best zoology school on the West Coast was at the University of California at Davis.

"Dad, I want to go to UC Davis," I announced shortly after getting home. The state university was located twenty miles west of Sacramento in Northern California.

"You're not going to be able to play any of that silly football, are you?" he asked.

"I don't think so, Dad. I know I'll have to spend a lot of time studying. Besides, UC Davis doesn't even offer athletic scholarships. I don't think sports are a big deal at that school."

Well, wouldn't you know it: Not only did I end up playing football, but I *also* played soccer my last three years as well. Yet I had enrolled at Davis with no intention of participating in collegiate athletics. It took an unexpected phone call from Jim Sochor, the head football coach, to change all that.

"I was talking to a coach at the University of Southern California," began Sochor, "and he told me a good kicker had enrolled in my school. When I saw you hadn't signed up to play football, I thought I'd call to see if I could talk you into joining us."

I thanked Sochor for the offer, but I informed him that football wasn't in my plans. But Sochor was a persuasive guy. I appreciated his no-pressure approach, and after several more discussions, I agreed to play on the JV team my freshman year. That experience helped me make the transition from high school to college ball much easier.

When I returned to Davis for training camp the following summer, however, a dilemma had developed. While it was true I did enjoy football, I had also gotten to know many of the players on the UC Davis soccer team. I realized I missed the sport.

At the same time we were in full pads, grunting it out in 100-degree heat, I would watch my friends on the adjacent fields, clad only in their shorts. Something was wrong with this picture.

The draw to play soccer grew stronger until one day I decided to bring it up with Coach Sochor. I explained how I felt, and he nodded understandingly. "I can appreciate your situation, Rolf," he said. "Tell you what. Let's play the upcoming game this Saturday night, and we'll talk about it Monday."

I didn't see any harm in that, so I agreed. When Saturday rolled around, we were all excited to play our first game of the season, and we ended up destroying our opponent. I had a good game with plenty of chances to kick.

On Monday, I walked into Coach Sochor's office and was surprised to find Will Lotter, the soccer team coach, sitting in a corner.

"Will and I have been talking," began Sochor, "and we think we can come up with a solution that will make everyone happy. What would you think if we 'share' you this season? Could you play for both teams?"

The idea blindsided me. Of all the possibilities, I certainly hadn't considered this. How could I play both sports in the same season? There has to be schedule conflicts. And what about the guys on both teams? What would they think?

"I'm not sure," I answered hesitantly. "The last thing I wanted to do was set myself apart from my teammates, or be considered a prima donna."

The two coaches explained why they liked the idea. Will Lotter said he favored it because it raised visibility for the soccer team and added a good player. Jim Sochor gave his blessing because by training with the soccer team, I could actually get stronger and become a more reliable kicker.

The arrangement made for some interesting Saturdays. It was not unusual to compete in a soccer match in the afternoon, and then either drive or get flown to a UC Davis football game later that evening.

What a crazy schedule! On one occasion, the soccer team was playing in the All-Cal soccer tournament in Santa Barbara. During the last game of the three-day event, I scored the winning goal in the consolation final. Immediately after the last whistle, I was whisked to the Goleta airport to catch a flight to Los Angeles. A connecting flight put me in Sacramento thirty minutes before game time. My roommate picked me up at the airport with two Jack-in-the-Box hamburgers and a map to the stadium. I ate while he raced across town to Sacramento State College, where the football team was playing that night. Sac State was a cross-town rival, so this was usually the biggest game of the season.

We arrived just before kickoff, but the security guard wouldn't let me into the locker room. Meanwhile, Coach Sochor was pacing the sidelines, wondering if his kicker was going to show.

"But I'm a player," I protested to the security guard. "You gotta let me in. Look, here are my kicking shoes. I'm just late for the game."

He wasn't buying it. Fortunately, one of our trainers heard the commotion, and he came over to vouch for me. The guard finally opened the door, and I rushed into the locker room to change into my uniform. I missed the opening kickoff, but I got into the game in time to kick three field goals in the first quarter. Those field goals were the difference when we won the game by five points.

Something special was happening here.

CHAPTER 3

The Next Step

Although I kicked pretty well at Davis, I didn't consider my college-playing days to be anything extraordinary. I certainly never entertained any serious thoughts about kicking in the NFL. But the summer before my senior year, I started receiving letters from quite a few NFL teams.

For the most part they were form letters, but many of them were quite humorous. Dallas Cowboy coach Tom Landry wrote, "An outstanding football player such as yourself usually watches his college career wind down to a close with mixed emotions. You may be experiencing feelings of accomplishment, frustration, and relief. But in your case, you may be feeling a sense of deserved optimism for a bright future in the National Football League."

Yeah, right. I couldn't believe these guys were serious. Another coach sent me this note: "For the past two years, we've received scouting reports confirming your ratings as a fine professional football prospect. Since we are in the football business, and since the game is not healthy without new, young talent, we are naturally quite interested in you."

When draft day came the following spring, I didn't know what to expect. The Oakland Raiders, who had been following my progress (UC Davis was 100 miles northeast of the Bay Area), gambled their very last pick on me. I was taken in the twelfth and final round of the 1977 NFL draft—the 334th player out of 335!

Although I was graduating on time with a degree in Zoology, I hadn't been accepted to Veterinary School. Thus, my options were to go to graduate school and re-apply for vet school in a year, or give the NFL a try. The more I thought about it, I decided *What the heck? Why not see what pro football is all about?* If I didn't make the Raiders, at least I would have some interesting stories to tell.

Colorful Characters

Back in 1977, the Raiders were reigning Super Bowl champs. They were the feared Silver and Black with such personalities as Ken "The Snake" Stabler, Jack Tatum, John "The Tooz" Matuszak, Ted "The Stork" Hendricks, and Otis Sistrunk, who, as one TV colorman described him, had graduated from the University of Mars. Colorful characters, all of them.

It was traditional for all first-year players to report to training camp a week ahead of the veterans. Remember, I was a wide-eyed, twenty-two-year-old rookie from little UC Davis—a Division II school that didn't even offer athletic scholarships. Our biggest crowds were about eight thousand, if you counted the cows in the nearby barns. We certainly never played on TV in those pre-ESPN days.

Most of the other rookies in camp came from football powerhouses: USC, Michigan, Ohio State, Notre Dame, Nebraska, and Texas A&M. Was I good enough to compete with these guys? I didn't know.

When the veterans finally reported, the mood in camp changed perceptibly. The big boys were back in town. We rookies suddenly felt like insignificant little kids as the veterans began renewing old acquaintances. It had been six months since they had all been together at Super Bowl XI.

Inside the locker room, the dressing stalls were

numerically ordered to match our jersey numbers. I was assigned number 6. Next to me was Ray Guy, a perennial All-Pro and perhaps the best punter in NFL history. On my other side was legendary quarterback Kenny Stabler with his familiar number 12.

When I walked into the locker room on the first morning, I was startled to find Stabler already suiting up. I had spent my college years watching this guy perform his magic for the Raiders. He was a gutty competitor, the master of the two-minute drill, and someone you could never count out. On dozens of occasions he had rallied the Raiders from the brink of defeat. Now he was sitting right next to *my* locker. What should I do?

Careful not to make eye contact, I quietly dropped my bag into my locker and began to change. I hadn't finished unbuttoning my shirt when Stabler, a grizzled good-ol' boy from Louisiana, looked up and noticed me. "Hey, Rolf!" he drawled. "How ya doin'?"

Did I hear right? Was Ken Stabler actually talking to me? I didn't know what to say.

"I'm fine, Mr. Stabler. Nice to meet you."

Ken smiled at my formality. "Hey, I'm not that old. Please call me Ken. We're teammates now. I've read a lot about you, and we're excited you're here."

Wow!

John Madden was the Raiders coach back then. (Today he's a color commentator in the broadcast booth with Pat Summerall for the Fox network). Madden had a reputation for not liking rookies *or* kickers—which made me just about his least favorite player on the team. It was nothing personal; he just didn't care for players who didn't get their uniforms dirty.

Madden seemed to enjoy making life miserable for kickers, and he was famous for his little "tests." My first exam came one week into training camp. As morning practice was coming to a close, Madden pulled the whole team together.

"As you all know," announced Madden, "we end each practice by running ten 100-yard wind sprints. Today, we're going to find out how good our rookie kicker is. Benirschke, you've got one shot from 45 yards. If you miss, everyone runs. If you make it, everyone hits the showers."

I was totally unprepared for this. Why didn't he give me some warning? I felt my heart begin to pound as 100 players began to scream and cheer. My legs felt like jelly, and I could hardly breathe.

"Hey, rookie, you better not miss this @#$$% kick!" yelled John Matuszak.

"You miss this and you'll be walking back to Davis," chimed in Ted Hendricks.

Madden cleared the field except for the defense and the field-goal unit. Then he spotted the ball. As if taking pleasure in the situation he had created, he looked at me and blew his whistle. The countdown had begun. I was still trying to quiet my nerves as I searched for a good spot on the field.

With the players going crazy on the sidelines, my holder, backup quarterback Dave Humm, took a knee seven yards behind the line of scrimmage. We had become friends in camp, and I had relied on him not just to make good holds, but also for moral support. Once again, he had the right words of encouragement. "You can make this sucker," he said quietly.

As I paced off the steps for my approach, the noise level rose. I knew why Madden was doing this, but I still hated it. Thinking about it changed my fear to anger. *I'm going to show this guy*, I vowed.

As I began the routine I had developed in high school, the distracting noise seemed to fade away. I was in my little world now, comfortable and in control. The ball was snapped, and I watched Dave catch it, put it down, and spin the laces. At the same time, I was already moving toward the ball. I planted my left foot and kicked with my right . . . effortlessly. The ball went spinning end-over-end toward the goalposts and easily cleared the crossbar. I made it!

The players whooped and hollered, ecstatic that they didn't have to run their wind sprints. I was just relieved Ted Hendricks wasn't going to kick my butt all the way back to Davis.

Making that kick is one reason why I'm alive today to tell you this story. But seriously, that field goal gave me the confidence to compete for a job in the NFL. Madden made me go through that same agony many times before training camp was over. I despised him for it, but he prepared me for the kind of pressure NFL kickers face every Sunday.

The Waiver Wire

The Raiders training camp was loaded with veterans. I was one of three kickers fighting for a job. By the final preseason game, I was the only one left on the roster. I had won the job! But I was to learn that nothing is certain in the NFL.

Raiders' owner Al Davis, known for taking chances, tried to pull a fast one on the final cut day. The Raiders needed to clear a player on waivers and then re-sign him to comply with league rules. They were unsure, however, who to put on the wire because the final waiver is irrevocable, meaning any player put on waivers could be claimed by another team.

With this dilemma in mind, Al Davis decided to protect another player and gamble that a little-known kicker from UC Davis wouldn't be claimed. His plan was foiled, however, by the San Diego Chargers, who had scouted me in the preseason and were looking for a kicker.

When John Madden called me into his office to tell me I had been claimed by San Diego and was no longer a Raider, I couldn't believe it. In fact, I was devastated. I had just endured nine weeks of training camp. I had won a job with the defending Super Bowl champions. I had passed all the tests thrown my way. I had even sung my college fight song at dinner—a dozen times. More than that, I had earned the respect and friendship of a great group of guys. Now I was being told I had to leave.

Although I was going to play in my home town, I was also joining a last-place team and players I didn't know. When I climbed into my green '62 Volkswagen Beetle and left the Bay Area for the nine-hour drive south, a huge emptiness filled my stomach.

Signing On

I drove all night to San Diego, arriving at my parents' house at 4 a.m. Three hours later, I was up and on my way to San Diego Stadium. After parking my car and checking in at the security gate, I was directed to the elevator to the Charger offices. I was carrying my football cleats and the rest of my gear in a small box. The receptionist greeted me with a smile.

"Young man, who is the delivery for?" she asked, noticing the box.

"No, this isn't a delivery. This box is mine. I'm looking for Coach Prothro."

"I'm sorry. He's getting ready for a team meeting in fifteen minutes.

"I know, I believe I'm supposed to be in that meeting."

The club had released veteran kicker Toni Fritsch and decided to take a gamble on me. Of course, I was cheaper, too. I signed for $26,000 that first year—tall cotton for a kid out of college, but not even a game check for most NFL players today. The Chargers were in disarray when I arrived, but had a lot of young talent ready to come together and mature.

Eight games into my rookie season, however, I was the worst kicker in the NFL. I was still adjusting to kicking without a tee, the narrower goalposts and the *intensity* of pro football. In addition, the Chargers' special teams weren't very special, and we soon became regular features on the "NFL Bloopers" films.

As one disappointing game followed another, I found myself wondering what I had gotten myself into. The way it was turning out, each week was a new chance to embarrass myself on national television. Not only was I making a fool of myself, but my Dad became the unwitting target of our team's poor play.

This pro football thing was a whole new world for Dad. When I had been drafted, a colleague called him from Boston and excitedly asked, "Did you hear the news? Your son's been drafted!"

"What?" replied Dad. "Didn't the draft end some years ago?" Dad thought I was being drafted into the U.S. military!

When I first started playing for the Chargers, Dad suddenly found doctors, nurses, and orderlies he didn't know coming up to him in the hospital and asking him to give me their best. "Tell Rolf we're behind him all the way," they'd say.

Dad had a hard time understanding why everyone was making such a big fuss about his son playing such a foolish game. He shrugged it off, but when I started spraying kicks, friends and colleagues suddenly made it uncomfortable for Dad. They began avoiding him in the hospital hallways, not wanting to make eye contact. *Strange*, my dad thought.

Meanwhile, I was thinking different thoughts. *I didn't go to school to do this. What am I doing trying to be an NFL kicker?* It was then, quite by chance, that I received my first fan letter. For some reason, a twelve-year-old boy from Ft. Wayne, Indiana, decided to write and encourage me at a time I was at my absolute lowest.

As I opened the letter, I couldn't imagine why anyone would be writing me. Then I read the first sentence. "My name is Dean Meier, and I think the Raiders made a mistake when they cut you," he wrote.

I laughed out loud. The Raiders were *glad* I was kicking for San Diego. They were *congratulating* themselves for putting me on waivers.

"I know things haven't gone like you would have hoped in San Diego," he continued.

That's the understatement of the year, I thought. *Doesn't this kid know I'm the worst kicker in the league?*

But then he added, "If you just hang in there, things are going to work out."

I smiled at his optimism and put the letter in my locker. Then it dawned on me. A twelve-year-old boy actually knows who I am, cares how I perform, and took the time to encourage me with a letter. Amazing!

Then I looked at the schedule. Our next game was at home against—irony of ironies—the Oakland Raiders. The Raiders were hot and headed back to the playoffs; meanwhile, the Chargers were going nowhere. To make matters worse, both our starting and backup quarterbacks—James Harris and Bill Munson—had been injured the previous week and would be unavailable for Sunday's game. We were going to have to start a rookie named Cliff Olander. Our prospects were not good.

On Sunday morning as I was dressing for the game, I couldn't help but think about Dean's letter—"Hang in there . . . just hang in there." It rang in my ears as I jogged onto the field for warm-ups.

The Raiders fought valiantly, but on this day, our defense played magnificently before a wild sellout crowd. Our offense did just enough to get me in position to kick two field goals. We won 12-7!

If you add the score up, however, you will realize we had a PAT blocked (in keeping with the rest of the season), but the difference was the two kicks. We had pulled off the biggest upset of the year and won a game against our biggest rivals— a win that would turn the Charger franchise around.

A few days after the Raiders game, I received my second fan letter from my new friend. I slowly tore open the envelope. On a piece of yellow-lined paper, Dean had written, "See, I told you so. If you just hang in there, things are going to work out."

As I read those words, a smile crept across my face. He was right. I'm embarrassed to tell you today that it took a twelve-year-old boy to teach me an important lesson about life: *Even though we may not understand why things are happening, we must always hang in there . . . because things change!*

I couldn't help but write Dean back, and we started a pen-pal friendship that continued for the rest of the season. He'd write me before a game, and I'd reply on Monday. I didn't miss the rest of the season and finished kicking twelve consecutive field goals, breaking the club record.

Dean and I continued to exchange letters as he entered high school. He explained that he had followed me because it was his dream to become a placekicker. We even met before a game in Detroit the following season, and I was able to explain to him how much his letters had meant to me.

Several years later, I received an unexpected note from his father. It seems that Dean had been standing on a street corner on a snowy, windswept day when a car skidded on the icy street and plowed into him, breaking his leg. The accident devastated everyone in his family and appeared to end Dean's dreams of becoming a placekicker.

Now it was my time to offer Dean some hope for the future. Sure enough, Dean hung in there, and ended up becoming a successful placekicker for his high school team.

But Dean, wherever you are, you were a twelve-year-old boy I'll always remember. You gave me a lift when I needed it most, and for that I'll never forget you.

CHAPTER 4

Storm Clouds

September 9, 1978
San Diego

I opened the door to Doc Brooks' home and stepped inside. Doc, the Chargers longtime equipment manager, had invited several players over for a "Monday Night Football" cookout. It was the day after our season-opening win against the Seattle Seahawks in my second season, and I was still on a high. I had tied a Charger team record by kicking four field goals in our 33-16 victory.

I walked in and said hi to my mates huddled around the TV set. The game had just started, and already the guys were complaining about some outrageous comment ABC's Howard Cosell had made. Players often disagreed with his opinions, but they knew Cosell could make or break a reputation.

During a commercial, one of the guys wondered if it was true what our head coach, Tommy Prothro, had asked me before the Seahawk game. We were playing inside the enclosed Kingdome, and I had come back to the bench after practicing kickoffs. Coach Prothro, who liked to know all the variables, actually asked me which way the wind was blowing!

Not sure how to reply, I smiled and looked up at the ceiling. "Coach, there doesn't seem to be much wind today."

My teammates howled upon hearing the story, and then we made a beeline for the food. Doc's wife, Jeri, always laid out a wonderful spread, and she made us feel like part of the family. On the dining room table were french fries, tossed green salad, corn on the cob, fresh bread, and the best barbecued chicken you've ever tasted.

Doc, a dutiful husband, was just finishing a few more chicken breasts on the barbecue as we worked our way through the buffet line and took our seats near the TV. For a bachelor, it didn't get much better than this.

Suddenly, a wave of horrible cramps rippled through my abdomen. I doubled over in pain, and for a long minute I couldn't straighten up. The game was getting exciting, so nobody noticed me get up and go to the bathroom—the third time in the last hour that I had to go. *Must be that fast-food burger I ate at lunch time*, I thought.

After relieving myself, the stomach cramps subsided for several minutes. Thankfully, no one had seen my painful grimaces. I shrugged off the lingering cramps, figuring it had to be mild food poisoning or a nasty flu bug. Several teammates had been feeling under the weather, including Coach Prothro. Something was making the rounds.

A couple of days later, I still wasn't up to par. My teammates had gotten well, and even Coach Prothro said he was feeling much better. I decided to see the team doctor, who told me it was probably the flu. I didn't press the issue. I had already learned in professional sports that you didn't want a reputation of being prone to injury or sickness. The Chargers would have to carry me off the field before I pulled myself out. Besides, our next game was against the arch-rival Raiders— at home.

When game time came around, I was running a fever, and my diarrhea still hadn't gone away. I was worried that once the game started, I wouldn't be able to leave the bench to go to the bathroom if I needed to. You never know when the coach will yell "Field-goal unit!"

Late in the first quarter, I slipped on the dirt infield (the Padres baseball team hadn't completed their season yet) and pulled a field-goal attempt wide, breaking a string of thirteen without a miss. Then I flat-out missed an extra point.

The errant kicks weighed on my mind as we nursed a 20-14 lead late into the fourth quarter. I was worried about Oakland's reputation for heroic comebacks. With only a few minutes to play, Raiders quarterback Ken Stabler was given the ball deep in Charger territory. Would he put together another one of his patented game-winning drives?

The Snake wasted no time and quickly drove the Raiders down the field. With nine seconds remaining, he had his team with a fourth-and-goal from our nine-yard line, down by six points. The Raiders had to go for the touchdown.

In the face of a ferocious rush, Stabler dropped back to pass, but found everyone covered. He avoided the pressure, stepped out of the pocket, and started scrambling toward the goal line. But he wasn't fast enough, and a couple of Chargers caught him from behind at the line of scrimmage. Just as he was about to be pulled to the ground, Stabler intentionally sidearmed the ball toward the end zone.

The ball bounced twice—like Vegas dice—into the arms of Raider fullback Pete Banazak, but Banazak was still a good five yards from the end zone. He was hit immediately, but just before *he* went down, he intentionally batted the ball toward the goal line, where Raider tight end Dave Casper kicked it once and fell on it in the end zone. The referees raised their arms, signaling touchdown.

Both benches erupted, and 52,000 Charger fans rained boos of disbelief and anger on the Raiders and the referees.

"He can't do that!" screamed Prothro, who had to be restrained. "That was an incomplete pass! The play should have been dead!" The enraged fans continued to boo lustily. The refs could have opened their rule book and called just about anything: incomplete pass, illegal forward pass, illegal batting the ball, or intentional fumbling.

But after conferring for several minutes, the referees allowed the touchdown to stand. The Raiders tacked on the extra point, and we slowly trudged to the locker room with a devastating defeat, 21-20. We couldn't believe what we had just witnessed. This one was stolen from us, and everyone in the stadium knew it.

Stabler's resourcefulness would live in infamy and become known as the "Holy Roller" play. Clearly a travesty of justice, the NFL changed the rulebooks the following season to disallow forward fumbling in the last two minutes of the game. But at the time, we had to live with a bitter loss to a hated divisional rival.

That week, much frustration was vented in the "Letters to the Editor" page in the *San Diego Union* sports section. Most letter-writers criticized the referees who, by unanimous verdict, blew the call. But one person pointed out that the refs' call wouldn't have mattered if the Chargers had someone who could kick field goals and extra points.

I put the newspaper down. It felt like someone had kicked me in my already tender stomach. It was a low blow. Reading those letters didn't make me feel any better.

The First Office Visit

The next day, Mom was concerned about how I might be feeling after the game. After chatting for a few minutes, she invited me for dinner. Mom's German cooking was the best. I loved her *Wienerschnitzel mit Nudeln*. Maybe some home cooking would get me over the hump.

As I walked into the old house, I found Dad opening mail at the kitchen table.

"How's it going, Rolfie?"

"I don't know, Dad. Never mind the Raider game, I just don't feel well."

"Are you still feverish?"

"Yes, but the worst thing is the cramps."

"You still having diarrhea?"

"Yeah, and what worries me is that it's not getting any better."

Dad stared off into space for a moment.

"We need to look into this," he said.

"What do you mean?"

"I mean you should see a doctor. I can find out who the top gastroenterologists are in the area. I'll give you a call with the names tomorrow."

The next day Dad arranged for me to see a doctor. I'll call him Dr. Jack Diamond, though that isn't his real name. From the first moment I shook hands with him, I did not connect with the man. He never looked me in the eye, and his uncertain manner didn't instill any confidence in me. Dad said he had a good reputation, but his indecisive manner proved to be frustrating for me.

He started poking here and pressing there, and then he drew blood for some tests. Man, I hate needles! Dr. Diamond closed his file and told me to not to eat the rest of the day. His final instructions were to return the next morning for an X-ray series. They would do an "upper GI," also known as a barium swallow.

Later that night, I asked Dad, "What's a barium swallow?"

"It's a procedure that requires you to drink a milkshake-like liquid that is radio opaque. As the barium progresses through your digestive system, a series of X-rays are taken that allow the doctors to examine the lining of your intestinal tract and see if there are any irregularities."

When I arrived the next morning, a nurse asked me what flavor "milkshake" I wanted.

"I'll try strawberry," I answered. Just one sip from the cold tin told me this concoction wasn't prepared at Dairy Queen. The heavy liquid tasted metallic, and it was all I could do to get it down.

As the barium shake passed through my intestinal tract, Dr. Diamond and a technician took an X-ray every few minutes, looking for any abnormalities. The awful-tasting liquid intensified my intestinal bowel distress.

"Well, what did you find?" I asked Dr. Diamond when we were done.

"Based on these X-rays and your fever, your tender abdomen and bloody diarrhea, you may have an inflammatory bowel disease known as Crohn's disease," he replied unemotionally. He might as well have been reading a Dow Jones stock quotation.

"What the heck is Crohn's disease?"

"Well, it's a chronic disease we don't know much about, and at the moment there is no known cure."

No cure! I hardly heard anything else he said as my mind struggled to imagine living with this the rest of my life.

That night, still in shock, I relayed Dr. Diamond's diagnosis to Dad.

"Well, now we know," he said, "and it'll be easier to figure out what we're fighting. I really don't know much about Crohn's disease, Rolfie. Let's go see if we can find out more about it."

With that, we walked into Dad's study, lined with several hundred medical texts. He pulled a half-dozen from the shelf, gave me a couple, then set the rest down at his desk. We began poring over the volumes, but it didn't take Dad long to find what he was looking for.

What he discovered was not very comforting.

Learning Curve

According to Dad's medical texts, Crohn's disease can affect any portion of the digestive tract, but it typically affects the small intestine and/or the colon. Symptoms include vomiting, fever, night sweats, loss of appetite, general feeling of weakness, severe abdominal cramps, and diarrhea (often bloody). Weight loss is common. Cause: unknown.

Clearly, most of those symptoms fit me. I couldn't believe what I was reading. My face flushed, and sweat began to form on my upper lip.

Dad, meanwhile, became engrossed in his medical books. He had his researcher's hat on.

"It says here that some people go through a bout of Crohn's, and then sometimes it can go into remission forever, or at least for long periods of time," said Dad encouragingly. "But the other end of the spectrum is surgery, or multiple surgeries . . . some requiring the patient to end up with an ostomy."

Surgery? Not me. No way. I'd only felt sick for a couple of weeks.

Dad saw the distressed look on my face. "Let's not jump to conclusions," he soothed. "We don't know that this is it."

At my next visit, Dr. Diamond drew more blood and started me on the standard treatment for Crohn's disease. He prescribed Prednisone (a powerful anti-inflammatory corticosteroid drug) and Azulfidine (an anti-bacterial drug). He told me that I could also expect another test—the dreaded colonoscopy.

"A visual exam will help make the diagnosis more conclusive," explained Dr. Diamond.

A colonoscopy is where the doctor inserts an instrument up the rectum and into the colon, which allows viewing of the colon's lining for inflammation or ulcerations. That sounded painful and like the most humiliating medical test a human being could be asked to endure.

I was right. When I returned for the procedure a few days later, I put on a gown and was told to lay on the examining table face down. My gown wasn't tied, leaving my backside open for the whole world to see. Just then, a nurse strode into the room.

"So, this is what a pro football player looks like," she said, trying to be funny. I was in no mood for humor and gritted my teeth until I was given the mild anesthesia.

Although I couldn't feel much, I had a vague sensation that I was being "plumbed" by an invasive device traveling way up my rectum. Let's just say the scoping procedure did not build my self-esteem.

Afterward, I asked Dr. Diamond the question that had been gnawing at me since the diagnosis: "Can I still continue to play football?"

He hesitated for a minute. "I don't see any reason why you can't, at least for the time being," he answered. "We'll just see how it goes."

I gingerly walked to the parking lot and climbed into my green VW bug. As I drove home, my thoughts were racing. I feared this illness and what it might mean for my future. I feared more tests and possible surgery. I feared telling the Chargers that I was sick and might not be able to kick. I feared they might not want to take any chances and would release me and bring in another kicker.

No Guarantees

The sobering reality about pro football is that you live from game to game. Contrary to what most people think, the vast majority of contracts are not guaranteed. That means that if your performance level drops off, the team can cut you in a heartbeat and not be obligated to pay the rest of the contract. It happens all the time.

The same can happen to coaches, although their contracts are usually honored. The Chargers fell into a tailspin after the "Holy Roller" loss, and Coach Prothro "resigned" when the club was 1-3. Don Coryell, who had tried to recruit me to play at San Diego State, was named the new coach. I soon discovered that Coach Coryell, with his sharp nose, piercing eyes, and excitable lisp, was an *intense* guy. But he was also an inspirational coach who brought out the best in his players. We all developed an instant liking for him.

Back in college, there were lots of things to take our minds off football. If it wasn't classes, homework, or exams, there was always some campus activity going on. In the pros, Coryell reminded us, we were expected to concentrate on football six days a week. As for himself, he took *no* days off, often sleeping at the stadium while preparing for games. Even when he was at home, his mind never strayed very far from football.

One morning, Coach Coryell's wife asked him to take the garbage down to the street on trash pick-up day. The Coryells' house was at the end of a long driveway, so to save time, Coach would often put the trash bags in his trunk and drive them down to the curb. On this particular day, he tossed the smelly bags into his trunk, but by the time he reached the street, his mind was already engrossed with our next opponent.

After the trash baked in the back of his car all day at San Diego Stadium, a curious security guard sniffed something amiss. He decided to investigate and alerted Coryell to his blunder.

As for me, the way I liked to prepare for Sunday's game was to kick hard on Wednesdays and Thursdays, taper off on Fridays, and not kick at all on Saturdays. By the time game day rolled around, my leg had a lot of pop, and I was ready to go.

Saturdays were always one of the fun days of the week for the players. If we were playing at home, we'd have an early meeting and then a walk-through practice in the stadium. While the offense and defense went through their game plan, the punter, Jeff West, and I would get some exercise by playing catch and running imaginary pass patterns. The fun exercise helped burn off the nervous energy that was already building and give us a good stretch.

If we had an away game, we would have our short Saturday practice in our stadium, and then the players would hurry off to a nearby deli or taco shop to grab something to eat before boarding the team buses for the airport. By the time the chartered 727 lifted off from Lindbergh Field, however, it was no longer fun and games. This was a business trip, and each player was beginning to focus on the upcoming battle.

When I began feeling ill, the fun Saturday morning practices were now something to be endured. Any quick movements brought sharp pain to my stomach, and I found it difficult to run. A malaise fell over me, and I no longer felt like laughing or eating with the guys.

As an athlete who knew his body like an Indy mechanic knows his race car, I felt myself changing. I began to lose weight. My leg strength was ebbing. My kicks didn't carry as before. Dr. Diamond told me the medications broke down muscle protein, so I had to be careful not to work out too hard. Trying to balance all that and remain in good condition was becoming impossible.

Complaint City

Statistically, I was still performing well, but I knew my kicks didn't have the same pop. I was relying on timing and technique to get me through. I feared the afternoon when I would be called upon to kick a 47-yarder, and I wouldn't have the leg strength to reach the goalposts.

I confided my doubts to Jeff West, my roommate on the road, and Wayne Sevier, our special teams coach. But the only people who really knew were my parents.

I was eating more and more often at my folks because I couldn't find the energy to prepare meals myself. Just the thought of cooking made me nauseous. At home, Mom and Dad could see the changes in me. They were also on the receiving end of my complaints, which were starting to come more frequently.

"I don't know what's going on," I moped one evening. "It's been six weeks, and I'm not feeling any better. Why can't I improve? This Dr. Diamond doesn't know my @#$ from a hole in the ground. Are you really sure he knows what he's doing, Dad?"

Dad didn't know how to respond, but he was frustrated with his inability, and with science's, to explain what was happening to me. After listening to another twenty-minute ode to self-pity, he had had enough.

"Quit bitching and get better," he said sharply. "Take control of this. Maybe you should get out of this stupid football anyway. Get a real job. Then maybe you can get away from the stress of all this."

His comments unglued me.

"This isn't stress-caused!" I yelled back. "Everything we read says it isn't stressed-caused. What if I'm not playing football? What else am I going to do? Do you think it will go away then? I'm fighting as best I can. I'm doing everything I can. Do you think I *like* being sick?"

I stormed out of the dining room and ran up to my old bedroom. Mom came up ten minutes later, as she often would after a disagreement in the family. She found me lying on my bed, curled up in a fetal position. The pain was so bad that the only way to relieve it was to lie down and distract myself, usually by watching TV.

"Are you okay, Rolf?" Mom asked, stroking my forehead. "You know Dad didn't mean what he said. He's just worried, too. He doesn't know how to handle this, and we both wish there was something we could do for you. You know how Dad is. He feels things so deeply, but he sometimes doesn't know how to express his own emotions."

"Mom, it's not fair for him to do that. Doesn't he know I don't want to be sick? I'm doing everything I can to fight this thing. I'd do anything to get rid of it."

"I know," said Mom. "It's hard on all of us, but I want you to know how much we love you. Let's all just keep doing our best."

Getting Nowhere

Each time I tried to get some specific information from Dr. Diamond, he seemed to evade me.

In my exasperation, I sought out other medical advice. I needed a doctor with a strong, confident personality. A take-charge guy. A doctor who would encourage me through this very rough time. My life was at a major crossroads. Should I continue to suck it up and play in pain? Would kicking put my life at risk? Was my promising football career about to come to a sudden end?

Dr. Diamond's indecisiveness frustrated me. When described my doubts to Dad, he reminded me that Dr. Diamond was a department head at UC San Diego, and he had heard his work was good. Nevertheless, Dad was beginning to have some doubts as well.

Meanwhile, my weakening condition was becoming more apparent to the Chargers—and the public. I went to Coach Coryell and explained my dilemma.

"Coach, the team has a chance to make the playoffs, and I've got to tell you that I'm struggling out there. If it ever comes down to the team needing a long field goal to win, I'm not sure I can do the job for you."

Coryell got up from behind his desk and walked over to my chair.

"Rolf, we've really come to depend on you, and there is nobody I'd rather have out there than you. How about if we have somebody else kick off and see if we can get through the season that way? You tell me how much you want to practice— or if you don't. Whatever you say is fine with me."

When I stopped kicking off, the media sniffed a story. There had been speculation that something was physically wrong with me, but now the truth came out. Readers of the *San Diego Union* and the *Evening Tribune* learned that I was suffering from Crohn's disease, an inflammation of the intestinal tract poorly understood by the medical community.

The newspaper articles prompted well-meaning letters from people suggesting various dietary cures: eat more roughage, lay off dairy products, add zinc to my diet, or mix bran with every meal. Some suggestions were bizarre: One person thought I should lock myself in a hotel room and watch Laurel and Hardy films and laugh until the disease went away.

I did start meeting with a nutritionist, thinking my bachelor diet might be the culprit. I also made my first contact with the Crohn's & Colitis Foundation of America, figuring it couldn't hurt to hear what they had to say.

The last month of the 1978 season was especially difficult. My health was deteriorating so quickly that after kicking on Sundays, the doctors would check me into a local hospital for treatment. In order to give my bowels a rest and ensure I was getting enough nutrition, I would be hooked up to an intravenous line in my neck for the entire week. Doctors forbid me from eating anything. I would be released on Friday, and then spend the night in the Chargers team hotel on Saturday night, home or away.

The weird thing is that I continued to kick well, so the Chargers *wanted* me to keep playing. At one point, I hit sixteen consecutive field goals, and the club was really coming together. Although we had lost too many games early in the season to earn a spot in the playoffs, we were making life miserable for a bunch of other teams.

Our last game of the 1978 season pitted us against the Houston Oilers. They were one of the best teams in the NFL with their star running back Earl Campbell and folksy coach, Bum Phillips. An hour before the game, I couldn't even zip up my football pants because the pain in my gut was so bad.

That afternoon in the Astrodome, quarterback Dan Fouts piloted "Air Coryell" to perfection, and we went out and crushed the Oilers. That meant a long day at the office for me. I had to kick six extra points and a field goal, and each time I jogged onto the field, I was in excruciating pain.

As for the Chargers, we finished the year on an absolute high. Our 9-7 record didn't qualify us for the playoffs, but with Fouts learning the new passing system and Coryell establishing himself on the sidelines, the Chargers believed 1979 could be their year.

But just as the Chargers' future appeared bright, my future was increasingly uncertain. I, too, wondered what 1979 had in store. But for me, I wasn't as optimistic as the team.

CHAPTER 5

Slowly Sinking

Chargers Training Camp
July 1979

When I reported to the Chargers training camp at UC San Diego, my ongoing medical problems arrived with me. All through the spring and summer, Dr. Diamond and his medical team had tried to stabilize my Crohn's disease so I could avoid surgery. Meanwhile, I was still experiencing piercing cramps, bouts of nausea, and nonstop diarrhea. Clearly, the treatments were not working.

When we started two-a-day workouts, I began to quickly shed the pounds I had worked so hard to put on during the off-season. To make matters worse, I was having a hard time eating, never a problem for my teammates. Three times a day, I watched these mammoth athletes devastate the buffet line, going back three or four times at each sitting. They ate everything in their path. As for myself, I was lucky if I could keep down two pieces of dry toast and a banana!

Since it was obvious I wasn't 100 percent, the Chargers team doctors were brought back into the picture. They struggled to treat me, too. To try to compensate for my poor appetite, we came up with a plan: I would drink special high-caloric "milkshakes," brimming with amino acids and carbohydrates. They tasted better than the barium shakes, but not much!

When I braved regular food, violent cramps would attack me, and the diarrhea worsened. I always had to know where I could quickly find a bathroom. When the Chargers broke camp at the end of August, the team doctors and nutritionists decided to cut out solid food altogether and put me on an amino-acid drink diet.

In order to take in enough calories to maintain my weight, I had to drink *fifteen* of those vile purple-colored concoctions each day. I was spending much of my free time at home, so Mom learned to make the drinks in the family blender. The taste, however, was so bad that I had to literally squeeze my nose when I drank one. If I didn't, I would gag and the contents would come right back up.

I was one sick puppy when the 1979 NFL season finally opened.

Late Hit

Like the year before, we opened again in Seattle, and once again I kicked four fields goals in a big Charger victory. But after each field goal, I returned to the bench and endured waves of pain through my abdomen.

In the jubilant locker room following the game, with my teammates whooping and hollering around me, I sat in front of my locker with my head in a towel, crying my eyes out. I knew something had to happen. I couldn't go on much longer like this.

It happened the next week when the Oakland Raiders came into town. Emotions ran high on both benches, since memories of the "Holy Roller" game were still vivid in everyone's mind.

Late in the first half, we scored our third touchdown of the day, and I ran out to kick the routine PAT. My kick sailed through the goalposts, when suddenly, I was blindsided and knocked to the ground. The Raiders' Lester Hayes, a defensive back known for his "in your face" play, had slammed into me and delivered a forearm shiver to my ribs. The violent blow sent me flying, knocking the wind out of me. The team physicians and trainers sprinted out to the scene of the crime, where they found me flat on my back fighting for breath.

After what seemed like ten minutes—but was probably just a minute or two—I was gingerly helped off the field. A team doctor escorted me to the locker room, where preliminary X-rays were taken. My ribs hurt terribly, and when I couldn't take a deep breath without pain, the doctors feared I might have broken some ribs. Either way, I knew I was finished for the afternoon. I showered, was handed an ice bag for my ribs, and returned to the sidelines to watch the rest of the game. After the Chargers won, a team doctor drove me to the hospital for more X-rays. The results: three cracked ribs on my left side.

Wrapped with a belly band that seemed to do absolutely no good, I spent the rest of the week recovering at my parents' home. I would go in for treatment and attend team meetings, but practicing was out of the question.

One morning, on my drive to the stadium, I was listening to a sports report on the radio. I was daydreaming and wondering what I was going to do on Sunday when I heard the sports guy announce that he would be returning in just a moment with a special interview with Coach Coryell.

I turned the volume up.

"Your kicker, Rolf Benirschke, was injured last week and didn't return for the second half," began the reporter. "What's his condition like? Will he play Sunday?"

"Rolf's a tough guy," replied Coryell. "There's no problem. We expect him back this Sunday."

I nearly drove off the road. *Holy cow, what am I going to do?*

I played.

Still Kicking

The pressure to play was constant. We all felt it, and I felt it perhaps more than others. Since Dean Meier's first letter back in my rookie season, I had converted 34 of my last 38 kicks. Despite my health problems, I was still enjoying the challenge of producing in the clutch.

The media was writing complimentary stories about me, and I had become an integral part of the Chargers' success. Three weeks into the season, we were undefeated and one of the league's marquee teams.

Week four sent us to Boston to play the New England Patriots. My physical condition was getting worse, and I was still suffering the aftereffects of Lester's late hit. The timing and technique that had kept me playing for the last month were suddenly gone. During warm-ups, I could barely kick a 35-yard field goal with a stiff wind at my back. Behind me, kicking toward the same goalpost, New England kicker John Smith was air-mailing 50-yarders high into the net. And Smith wasn't known for having a strong leg! I was totally demoralized.

The Patriots won the coin toss, elected to take the wind, and put three touchdowns on the scoreboard in the first quarter. We never recovered and lost 27-21. I couldn't wait to board the team plane for the long, cross-country flight home. As I settled into my seat, all kinds of thoughts were going through my head. I knew the end was almost here. I had to tell the coaches I could no longer kick. I had become a liability. My illness had worsened, and it was clear I could no longer play professional football.

Not long after the flight took off, I began to feel feverish, and cramps began to assault me. I was exhausted. *Perhaps if I sleep, I'll wake up and this nightmare will be over*, I thought. But after an hour of restless sleep, I was jolted awake by another wave of cramps. I knew what they meant, so I hurried back to the lavatory, sat down, and relieved myself.

When I returned to my seat, my world suddenly started

spinning and turning black. When I came to I was on fire—103 degrees! Despite my high temperature, my body shivered with chills, so the team doctor quickly ordered my teammates to carefully lay me across three seats and wrap me in several blankets.

That's when a Charger official asked the pilot to relay a message to my parents in La Jolla: *Rolf is very sick, and he may have to be hospitalized. Please meet the plane when we land at 9:30 p.m.*

When the chartered jet touched down at Lindbergh Field, I had regained a little energy. I convinced my parents that we could bypass the hospital. They asked me to come home with them, and I agreed.

In my heart, I knew I should have been hospitalized, but I thought if I gave in to this disease and admitted defeat, then it would consume me. All night and into the wee hours, I tossed and turned in my bed. The pain in my gut felt like someone was sticking me with a hot poker. I regretted talking Mom and Dad out of a trip to the hospital.

When Mom came in to check on me on Monday morning, the soaking-wet sheets immediately told her the fever had broken, but I was weak and worn out. Mom helped me out of bed, and after a meager breakfast, drove me to Dr. Diamond's office.

Before I left, I called Coach Coryell and told him I would be missing the team meeting and would report back to him after meeting with the doctor.

At University Hospital, Dr. Diamond looked me over and suggested that we had waited long enough.

"Rolf, we've tried everything. We've tried medication, we've tried diet, and we've tried rest. Things seem to be getting worse. I don't know how you've been able to play as long as you have, but Rolf, you're really sick. Your life is in danger. I'm going to talk to the surgeon as soon as you leave. I think surgery is our only option."

In a sense, I was relieved to have the decision made for me. On the way back from the hospital, I asked Mom to swing by San Diego Stadium. I needed to break the news to Coach Coryell so he could find another kicker. He had been so good to me during this ordeal, and now I had to tell him I couldn't kick anymore. I knew that on a lot of other teams, the coach would never have been as understanding as Coryell.

As I expected, Coryell was more concerned about me than his football team.

"We'll find another kicker," he said, "but more importantly, Rolf, you do what you have to in order to get well."

"Thanks, Coach. That means a lot to me."

"Well, good luck and Godspeed. We'll all be pulling for you."

As Mom and I drove out of the stadium parking lot, a thousand thoughts flooded my mind. I wondered if I would ever wear the blue-and-gold Charger uniform again. But lurking deeper were thoughts of the upcoming surgery. Would I ever be healthy again?

University Hospital
Tuesday, October 2

I had put off the inevitable long enough. One year of debilitating diarrhea and stomach cramps had taken its toll. I was worn out; I couldn't take it anymore. I had exhausted my reserves. I was ready to submit myself to whatever medical solutions the doctors presented to me.

I sat at the nurse's admitting station, squeezing my hands tightly together. Then I tapped my fingers on the table. Anxiety was oozing out of every pore.

When my head strayed a bit too far to the right, my eyes met Mom's. For lack of anything else to say, I blurted, "Mom, can you believe this is happening?"

At this point, the seasoned hospital admitting clerk knew she had a problem patient on her hands. "We don't have to finish this work-up now," she said sympathetically. "We can complete it later."

She smiled and turned to the orderly standing at the door. "Carlos, you can take Mr. Benirschke to 11 West."

I stepped into the elevator, but then another shot of intense pain tore at my insides. I closed my eyes tightly—as though that might shut out the severe pain—and felt Mom squeeze my arm gently.

"We're doing the right thing, Rolf," she soothed. "We're doing the right thing."

After finding my room, Dr. Diamond and several other doctors came in to poke and prod me. Their verdict: *You need surgery, but you may be too weak to survive the procedure. We need to build up your strength for two weeks before we can operate. To do that, we are going to keep you in the hospital and put you on TPN— Total Parenteral Nutrition.*

I learned that TPN involved putting a central IV line in the jugular or subclavian vein in my neck. Large amounts of fats, concentrated dextrose, amino acids, and other essential minerals would be administered around the clock.

Dr. Gerald Peskin would be the lead surgeon, and once the reins were handed over to him, I saw or heard little from Dr. Diamond. It was as though he disappeared from the radar screen. I sensed he was a little embarrassed that he hadn't taken more control of the situation. In fairness, there may not have been much more he could have done, but we'll never know.

Either way, I was happy to have Dr. Peskin leading the medical team. He told me he would most likely perform a resection, or the removal of the diseased part of the bowel.

"You should be able to function very nicely with only a small part of your intestine missing," Dr. Peskin said. "In fact, I think you'll play football again."

Getting the huge IV needle into my jugular vein was not fun. I had to hang my head over the end of the bed so the nurse could expose the large vein. It was uncomfortable, to say the least, and when she missed the vein, blood spurted everywhere.

This disease has been a pain in the neck since day one, I murmured with grim humor. But I was in so much discomfort that I didn't care about the details. I just wanted to get well.

University Hospital
Thursday, October 4

The west wing of University Hospital's eleventh floor was reserved for VIPs. Rooms were decorated with a little more flair, a bit more pizzazz. The food was not only better, but it was served on fine china. Perhaps this was the floor where hospital authorities thought the younger son of Dr. Kurt Benirschke, head of UCSD's pathology department, should go. Or perhaps they sent me to the eleventh floor because I was a San Diego Charger.

But the eleventh floor was not really set up for critical cases; the sixth floor was.

Down on sixth, registered nurse Colleen Holt was talking with Bertha Robles, the floor's nursing supervisor, about the hospital's new celebrity patient.

"Why would they put him on eleven?" Colleen asked. "He should be one of *our* patients. All the IBD cases are here. We're the ones who are supposed to take care of him."

"You're absolutely right," Bertha responded. "He really should be here with us."

Colleen called the ward clerk, who called Dr. Peskin, and the matter was resolved. I'd be transferred to the sixth floor the next day.

For the rest of the day, however, I stayed on the eleventh floor, where the hyperalimentation entered my body at 40 cc per hour.

Mom continued to comfort me, and Dad stopped by three times. He didn't have to travel far; he worked in the pathology lab on the second floor.

"How are you, Rolfie?" he asked in his upbeat voice each time he came in.

I could hardly look him in the eyes. I didn't want to cry in front of Dad. For one of the few times in my life, I recognized that no matter how much Dad knew, he couldn't control the situation in which we found ourselves. That had to be difficult for him, especially since he had devoted his life to medicine.

"Just a few more days . . . you've got to hang in there, Rolf," he said in his soft German accent. I could feel the resolution in his voice, born of a man who had achieved what he set out to do with life. He bent over and touched my shoulder. "We can get over this thing. We must!"

"Why do I feel I can't?" I pleaded. "Why do I feel so absolutely helpless?"

Dad's eyes never left mine. "It's okay. We're finally getting somewhere. You've got to keep fighting just a little longer."

"I feel . . . so out of control. I'm worried about what's going to happen with my life, with football. I'm scared about the surgery. I'm worried that maybe. . . ."

I couldn't bring myself to finish the sentence. The unthinkable was unsayable.

Dad thought for a minute. "I know, Rolfie. We've got to take this one day at a time. We'll find a way to get through this. Don't worry about football. It's just a game, something you do for now, but not forever. Who's to say the stress of football didn't cause all this to happen?"

I turned my head to the window. "C'mon, Dad. We both read the same books. We both know the research says that stress is not the cause of this."

It was an old, familiar argument between Dad and me . . . and now it was starting again. For years, Dad believed sports were a diversion, something not to be taken seriously. Skiing and tennis made sense, he said, because they were recreational sports. "You could do those things on the weekends, and still busy yourself with the rest of your working life. Football is playing, not working!"

In my hospital room, Dad decided not to reopen the argument, but his comment about stress causing my health problems hung in the air.

Mom rose from her chair. "Kurt, you're only upsetting him. He doesn't need that now."

"I suppose you're right, Marion."

Dad got up from the edge of the bed. "And now I must tell you that I have to leave for New York tomorrow to give a speech at Cornell University. I'll be back Sunday night. And Rolf, I'm sorry if I upset you, but that was not my intention. I want so much for the pain to be gone for you . . . for you to find peace. Believe me, Rolf."

"I know, Dad, I know. But please understand that football and sports are important to me."

"I'll try, Rolf."

Later, when I was alone, I tried to drink some water. That was all I was allowed to take orally, and even a simple glass of water didn't sit well on my stomach. I was still grimacing when Dr. Peskin breezed into my room with two nurses on his heels.

"How's my football hero doing?" he asked.

"Lousy, really lousy," I answered.

Despite my poor attitude, I liked Dr. Peskin's cheerful manner. *At least he looks me in the eye and asks how I'm doing, not like Dr. Diamond.*

"The good news is that we're going to move you down to the sixth floor tomorrow. Not that you aren't getting good care up here, but it'll be better on six."

I thanked him for the news, then Dr. Peskin stopped at the nurses' station and wrote the following note on my chart: "Dx of Crohn's disease of the terminal ileum, ascending transverse colon. Admitted for HAL, then resection of involved segment of the bowel. Also has oropharyngeal candidiasis for past two weeks."

Oropharyngeal candidiasis is a yeast infection of the mouth and throat, relatively common in people taking Prednisone regularly. Prednisone is a wonder drug when it comes to reducing inflammation, but it has a legion of side effects, including yeast infections.

Another side effect of Prednisone is that it causes the body to retain water. On the morning of my second day at University Hospital, I weighed more than 150 pounds, down from my healthy weight of 178, but up from my admittance weight of 147 pounds. That was a deceiving figure, however. I felt like a football filled with fluid.

Dr. Peskin visited me the following morning, a Friday. He didn't like what he saw, so when he left, he ordered two units of blood by transfusion. In addition, he increased the hyperal solution intake to 50 cc per hour.

Peskin was also disturbed by my lack of motivation and feelings of depression. He arranged for hospital psychologist Dr. Harvey Ward to visit me after I was transferred from the eleventh floor.

At one o'clock that afternoon, I was taken by wheelchair to the sixth floor. Nurses Colleen Holt and Bertha Robles greeted me at the elevator and escorted me to Room 9. I was agitated, and my eyes darted everywhere. I must have looked like a scared deer staring at onrushing headlights on a lonely highway.

Later, over a cup of coffee, the two nurses discussed their new patient.

"It's been a long time since we've seen anybody that frightened," Colleen remarked.

"Terrible," answered Bertha. "His eyes are almost scary. They're so full of fear."

Dr. Ward, the hospital psychologist, came to my room and discovered a patient who wanted nothing to do with him. I was moody and uncommunicative.

"How come you have all this built-up hostility?" he probed.

I didn't answer. *You're not going to make me talk.*

"Rolf, tell me what's bothering you."

I remained uncooperative, and just then my parents walked into my room. They were on the way to the airport, where Dad would fly to New York for his speech. Two friends also appeared within moments.

They sat in the back of the room and listened to Dr. Ward's questioning. I finally spoke to him, but more out of politeness since guests were in the room.

Finally, I had enough of this psychobabble. "Please leave us alone," I said. "Please leave *me* alone."

The psychologist left and wrote the following on my chart: "Severely depressed. Fortunately, patient has a substantial social support system."

For the next few days, my hyperal intake was increased and my Prednisone dosage doubled. I kept dozing off, waking up only when nurses and interns came around. Mom was at my side most of the days, but we didn't talk much.

I had to undergo two exams—another upper GI and a proctoscope. The barium swallow, as expected, was merely awful. The proctoscope was humiliating.

Meanwhile, I met a new nurse, Helen Del Gado, who worked the 2 p.m. to 10 p.m. shift. She was a special woman full of kindness and compassion, but also capable of speaking directly to me.

The first evening, after listening to my "woe is me" litany, she chided my attitude. "It's not the end of the world, you know. Stop acting as if you think it is."

The rebuke stung, but it got me thinking. *Maybe she's right.* I opened up to her, something I hadn't done with Dr. Ward.

"It seems like I've been fighting this for so long. I just don't have anything left."

"What you've got to do is start trusting, start accepting a little help from all of us," she said. "We're here to support you. You've got to believe that."

Helen brought me crackers, the first solid food permitted by my doctors. Shortly after eating one, however, my intestines began to cramp and the crescendo of pain returned once again. I tried to put the crackers on my nightstand, but they fell to the linoleum floor. Helen picked them up and patted my arm.

"You tried. It didn't work. Forget it."

Friday, October 5
11 a.m.

University Hospital was associated with UCSD, and as such, was a teaching hospital. That meant a steady stream of residents, interns, and medical students flowed in and out of my room. The exams and discussions were never ending.

That morning, a swarm of interns invaded the premises, led by primary intern Cammy Mowery. Normally, I flashed a smile to strangers and tried to act civil. But this morning I was distant and rude, plainly not happy with the intrusion.

After the group had left, Dr. Mowery returned to my room for a visit. She talked about family support, about fear and tension, about my upcoming surgery. I felt better, then I looked up and confided, "Sometimes I think I'm *not* going to get out of here."

"You want to know the truth?" Dr. Mowery asked. She didn't wait for an answer. "The truth is you're not the first to go through this. We have a half-dozen other people on the floor with inflammatory bowel disorders, and across the nation, there are hundreds—make that thousands—of other people in hospitals with exactly the same thing you have. The point is, you're not unusual. And knowing a little bit about your background in football, I have confidence you can get through this."

I chewed on that one for a while.

Dr. Peskin walked in a short time later with good news.

The proctoscope and upper GI showed nothing unexpected.

"Now, I want to do an IVP," he said.

I knew what an IVP was. "Are you doing this to see if I have kidney stones?" I had had an intravenous pyelogram in college when I had surgery to remove a painful kidney stone.

"No, we'll check to see if you have stones, because as you may have learned, stones are often associated with inflammatory bowel disease. But what we're really doing is locating your ureters, which extend from your kidneys to your bladder. We want to make sure we don't snip them when we open up your abdomen."

I stared at Dr. Peskin. "You mean, there's no chance of avoiding surgery?"

"Almost none," he replied. "We've scheduled your resection surgery for ten days from now, Monday, October 15."

A couple of days later, the Chargers played the Broncos in Denver. It was a frustrating game to watch from my hospital bed; we lost 7-0 as my replacement, Roy Gerela, missed three field goals inside 35 yards.

After the game, I turned on the radio and listened to the Chargers' call-in show. I wasn't prepared for what I heard.

"What this team needs is a placekicker," stated one upset fan.

"Gerela stinks! When is Benirschke coming back?" asked another.

"This Gerela fellow is going to really cost us. Even a sick Rolf wouldn't have missed those kicks."

At first, the comments bolstered me, but it hurt to hear the anger expressed toward a guy who was trying his hardest. Gerela, who had kicked for years with the Super Bowl champion Pittsburgh Steelers, had been a good kicker his whole career.

I couldn't take it any longer. In frustration, I picked up the phone and called the station. They put me on the air immediately.

"This is Rolf Benirschke," I said to the startled host. "I just want to put in a word for Roy Gerela. He's doing the best he can. You can't imagine what he's going through. The grass in Mile High Stadium is extremely long, and it's a tough place to kick for anyone, much less a guy who's just getting familiar with the snapper and holder. So go easy on Roy, will ya? I promise you there's nobody who wanted to make those kicks more than he did."

Sunday, October 7
10 p.m.

Out-of-bed activity is mandatory for IBD patients—or anyone confined to extended bed rest—because it keeps the lungs from collecting fluids, which can cause pneumonia. Any movements for me, however, triggered painful consequences. I preferred to remain quiet in bed and distract myself with TV. But my nurses had other ideas; they insisted that I walk around.

Dad returned from New York on Sunday night and stopped by the hospital. He had been away for just a weekend, but in forty-eight hours, he could see pronounced changes in me. I was pale and wan, and the effects of Prednisone and hyperal left me with a bloated look around my neck and face.

I looked at my father. "It hasn't been a fun day. The Chargers lost in Denver. . . ."

"Never mind," he whispered. "How are you doing?"

The next morning, senior resident Lee Griffith led another group of interns into my room.

Dr. Griffith lifted up my hospital gown and touched my right side, pressing his fingers into my intestines.

"Ouch! That hurts like hell!" I screamed, pushing his hand away. "Do you have to do it so hard?"

Ignoring me, the doctor addressed the four interns gathered around my bed. "Did you hear that? The surest sign of intestinal distress."

Glad to be of help.

I received permission to eat limited quantities of neutral solid foods, and chose one of my favorites: pretzels. A couple of handfuls, add one hour, and I had the recipe for pain. The cramps were incessant.

Dr. Peskin informed me that my kidneys looked good and that I had no stones, but my white blood count was very high: 13,400. (The normal range is 4,000 to 10,000.) A high WBC indicated an infection somewhere.

Then came more jolting news for the Benirschke family. My parents received a phone call from my younger sister, Ingrid, who lived in New York City. Ironically, Ingrid had developed her own set of kidney stones and needed surgery immediately.

The news was very discouraging for my parents.

"What next?" Mom asked Dad sorrowfully.

"Yes, Marion," replied Dad. "What next, indeed."

When they told me the news, I felt sorry for what my folks must be going through. Now they had two of their children with serious medical problems. The decision was made to fly Ingrid to San Diego and join me at University Hospital. The only silver lining was that we would be a couple of floors apart, easy for my parents to visit us.

That night Ingrid arrived and dropped in to say hi.

"Hey, big guy," she said. "Are they treating you okay?"

"Ingrid!"

"Isn't this crazy? I almost feel like I'm having sympathy pains," she smiled.

I could tell by her face that she was shocked by my appearance. I was only fourteen months older than my sister, and we had always been close, united by our common sensitivities and values. We chatted for a short time before Ingrid had to head home and get some rest.

Meanwhile, my abdominal cramps returned and were again followed by explosive diarrhea. Another blood work-up was ordered.

The endocrinologist reported: "Patient is getting toxic, although it's unknown if the infection is due to an abscess or to the CVP line."

Toxic shock is generally caused by the presence of bacteria or their toxins in the bloodstream. Dr. Griffith was called in.

While he studied my chart, I asked him why I couldn't have the surgery now instead of waiting another week.

"Understand that we're trying to build up your strength and resistance," he informed me. "But I will talk this over with Dr. Peskin, and if he feels the resection should take place now, we'll proceed."

The old saying—*Be careful of what you ask for. You might just get it*—came to mind. A deep sense of fear shivered through my body. My eyes darted around the room, and suddenly, I never felt more alone in my life.

CHAPTER 6

Early Call

University Hospital
Friday, October 12
8:30 a.m.

Thursday night was a horror show. My temperature never dropped below 103 degrees, my pulse raced at 150 beats per minute, and my blood pressure was dangerously low.

Early Friday morning, Dr. Peskin felt we couldn't wait six more days for surgery. It was time to take action.

"Rolf," he said. "Wake up."

I opened my eyes and turned my head.

"We're going to move the surgery up to tomorrow. We can't wait any longer."

I thought for a long moment. "Will you have to do an ileostomy?"

I knew that ostomy surgery was a possibility, but we had hardly discussed it. It had been my unspoken fear since first reading about Crohn's disease and ulcerative colitis in my dad's library. Many times, patients requiring IBD surgery ultimately end up wearing an ostomy appliance—a bag attached to a stoma, or opening, in their abdomen to collect fecal waste. As a professional athlete and a single twenty-four-year-old guy, I couldn't imagine living with a bag permanently attached to my side.

74

"We don't know yet," replied Dr. Peskin. "We think we just need to do a resection. Your disease appears to be localized to one area of the colon."

Nurse Colleen Holt drew her usual four test tubes of blood from me at 8 a.m. By now, my arms were black and blue from the needle sticks, and she was having difficulty finding a vein. Colleen didn't like the way I looked, so she had a student nurse stay with me while she finished her rounds.

A short time later, as Colleen came out of another patient's room, she noticed the call light on for Room 9. Sensing trouble, she ran to my room, where she found me draped over the toilet. The young student nurse, who couldn't have weighed more than 105 pounds, was trying to lift me. The odor was awful!

"He had to go," the young nurse explained almost apologetically. "But when he got in here, he began getting lightheaded and started going to the bathroom standing up. I didn't know what to do."

Colleen ran to the door and called for help. Two other nurses came running, and together the four of them dragged me out.

I had another violent bowel movement about three feet from the bed, soiling the front of Colleen's uniform. The nurses cleaned me up and lifted me into bed as best they could.

With tears of shame in my eyes, I tried to apologize to the nurses. "I'm so sorry," I stammered. "I couldn't control myself."

"Don't worry," said Colleen, as she began changing my gown. "It's not the first time, and it certainly won't be the last time for us. Accidents happen."

The nurses took my vital signs. My temperature was 104, my pulse was 180, and my blood pressure was a shockingly low 80/60. Prednisone intake was increased to 40 mg., and antibiotics were added to my IV in preparation for the surgery.

When my parents got the news of my accident, they came as quickly as they could. I complained about blurred vision.

"My head aches, too, but that's good because it takes my mind off the other pains," I said.

I went back to sleep with Mom at my side, squeezing my right hand.

Meanwhile, four floors below, Ingrid was just coming out of her own surgery. The word was she was extremely sore, but recovering nicely. Mom and Dad asked nurse Helen Del Gado to stay with me while they went downstairs and checked up on Ingrid.

I awoke and smiled at the angel in the white uniform.

"Hi, Helen. Is it morning already?"

"Morning? It's afternoon. You've had a rough day so far, in case you didn't know."

For a week, I had kept the unmentionable deep within, but I had to ask The Question.

"Helen, am I going to die?" I blurted out. "Am I going to wake up after the operation?"

She smiled and nodded, almost as relieved as I was that the subject had been raised.

"No, Rolf, you're not going to die. And yes, you *are* going to wake up after your operation."

"It's so awful, Helen. The bad dreams I've been having about having a bag around my stomach. A bag! Can you imagine going through life like that? I can't."

"Let's not worry about that now," she soothed. "Let's try to get some rest. You have a big day ahead of you."

"I could die, though, right? Something *could* go wrong and that would be it, right?"

"We hope and pray that won't happen. You need to think good thoughts, not bad thoughts."

"When are they going to do it?"

"It's all set for 8 a.m. tomorrow. I know it's hard to imagine but believe me, you'll feel much better after it's done."

That afternoon, alone in my room, I began to think about what lay ahead. *What happens when you die? Where do you go? Is that all there is?* For months I had been reading my Bible, rekindling my faith in God. As if an answer to prayer, Jim Adkins, the youth pastor of the church I was attending, walked into my room.

"Jim, what are you doing here?" I asked.

"Well, I've been thinking about you ever since I heard you were admitted," he said. "I wanted to come by and let you know everyone at church is praying for you. I know this is a tough time, but perhaps I could just take a moment to pray for you and your surgery tomorrow."

By now, tears were flowing freely down my cheeks. I could only answer with a nod of my head. Jim squeezed my hand while he bowed his head and prayed that the Lord would guide the doctor's hands during the surgery, and that the Great Physician would work through all the medical people to bring a healing to my diseased body.

In the back of the room, my father had slipped in while Jim was praying out loud. Although he had never been a churchgoer and had never heard someone pray like that, the emotion and concern he heard in Jim's voice caused him to well up, too. I felt the Lord's presence in that lonely hospital room, and I knew I was prepared for whatever the next day would bring.

The calm did not last long, however. Shortly after Jim left, intern Cammy Mowery came in and began explaining the upcoming surgery to me. Suddenly, I was confronted by the reality of a major abdominal procedure; I was heading down a road in which there was no turning back. When Dr. Mowery held out a pen for me to sign the medical consent forms, she noticed my body suddenly tense up. I had just read in the form that I was giving permission for the doctors to perform an ostomy if they felt it was necessary.

"Cammy, what's the probability of an ostomy?"

"Rolf, very low. It's routine to include it in the consent form though, just in case."

Friday, October 12
5:30 p.m.

Dr. Larry Saidman, the anesthesiologist, dropped by for his routine pre-op visit and became concerned immediately. He didn't like what he saw at all. Sweat was beading up on my forehead and running in rivulets down the sides of my face. My hands trembled, and I had trouble focusing on his words. Dr. Saidman checked my blood pressure; it had dropped to a perilously low 65/30. The evidence was clear to him: My body was experiencing severe septic shock. The colon must have ruptured, causing bacteria to leak into my system. I was on the edge of delirium, and my situation was now critical.

Dr. Saidman raced to the desk and called Dr. Peskin at home. "Gerald, we can't wait until morning. Rolf's become septic, and his condition is serious. We have to operate now!"

"I'm on my way," Dr. Peskin said. "Maybe thirty minutes at most."

Nurses and a host of doctors sprang into accelerated action, and by 6 p.m., I was lifted on to a gurney for the trip to the second-floor operating room. I didn't know it, but my life hung in the balance.

An orderly wheeled me to the elevator, followed by Helen and Colleen. As we waited for the elevator doors to open, a young intern joined the group. He gripped a piece of paper and a pen in his hand.

"I hate to bother you at a time like this, but my dad's a big fan of yours," he said, thrusting the pen and paper at me.

Helen couldn't believe his presumption. "For goodness sake, can't you see this isn't the time?"

Instinctively, I reached out for the paper and scribbled something that resembled my name just as the elevator doors opened.

Dr. Saidman began the anesthesia procedure at 6:15. Because of my weakened condition, he supplemented the usual assortment of anesthetic drugs with Dopamine, a drug that raises blood pressure.

Dad and Mom, barred from the operating bay, found solace in Ingrid's room on the fifth floor.

Dr. Peskin arrived at 6:30, running from the parking lot. The five-man surgery team cut a long incision in the middle of my stomach and opened me for the first look-see. After some discussion, the decision was made to proceed with the resection. Approximately ten inches of my large intestine were snipped out, and doctors sewed the end of the ileum to the end of the transverse colon. It took three hours and forty minutes until the final stitch was done.

I had dodged the ostomy bullet. Mom and Dad were there when I was rolled out of surgery and into the Intensive Care Unit at midnight. I, of course, was still in dreamland. My parents were glad to see me alive and were grateful to hear everything went well.

In the ICU, Mom and Dad stood on either side of the bed, each holding one of my hands. Although they knew I would not wake up for some time, they stayed by my side until 1:30 a.m. Finally, exhausted, they headed home. It had been a trying day.

As anticipated, I slept through the night, the anesthesia bringing a few hours of drugged peace. Little did I know that my medical problems were just beginning. The worst was yet to come.

Saturday, October 13
8:35 a.m.
In the Trauma Unit

When I struggled to open my eyes the next morning, I could hardly move. At first, I was aware of the intense pain in my abdomen, but then I realized I was hooked up to more tubes, bottles, and IV bags than I could count. Strange clicking-like sounds distracted me, as the blood pressure monitor and respirator recorded my vital signs. I had an oxygen mask over my face and IV lines running from both arms and my neck. I felt like a marionette, connected to a bunch of strings.

The Trauma Unit was one big room, filled with a half-dozen patients, each separated by a curtain—much like an emergency ward. There was twenty-four-hour supervision and monitoring machines everywhere. Because the patients received round-the-clock care in the well-lit room, it was difficult to tell night from day.

The shift nurse noticed I was awake and came over from her monitoring station to check on me.

"Good morning, Rolf," she said with a strong European accent. *She must be German or Czech*, I thought. "How do you feel?"

I wasn't sure. One thing was certain: I didn't feel like moving.

Nurse Carla Van Hooten lifted the clear plastic oxygen mask from my face.

"Where am I?"

"You're in the Trauma Unit of the ICU," answered Van Hooten. "It's a stop after surgery until you can go back to your regular floor."

"What's that groaning? It sounds like someone dying."

She leaned over and whispered in my ear. "It's a very sick lady. There are four other very sick people in this room."

The nurse took my vital signs. Temperature was high: 102 degrees. Pulse was also high: 130.

"What's this tube in my nose?" I asked.

"That's an NG tube, or nasogastric device. It extends through your nose and into your stomach, draining the stomach's contents by suction. You see, the bowel usually stops working after surgery like yours, at least for a while. The NG tube will prevent nausea and vomiting," said the nurse.

She continued speaking. "You have several more tubes, brave young man. A couple of Penrose drains are connected

80

to the side of your abdomen. They're collecting incisional drainage from the resection area. A Foley catheter is catching your urine. You just might qualify for some award," she quipped.

I managed a faint smile. Nurse Van Hooten repositioned the oxygen mask. *Is this really happening to me? I'm a professional athlete in my early twenties. How did I end up here?*

Before I could think further, I saw Nurse Van Hooten with her blood-drawing kit. *Not again,* I thought. I was aware of several needle stabs as she probed for an artery deep in my right wrist. She needed arterial blood this time to check my blood gases, and she would repeat the unusually painful procedure daily over the next week.

"There you go," she said, as she pocketed the vial. "I'll be over at the nurses' desk. We're here to help you twenty-four hours a day."

Dad and Mom returned to the hospital at 9 a.m., still exhausted after only a few hours of sleep. When they were at home, they had to answer numerous phone calls from friends and the media about my condition.

In the meantime, Dad was supposed to prepare for a medical conference in Copenhagen the following weekend. In many circles, Dad was better-known than me. In addition to heading the pathology department at UC San Diego and directing the Center for Reproduction of Endangered Species at the San Diego Zoo, he was the world's authority on the human placenta.

Dad slipped out of the ICU and headed toward his basement lab. He knew that my specimen would be waiting for him, and he was anxious to see what it would tell him. Dad was on a first-name basis with most of the lab techs.

"Hello, Kurt, nice to see you," said one of the older techs. "We heard about Rolf. We're so sorry. How's he doing?"

"He made it through the night okay, and he's resting right now," answered Dad. "Are the tissue samples ready?

"Yes, they are, Kurt. You can view the slide of Rolf's colon under this microscope."

Before Dad examined the slides, however, he looked at my removed colon. The extent of the lesions on the inside lining of the intestinal wall horrified him. There was virtually no healthy section anywhere.

Next, Dad placed the slides under the microscope. He bent over and looked through the lens. He glanced up, thought for a minute, then peered inside again.

"Anything unusual, Kurt?"

"Yes," he replied. "Rolf doesn't have Crohn's disease. Those tissue samples are consistent with ulcerative colitis."

My father groaned. Dr. Diamond had blown the call.

Wednesday, October 17
9:15 a.m.
First Steps

After major abdominal surgery, it's vital to keep the lungs clear to avoid collapse or pneumonia. That's why I was connected to a respirator, which forced me to take deep breaths.

With each heave, my lacerated stomach muscles ached terribly. There was no way I could splint the discomfort, and I found myself anticipating each breath knowing a shot of pain would follow immediately.

Dad returned at noon and waited for me to receive my much-anticipated morphine injection. The shot helped take the edge off the pain and allow me to get out of bed and take a few steps—standard post-op procedure.

"First comes sitting up," he said, as he gingerly lifted me.

"Oh!" I moaned.

"I know it hurts, but you have to do this."

Dad and a nurse lifted and slid my legs over the side of the bed. The floor looked like it was at the bottom of the Grand Canyon.

"Easy does it," said Dad, as he slowly eased me down.

I caught my breath and wondered what to do next.

"Take a few steps," Dad directed.

I grabbed an IV pole in one hand and Dad's arm in the other and shuffled my foot, taking my first step. Then came a second . . . and a third . . . and a fourth.

Those four steps felt like four laps around the track.

"I can't do it anymore," I protested. "I'm getting dizzy."

"That's enough for now," said Dad. "Time to get back into bed."

Later, under Dad's watchful eye, Dr. Peskin came by to examine my incision. He lifted the pus-filled dressing, and for the first time I saw the incision. My chest and belly had been shaved smooth, and now a neat line ran down the middle of my stomach and was secured with nice tight sutures.

"It looks good," said Dr. Peskin proudly. "You're going to heal nicely, Rolf."

Mom stepped in the room. She had good news and bad news regarding my sister. Ingrid was fighting a fever, and she had to be catheterized. Despite her pain, however, she had written me a note: "I know what I've been going through hasn't been any fun, but it's certainly nothing compared to what you are going through. I'm thinking of you, and I hope I can come up and see you soon."

Just then, Dad was asked by a nurse to step outside for a phone call.

"Dr. Benirschke, this is Gene Klein," said the voice.

"Yes, Mr. Klein, what can I do for you?" Although Dad didn't know much about pro football, he did know that Gene Klein was the owner of the San Diego Chargers.

"We just want you to know that we're all hoping and praying for Rolf over here. I know you realize what a fine young man you have. Please tell him there will always be a place for him with our club as long as I'm around."

Early that evening, following another brief experience out of bed, my fever shot up to 103 and with it, the fear that perhaps something was wrong. Dad and Mom were also uncertain about my feverish condition, but Dr. Peskin, on his evening rounds, didn't seem alarmed.

"I don't think you have anything to worry about," he said. "The fever spikings are natural and should begin to dissipate. Nothing has happened here to warrant any undue concern."

Mom and Dad had a lot to talk about that night. Their youngest son and their only daughter were in the same hospital, two floors apart, both in severe pain following major operations. For several days, they had also known that Mom's father, Opa, lay in a German hospital, not expected to live more than a few months. On a non-medical note, Dad was scheduled to give an important keynote speech in Copenhagen, one that had been planned for over a year.

"Even though Omi says not to come, I feel I have to go," said Mom. "It may be the last time I see him alive."

"You're probably right, Marion. And I must fulfill my obligation to speak in Copenhagen. But. . . ."

"Yes, she agreed, "it's a difficult dilemma."

They were also parents, and they agreed that neither of them would leave me if things turned for the worse, which now seemed unlikely. Besides, my brother, Steve, who was still in medical school, had decided to fly in from Cleveland to bolster the family. He would be arriving in three days, and he would be here before my parents left and stay until they returned. That helped my parents make their decision. Unless I took a turn for the worse, Mom would fly to Munich and Dad would leave for Copenhagen as planned.

The night proved uneventful, and by early morning my temperature was returning to normal. Oddly, when I woke up, I noticed my right eyelid was drooping profoundly. In addition, my neck and chest also seemed very swollen.

A blood work-up revealed an astonishingly high white blood cell count of 44,500, and concern immediately mounted that there was an infection somewhere in my system. A chest

X-ray showed signs of a micro-lung collapse—the result of poor respiratory effort.

To take care of the latter problem, Drs. Peskin and Mowery ordered respiratory therapy to begin immediately and proceed every six hours. The therapy involved using a chest vibrator applied to my back to loosen mucus and fluids. I was instructed to cough as hard as I could to bring up any phlegm and expand my lungs with the regular use of blow bottles.

Early that afternoon, Mom helped me on my first significant exercise in more than two days. We walked the length of the Trauma Unit and back. It took nearly thirty minutes to cover the hundred feet. And this once professional athlete thought that was quite an accomplishment!

During my hall-long hike, I peeked at the patient who had been making all of the noise. I learned she was a Samoan princess who tipped the scales at 450 pounds. Her body, covered with tattoos, was filled with metastasized lymphatic cancer, and although she had undergone two successive major surgeries, the prognosis was not good.

Next to the tattooed princess was a young man who had been in a major motorcycle accident. His helmet had saved his life, but both sets of arms and legs had been broken, and they were now set in awkward-looking casts. Adjacent to him was another banged-up victim—a man who had plowed his car into a telephone pole.

"It kind of makes me feel like I have it pretty good," I said to Mom.

"Life isn't easy, Rolf, and it certainly isn't fair."

CHAPTER 7

Lightning Strikes

University Hospital
Saturday, October 20

Trauma Unit patients are supposed to be limited to visits from immediate family members. But that afternoon, an exception was made for a special visitor—Coach Coryell.

I looked up and saw a pained expression on his face. He probably didn't expect to see one of his football players hooked up to a half-dozen whirring machines with tubes running everywhere. It had to have been difficult for Coryell to make the hospital visit, but he felt it was important for him to be there representing the team.

"Hello, Rolf," he began awkwardly. "How are you feeling?"

I nodded, then whispered, "I guess all right."

"I want you to know, Rolf, that all the guys and I want you to hurry up and get out of here. We're pulling for you. We want you back with us where you belong."

"Thanks, Coach."

"I also have a little present here," said Coryell, as he reached into a small equipment bag and pulled out a white No. 6 Charger jersey. It was my jersey.

He held it up for me to see. All my teammates had

scribbled their names on the jersey, some adding notes of encouragement: "Hang in there Rolf" "We're thinking of you" "Get well soon" and "We need you back." Each player's signature brought a special memory, and I realized how much I missed them.

Coach and I made small talk for a few minutes, and then it was time for him to go. I could tell it was uncomfortable for Coach Coryell to see one of his players so sick, but for me, it was very special—a visit I will never forget.

The jersey was hung on the hospital wall next to my bed so I could see it without moving my head. It became a great source of inspiration even though I thought I'd never wear a Charger jersey again.

After Coryell left, Mom and Dad came by for their third visit of the day. When I pointed out my new prized wall hanging, they hardly noticed. I could tell something was troubling them.

"Should we really be going away next week?" Mom asked Dad. *Ah, so that was it.* By the way she phrased her question, it was obvious she was having second thoughts about the wisdom of her and Dad both traveling to Europe.

"I've been wondering, too, Marion," said Dad. "We can't make a final decision yet. Let's wait a few more days when Steve gets here."

Mom decided to change the subject.

"Some good news! Ingrid is feeling much better. She has gas pains and it still hurts some, but the doctors say she's turned a corner. She may come down to see you tomorrow."

"That would be nice," I said, trying to force a smile.

"And Steve is arriving Monday for sure," said Dad.

"That would be nice, too." *What would really be nice would be to get out of this ICU and back to my own room,* I thought. *The Samoan woman never stopped moaning and groaning all night.*

"We really don't know what we should do," said Mom, still wringing her hands. "I don't feel good about this."

I realized I could help put her at ease. "Mom, if Opa is in bad shape, you should see him."

My sleep was erratic that night—moments of peace interrupted by times of pain and chills. I'm sure I talked in my sleep, but it couldn't have been anything like the ghastly sounds coming from behind the neighboring curtain.

In the morning, nurse Carla Van Hooten noted that my face and neck appeared more bloated than usual, a sign that I may be retaining water. She checked my vital signs, but for the first time in weeks, my blood pressure and temperature were normal.

"Let's get you weighed," said Carla, pointing to the scale by the nurses' desk.

"Do we have to?" The scale was fifteen feet away.

"Yes, I'm afraid so."

With her help, I shuffled over to the scale and weighed in at 150 pounds—up nearly ten pounds in just twenty-four hours! Not a good sign.

Carla notified a doctor, and I was immediately hooked up to a bottle of Lasix, a diuretic that forces fluids to be expelled through increased urine output.

Upon returning to bed, I began perspiring profusely. Carla took my temperature; it had shot up to 102 in a matter of minutes.

Dad arrived at 9:30 a.m., just as Dr. Peskin was making his morning rounds with Dr. Lee Griffith, the chief resident. When they finished their examination of me, Dad followed them into the hallway.

Dad spoke first, uttering what had to be on all three doctors' minds. "He looks terrible, doesn't he?"

"The fluid infiltration is not good," answered Dr. Peskin. "But the Lasix should help. I think we still have things under control. Rolf is making as good progress as we can hope for."

When the doctors left, Dad bumped into Carla as she was coming out of the ICU.

Dad and Mom: Kurt and Marion Benirschke

The Children: Steve, Ingrid, and me. (1966)

All together in happier times. (Christmas, 1976)

I leaned on my parents a lot after my surgeries.

Playing soccer at UC Davis helped develop my football skills.

Steve interrupted his medical studies to be at my side in the hospital. (October 1979)

At the same time I was in the hospital, Ingrid needed emergency kidney stone surgery. (October 1979)

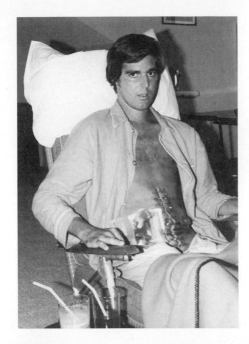

Recovering at home.
Wondering how
to deal with it all.

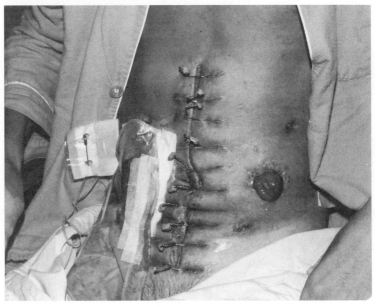

The realities of my surgery: wire sutures holding my
surgical incision together, with ileostomy appliance, left,
and colostomy stoma, right.

Photo: Teri Cluck

My biggest day, when I was honorary captain with
Louie Kelcher, soon after being released from
the hospital. I weighed 127 pounds and
still had wire sutures in my abdomen.

Kicking out of the hold of Ed Luther.

Above, left: Celebrating the kick I'll never forget with Ed Luther and Hank Bauer in the playoffs against Miami. (January, 1982)

Above, right: Mobbed by teammates and Coach Don Coryell after kicking a game-winner.

Left: Playing in the Pro Bowl in Hawaii with my ileostomy and a broken wrist. (January, 1983)

Above, right: Strength coach Phil Tyne helping me warm up before a game. Without his help, I never would have returned to the NFL.

"You look worried, Dr. Benirschke."

"Worried? Perhaps. I know I'm definitely concerned. This has been hard on all of us."

"I'm sure it has," she said sympathetically.

"Marion has been taking it extremely hard. She can barely sleep anymore. Last night was the worst. Thank goodness Ingrid is doing better, but poor Rolf. . . ."

Dad returned to my bedside. Seated in a chair, he tried to concentrate on some reading while I drifted in and out of consciousness, finding little peace in either state. It was difficult for Dad to just sit there and not be able to do more than read my charts and consult with the doctors. For one of the first times in Dad's life, all his knowledge and abilities couldn't help the one patient he cared most about—his son. He was powerless to do anything, and that had to be torturing him.

While tossing and turning, I suddenly blurted out, "Dad, I've got to get dressed!"

"Dressed for what, Rolf?"

"The game! I've got to get into the game. Coach just called for the field-goal unit!"

"That's not possible. Rolf, you're having a dream."

"But Coach needs me in there. He's depending on me!" I said insistently.

"Rolf, wake up, you're in a hospital bed."

"Who put me here?" I asked, a bit mystified.

"You're in the hospital. The Chargers are playing Seattle today, but you're not going to be there."

"Oh."

My head slumped back onto my pillow. I was really confused. The morphine was playing tricks with my mind.

Later that morning, I was taken for a chest X-ray. My lungs did not look good, which meant the diuretic was acting slower than the doctors hoped.

I looked into a mirror, and my dark eyes portrayed a sadness within my soul. My life had forever changed that evening when Dr. Peskin ordered emergency surgery. I had lost more than half of my colon; I had lost the innocence of youth. Instead of worrying about football games and Friday night dates and hanging out at the beach, I was worrying about IV lines and major surgery and pondering some frightening questions. *Will I survive? If I do, what kind of life will I have? Will I ever be able to play sports again? Will I ever enjoy a run on the beach or a swim in the ocean?*

The questions were overwhelming, and I dared not dwell on them. My thoughts returned to the present just as intern Cammy Mowery came over to check my vital signs.

"This is a total bummer," I said to Dr. Mowery. "I mean, look at me."

Cammy smiled. "You don't look so bad. You just think you do. The drugs are causing the acne, and we can wash your hair today. That should help."

Since the Trauma Unit had no television sets, Dad brought one in so we could watch the Chargers play Seattle. Mom joined us for the kickoff.

At halftime, Dad tried to help me out of bed for a short walk. But the pain of sliding off the bed and standing up was so excruciating that I asked to rest for a moment in a chair first. Dad picked up his camera again.

"Smile!" *Click.*

"Dad! Do you have to?" *Click.*

Those pictures still serve as a gruesome reminder of that difficult time and help me remember how lucky I am today.

"You look better, Rolfie," Dad said. "Remarkably better than five hours ago." The diuretic was starting to do its job.

Sister Act

At five o'clock, Ingrid and I saw each other for the first time since she had arrived at University Hospital five days earlier. An orderly wheeled her into the Trauma Unit, and she was clearly shocked by what she saw.

"Oh, Rolf! I. . . ."

"Ingrid!"

She held my arm against her cheek. "I was going to tell you some good news," said Ingrid, "I'm having my IV removed tomorrow, but after seeing you, what I'm going through seems like nothing."

She searched for a safe subject to talk about.

"Are they treating you okay?" she asked.

"Sometimes yes, sometimes no. It's mostly this place," I said, jerking my head toward the other patients.

We talked for a short time before the orderly arrived to take her back to her room. "If there is anything I can do for you, I should be out soon," said Ingrid.

"Just coming to visit was wonderful," I replied.

Later, Mom and Dad helped me out of bed and into a wheelchair. Dad pushed me around the hospital halls, tubes and bottles accompanying us all the way. The journey lasted ten minutes. *Rolf looks weak, but he's steadily improving*, Dad thought, trying to convince himself.

Dr. Peskin was thinking along the same lines. "I think the best thing we can do is to let nature take its course," he told Dad in the hallway. "We still need more time."

"What do the latest blood and urine samples show?" asked Dad.

"Well, actually there are some disturbing lab results," said Dr. Peskin. "It appears *E. coli* and several other bacteria are present in abundance in his bloodstream. We're still trying to find the source of the infection."

Monday, October 22
10 a.m.

At mid-morning, the sutures were examined by Dr. Peskin, and my twelve-inch incision was irrigated and cleaned with Betadine. To me, the ugly wound still appeared open, up to a half-inch in some areas. But Dr. Peskin pronounced it fine and explained that it would granulate in.

After the surgeon left, I found myself behind the curtain wall with nurse Carla Van Hooten. Several questions had been spinning around my mind for several days, but now I needed to voice them. Carla had earned my trust, and I really needed someone to talk to.

"Is there hope?" I asked. "Am I going to make it?"

"What do you mean, is there hope?" she replied, feigning annoyance.

"They're talking about taking out the stitches. That must mean I'm going to get out of here soon."

"Could be."

"But Carla, if that's true, then why do I still hurt so much?"

"Time," she said emphatically. "It takes time to heal."

I continued to receive Lasix, the diuretic that was purging my system of fluids. I was being weaned off Prednisone, but I still needed regular shots of morphine to take the bite off the pain.

The next morning, Dad came in just as I was completing my morning walk.

"You look distressed," said Dad.

"I'm exhausted," I panted. "We just walked fifteen yards, and if I can't do that without getting tired. . . ."

Mom interrupted my thoughts.

"Rolf, you're shaking."

She was right. Suddenly, my teeth began chattering violently and my body began shaking uncontrollably. My parents eased me back into bed while I cried out in pain. It felt like my incision was being ripped open from top to bottom.

Dad quickly called for the nurse while I begged Mom for more blankets. I was freezing. But when the nurse arrived, she recognized my symptoms and took a quick check of my temperature. It had risen to 103 degrees, confirming that I was spiking a fever.

Little did I know that I would repeat those horrible chills and fever spikes countless times over the next ten days. Although I would get very cold, my temperature would rise to 103 or 104 degrees—dangerously high. The nurses would labor to bring my temperature down as quickly as they could, but each episode lasted thirty minutes or more and left me physically exhausted—and terribly frightened.

What was happening to me?

I was given more morphine, and as my shaking subsided, I drifted off into fitful sleep. By afternoon, my white blood count had dropped to an encouraging 10,900, barely above the normal 10,000 and way down from 44,500 two days earlier. Whatever internal infection I had seemed to be under control.

Then Ingrid dropped by, all excited because her IV had been removed and because she was eating solid food again.

"But the really good news is that I get to go home tomorrow," she said.

"Great! I wish I was going with you." I really meant it.

Suddenly, my breathing became very labored, and I could sense Ingrid's concern.

"Rolf, are you okay?"

"I'm not sure. It's like I'm not getting enough air. . . ."

Ingrid quickly moved her wheelchair toward the nurses' desk, where Sheana Funkhauser had just come on duty.

"Nurse! Nurse! Rolf's having a hard time breathing!"

Sheana ran to my bed and immediately reinstalled the nasal prongs into my nostrils. The direct flow of oxygen slowly restored my breathing to normal.

"Easy to fix, fortunately," said Sheana. She looked at my chart and noticed that over the weekend my oxygen mask had been removed. "I wonder why they did that?" she asked out loud. "The surgery wasn't that long ago."

"Maybe they thought he was getting better," Ingrid offered.

"Rolf *is* getting better, but it's always a good idea to be a little conservative in these kind of things."

When the nurse left, I confided several thoughts to Ingrid.

"Oh, Ingrid, I hate this place. I can't tell if it's night or day. The lights are always on, and I always seem to have people checking up on me. I hate the noises, the smells, and being in the same room with all these sick people."

As if on cue, the Samoan woman let out a low moan, followed by a gasping shriek.

"Just like that!" I said. "I know she's in pain, but it's hard to have to hear it all the time."

That night, Mom called and said that my brother, Steve, had just landed at the airport and would drop by in the morning. She also called Germany and learned that her father was not doing well.

"Opa could die soon," said Mom. She paused as she considered her next words. "We're letting our consciences be our guides, so we won't decide until tomorrow night whether I'll be going to Germany and if Dad will fly to Copenhagen. If you or Ingrid need us, we won't go, even if that means not being able to say goodbye to Opa."

"I *want* you to see Opa," I pleaded. "And I *want* Dad to speak in Copenhagen because they're counting on him. I mean that. I'm getting better, and besides, Steve will be here."

When our conversation ended, I carefully placed the phone on the cradle and stared at the ceiling. I was messing up a lot of people's lives, and I didn't feel good about it.

CHAPTER 8

He Ain't Heavy

Tuesday, October 23
9 a.m.

Five days after my surgery, my brother, Steve, arrived at the
hospital and was escorted to the ICU. Even though we had
been competitive brothers as youngsters, we had matured and
put all that behind us.

"Thanks for coming, buddy," I said, as I put my left hand
over Steve's. "I appreciate you taking time off from med school
and coming all the way out from Cleveland."

"I *had* to come," said Steve. "There's no way I could have
stayed away, especially with Mom and Dad leaving for
Europe."

"You came just in time," I continued. "There are some
good people here, including a couple of the nurses, but it's been
no picnic. I've had it up to here with docs and nurses sticking
needles in me."

The worst was when they needed arterial blood to check
my carbon dioxide and oxygen levels. Normally when you give
blood, a nurse finds a vein in the crick of your arm, gives it a
quick stab, and then fills a syringe with blood. But arterial
blood must be drawn from an artery, and the best place to find
one is in your wrist, underneath a protective layer of tendons

and muscle.

I remember the first time a nurse drew arterial blood out of my left wrist. Instead of a fast jab, she poked the needle in my wrist and then moved it around until she found the artery. It felt like a thin poker was tearing my flesh apart. (The procedure left scars on both wrists that I carry to this day.)

After relating that story, I told Steve about the thrice-a-day examinations. It was getting to be a bit much.

"You have to remember, Rolf, that University Hospital is a teaching hospital. You've got to expect that residents and interns without a lot of experience will be coming by to see you."

"Yeah, I know. But why do I have to be the guinea pig? Why can't they coordinate their visits so I don't have to have my dressings taken on and off all day? Don't they know it hurts?"

"Tell you what," said Steve. "Let me see what I can do."

My brother used the telephone near the elevator to call Dr. Peskin.

When he finally got through, Dr. Peskin asked Steve for an evaluation. "He seems quite lucid, but he's awfully depressed," said Steve. "That worries me more than the way he looks. And he's complaining about the residents and interns dropping by all the time. Is there something you can do about that?"

Dr. Peskin said he'd try to minimize the intrusions. As for my depression, he was taking a wait-and-see attitude.

In mid-afternoon, I had to go to the bathroom. I put my arm around nurse Sheana and slowly hobbled over to the nearby toilet.

But just past the nurses' station, I lost control and had an accident. The smelly brown mess leaked down my leg and onto the floor.

"I can't stand it!" I said angrily. "I hate this!"

"Don't get upset," Sheana said. "You *are* sick, and when

you're sick, these things happen. It's nothing to get worried about."

"But Sheana, it's so humiliating."

When she put me to bed, I noticed that the front of her uniform was soiled. Enough was enough! I turned my face to the wall, tears streaming down my cheek, while I heard Sheana and two other nurses mop up the floor. *Dear God, when will this all end?*

At 9 p.m., Dad visited the Trauma Unit. Mom stayed home to finish packing, as both would be leaving in the morning on separate flights to Europe.

"I had kind of a shaky afternoon, Dad. But I'll be okay now that Steve is here."

"Well, you look pretty good now," he said, noticing that the puffiness around my face and neck had dissipated. The diuretics had done their job, and I was back to my "frail and gaunt" stage again.

"Since your condition has stabilized, Mom is going to Munich tomorrow, while I fly to Copenhagen. I hope you understand why we have to go."

"Dad, I do. I'll be fine. Really."

Wednesday, October 24
10:30 a.m.

The first key to the mystery of my unexplained fevers was revealed this morning. The results of the blood cultures, taken from the previous day, indicated the presence again of gram negative organisms. Somehow, *E. coli* bacteria were getting back into my bloodstream. The news raised two questions: From where were the organisms originating? And, what antibiotics would be effective?

Early that afternoon I started having a series of watery, green-colored bowel movements, most of which were followed by severe cramping.

I slept reasonably well that night, but when I got up in

the morning, I had another bad accident on the way to the toilet. Carla Van Hooten took my temperature, and it had risen three degrees (to 102) after my bathroom trek.

"What's the use, Carla? Tell me, what's the use?" I said, feeling sorry for myself again.

"This is a tough time, Rolf."

"I'm tired of being a bother and messing on floors. I must be such a pain."

"You're not a pain," she said. "We'll get through this. Just be patient."

"It's not easy from where I am."

"Look, it may seem like you've been in this place forever, but how long has it been since you were admitted? Two weeks? And how long since your surgery? One week?"

I didn't answer her. The pain in my gut felt as though someone was tickling me with a sharp knife.

A bit later, Steve arrived and read my chart while standing at the foot of my bed. He stopped when he saw the notation about the *E. coli* in my blood.

"Have you had any more fevers?" he asked.

"Yes," I answered. "Why?"

"Well, it says here you have bacteria in your system that you shouldn't have."

"What does that mean?"

"It means that you either have an abscess or there is a leak in the anastomosis line. Whatever it is, we need to find out right away. Rolf, this is the complication that causes people to die from this operation. If we can't get a handle on the bacteria, they will multiply so rapidly that they can overcome your body's defense system very quickly."

Steve added that it was critical to identity the organisms and find the appropriate antibiotics. He explained that the bacteria can quickly become resistant, and, as a result, the antibiotics must be continually changed. "This is where we really have to rely on the hospital's infectious disease department," Steve commented.

"Are they good?"

"Dad said they're the best around," replied Steve. "I also see here that Peskin has scheduled you for another ultrasound. I'm going to talk to him to see if he's considered doing a dye study on you. That's where they inject methylene blue into your system, and together with the ultrasound, they'll be able to find out if you have a leak in your bowel or if there is a pocket of infection somewhere."

I could tell Steve was very concerned, and his changed demeanor was unsettling for me, as well. He decided to escort me to the diagnostic room. Clearly worried, he kept a brotherly hand on my shoulder as the orderly pushed my gurney to the ultrasound room.

"This won't hurt, Rolf. I promise."

Three hours later, I was back in the ICU. The tests hadn't hurt much, but my stomach still felt awful. I was greeted by a doctor from the infectious disease unit and a new series of antibiotics for my IV. I was encouraged that they seemed to be on top of the situation, but what lifted my spirits more was seeing a sackful of mail in the corner. Although I was too weak to open any of the letters, just the thought of so many people taking the time to write a card and encourage me was something.

Thursday, October 25
8:30 a.m.

Drs. Peskin, Griffith and Mowery arrived together on morning rounds.

"The nurses tell me you won't take the Maalox, which could help your gas pains," said Dr. Peskin with a slight smile.

"I tried, but that stuff makes me gag. Ever since I was young, I've had a hard time taking pills or medication. Now that I'm sick, it's impossible."

"I understand, Rolf. I'm like that myself, but it could

really help," said Dr. Peskin.

"Doesn't matter. I still can't get it down."

Knowing he was licked, Dr. Peskin changed the subject.

"The ultrasound scan of your abdomen doesn't show anything, but we do know something's not functioning properly. Normally, at this stage after surgery, a patient's systems are beginning to return to normal."

But in my case, something was clearly wrong. Besides the very loose stools, I was spiking high fevers, and tests were detecting an increasing number of bacteria in my blood. Something had to be wrong with the anastomosis.

"Dr. Peskin, what's going on?" I asked.

"Well, we're going to have to go back in and find out," said the doctor matter-of-factly.

"You mean another surgery just like the first one? *Laying me open again?*"

"There's something clearly wrong. We have to find out what it is and fix it. I can only tell you that a week after surgery, you should be getting better, not worse."

As my surgeon left the room, a myriad of thoughts swirled through my mind. I couldn't understand—a full week after surgery—why I wasn't improving. Now I was going to have to face surgery all over again: general anesthesia, the scalpel, the dreaded NG tube—more morphine. It was back to square one again. I wondered if I could get myself up for a second operation.

Really wondered . . . but I didn't have a choice.

Later that afternoon, I was napping when Jim Adkins dropped by. Sheana Funkhauser motioned him aside.

"He's as down as I've seen him since he's been here," the nurse confided. "He keeps talking about dying. He's one depressed fellow."

"Did something happen?" asked Jim. "What caused him to start feeling this way?" asked the concerned minister.

"The doctors told him they need to operate again to find

out what's going on. But even without that news, it's not hard to figure out why he's so miserable. His white blood count has shot way up again, indicating there's still some major infection going on. Something is definitely wrong."

Jim shook his head. He had seen my faith grow over the past year, but he must have wondered if I was strong enough to survive this latest news. I had been attending Jim's church regularly during the off-season, and I never missed the Charger team chapels, where Jim sometimes spoke.

"Yesterday, he told me he was losing his will to fight," Sheana continued. "Now, he's telling me that he doesn't care anymore. He felt he had no dignity left, and he didn't want to be a burden to the nursing staff. He also said he had always felt in control of himself, until now. He believes that if this is the time that the Lord wants him, he is ready," said Sheana, who was a strong Christian herself.

They moved closer to my bed, and then Sheana leaned over. "Rolf . . . you have a visitor."

My eyes slowly flickered open. "Hey, Jim, how are you?" I muttered.

"The question is, how are *you*, Rolf? Sheana tells me you've been struggling a bit."

"Maybe so. There's not really much to feel good about these days." My voice cracked as I avoided eye contact with Jim.

"I hope you realize that a lot of people care about you and are praying for your recovery."

The tears were flowing freely down my cheeks, and I turned my head away. "Jim, I don't deserve those prayers. God seems so far away. I feel like He's left me alone to struggle against this disease by myself, and right now, I don't feel like fighting. I've also been a jerk to a lot of nice people."

"What do you mean?" asked Jim softly.

"Remember Helen, the nurse from upstairs? Well, she checked in on me during her break, and all I did was complain to her. I mean, she's one of the nicest, most caring people here, and I was just a jerk."

"I guarantee you Helen understands," said Jim. "She's seen hundreds of people experiencing the toughest things life has to offer. She knows exactly what you're going through, as does Jesus. He created us, and He knows exactly where you are, and He cares so much for you."

Jim then had a question for me. "Rolf, can we all pray together?"

"Sure," I replied. "And Jim, would you pray that I don't lose my will to fight? I need help right now."

I felt broken, and ahead of me I stared into a dark abyss. I really didn't want to die.

The Samoan princess was moaning loudly when Jim bowed his head and led the three of us in prayer. He had to pause several times to be heard, but it didn't matter. When Jim said "Amen," we gave each other a squeeze of the hand, and I thanked him for coming.

Lifting Dead Weight

Ingrid arrived about a half hour after Jim Adkins left.

"Good news," she bubbled. "I'm outta here. I got my walking papers a few minutes ago."

"That's not good news, that's *great* news," I said.

We chitchatted for a short time, and then I dozed off to sleep. I woke up a short time later with an urge to go to the bathroom. Sheana and another nurse helped me cross the room, but then I became dizzy and lost control of my bowels. Just before I slumped to the floor, the nurses carried my dead-weight, 135-pound body back to bed. They tried to comfort my fears and frustration, but I was humiliated and frightened, all at the same time.

My doctors were alerted to the latest episode, as was Steve. Just before midnight, San Diego time, Steve received a phone call from Dad in Copenhagen.

"Dad, I'm afraid Rolf has taken a turn for the worse. It looks like he has real bad sepsis. It appears his bowel is leaking somewhere into his abdomen."

"When are they going to operate?"

"It may happen as soon as tomorrow. His fever's been going up and down like a yo-yo. Right now, it's 102 degrees again, and he has those awful shaking chills. We don't think he's in any real danger, but who knows?"

"My God, Steve! I wish we hadn't gone. Mom will be very upset when she hears this."

After hanging up, Dad sat in shock, wondering what was happening to his family. Since it was early morning in Copenhagen, he had an hour before he was scheduled to talk to an international meeting of Zoo Directors, so he called Mom in Tutzing, outside of Munich, to tell her about my condition. Upon hearing the news, she wanted to return to San Diego on the next plane.

"But how is Opa?" he asked.

"Father is not good. Not good at all. He's not expected to pull through this. But what are they saying about Rolf?"

"He's stable at the moment, but they're not sure what the prognosis is," replied Dad. "Marion, there's nothing you can do at home. Why don't you stay there? I'm going to cut my trip short and head back tomorrow morning, right after my talk. That should put me back in San Diego by tomorrow night."

Friday, October 26
Early morning hours

The beginning of my fourth week in University Hospital was a miserable one. The pain was constant, and so were the cramps. The longest period of rest seemed like fifteen minutes.

"I can't take this much more," I told the night nurse.

"The morning is almost here," she said sympathetically. "Things will seem better when it's a new day."

When Drs. Peskin and Griffith came by in the morning, they quickly determined that surgery could not wait.

"We have to go in today," said Dr. Peskin. "Alert Said-man, and then have the operating room staff clear the way! The exploration should begin as soon as possible. And call Steve Benirschke and tell him what's happening."

Within thirty minutes, Steve rushed into the Trauma Unit, unshaven and not wearing socks. It was 10 a.m.

"What's the story?" he asked nurse Carla Van Hooten.

"We put Rolf on some new antibiotics this morning, which seemed to have stabilized him a bit. But he's not very coherent. He's talking a lot of gibberish. He thought I was Sheana when I first walked in."

Steve bent over my bed, his head just inches away from my face. He had to see for himself.

"How ya doing, Rolf?" he asked.

"No! No!" I moaned, violently shaking my head. "Oh, God!"

Steve tried to explain to me that they were going to have to do another operation, but my scrambled mind couldn't comprehend the words he spoke.

"Rolf, listen to me. The anastomosis must have broken down, so you don't have an option. We need to find out what's wrong and correct it right away."

I started to come in out of the fog. "I can't, Steve. I just can't go through all this again."

"It's not an option, Rolf. It just isn't." Steve was firm, but understanding. "You've got to get up one more time. A lot of this depends on your will to fight."

Dr. Peskin walked in and said hello, trying his best to sound cheerful. Then he lifted the surgical dressings and examined the eight-day-old surgical opening.

"I know it's hard right now, but you're going to feel a lot better when it's all done," he said.

"I've heard that before!"

"You will, Rolf," said Steve. "Believe me, you will."

I soon fell asleep, and Ingrid arrived at the hospital. She and Steve called Copenhagen to tell Dad about the news. Steve finally got through to the desk clerk at the hotel, but there was a language barrier. The clerk did speak German, however, so Ingrid, who is fluent in the language, took the phone.

Dad had left word that he was off speaking at the Zoo Director's conference. "It's urgent," Ingrid told the desk clerk. "Please leave a message that his son Rolf is going to go into surgery soon. Ask him to call Steve or Ingrid at University Hospital as soon as he can. *Danke schön*."

I was rolled into the surgery bay at 2 p.m., accompanied by Dr. Saidman, the anesthesiologist. "What, no autographs this time?" he quipped. "You must be losing your popularity."

I looked up at him and said, "Beat the Broncos."

The kid must be losing it, thought the doctor.

But then my autograph *was* wanted. Dr. Mowery handed me a pen and paper and told me to sign it.

"What for?" I asked.

"It's a medical consent form. Routine," she said.

"Okay," I said, as I feebly scribbled my name.

At the bottom of the consent form was a typewritten annotation stating the possibility that the surgery team may have to perform an ileostomy on me.

I was too drugged-out to read it, but if I had been lucid, I would have asked about the odds for such a procedure. I would have wanted to be mentally prepared for such a life-changing operation, just as I would for a game-winning kick. In my fleeting subconscious, however, I thought I was just going to have my gut re-opened to find out what was wrong with me.

The surgery bay—like a walk-in refrigerator—was cold. A nurse covered my shivering body with two blankets as I looked around at all the steel reflecting lights.

"We're going to start the anesthesia now," announced Dr. Saidman. "Name ten players on your team."

"Dan Fouts . . . Charlie Joiner . . . Kellen Winslow . . . Louie Kelcher . . . Hank Bauer . . . ."

I was under.

CHAPTER 9

One More Time

Friday, October 26
4:05 p.m.

The surgical team, headed by Dr. Peskin, didn't waste any time. Using the same incision, they opened me up and peered inside my abdominal cavity. They quickly found the problem. A small leak at the suture line where the ileum and the colon had been reconnected—the same place they had sewed me up eight days ago—had become a big hole. The bacteria that normally lived inside my gut and were useful in digestion were now spilling into my abdomen, creating a life-threatening situation.

No wonder I had been in so much pain and was spiking such high fevers. It was a miracle I had survived to this point; clearly any delay would have been fatal.

Steve was a surgical observer for the first half hour, but finally the tension became unbearable. He retreated to the waiting room to be with Ingrid.

At 5 p.m., Dad called from Copenhagen.

"He's in surgery as we speak," my brother said.

"Well, is there any more news?" My father was hoping for some sign of optimism.

"They appear to have found the problem, Dad. It's a good

thing they went in when they did."

"What did the doctors find?"

"It seems the anastomosis has broken down," said Steve. "From what Peskin says, when they sewed the two ends closed after the resection, it was like sewing two sponges together. Apparently, the combination of the disease and the long period of time on Prednisone must have caused the sutures to come apart. The last week must have been hell on him. I don't know how he's made it."

"My God," said my dad, mulling this bit of information around in his mind. My father and brother were thinking the same thing: *Rolf is going to come out of the operating room with an ostomy.*

Steve broke the long pause. "Dad, I think it's inevitable. If Rolf survives, he's going to be wearing a bag."

"That's okay; we can deal with that," Dad replied. "He just has to get through this operation, which is why the next forty-eight hours are critical. From what you've said, the situation is touch and go. You can't believe how far away and helpless I feel right now here in Copenhagen."

"I feel helpless, too, Dad, and I can see the operating room from where I'm calling you from. We'll get back in touch as soon as we have any news."

Down the hall, Dr. Peskin was continuing to probe my abdominal cavity.

"My God, look at the infection!" exclaimed Dr. Peskin. "We caught it just in time. Any longer, and the Chargers would have been looking for a new kicker."

"Nurse, more suction," said Dr. Griffith, as the ostomy procedure began.

The doctors carefully snipped another inch off the end of my ileum, then began plotting their next move: cutting an opening for the stoma into my right side. Normally, ostomy surgeries are well-planned, and careful attention is paid to where the stoma hole is cut on the body. Stomas are placed below the belt line so that the appliances collecting fecal waste are out of the way and the patient's belt does not restrict the opening.

For reasons I cannot fathom to this day, my stoma was inadvertently placed *above* my belt line. Perhaps the doctors weren't paying close attention because my surgery was performed under such emergency conditions, or perhaps the doctors just miscalculated. At any rate, the surgeons took the remaining part of my ileum and sewed it into the opening, creating the ileostomy.

The doctors had a second problem—what to do with the non-functioning colon. Rather than leave what was left of my colon floating around in my abdomen, they created a second small opening on my left side and attached the transverse colon to it. Although this second stoma looked the same as my ileostomy, it would become a non-functioning opening. I would, nonetheless, be obligated to wear a small bag to collect mucus sloughing off the lining of the remaining colon.

It took the doctors more than four hours to complete the complex and tricky surgery. When my midsection was ready to be closed up, they employed a novel way of suturing the stomach. In addition to the traditional string stitches, the doctors sewed me together with thirteen "piano wire" sutures. The heavy-gauge wire was inserted on one side of the wound, brought underneath the incision to the other side of the wound, and then twisted together. The tie-offs extended nearly two inches above my stomach.

Yet the wire sutures did not completely close the wound. A nearly one-inch gap still existed at the lower part of the incision, which doctors stuffed with dressing dipped in Betadine. These dressings would have to be changed twice a day, and the painful process would take my breath away each time the doctor repacked the wound.

Post-Op

At 8:30 p.m., Steve and Ingrid called my father in Copenhagen, where it was 5:30 a.m. It made no difference; Dad hadn't slept all night. He grabbed the phone on the first ring, but the connection was lousy.

"Dad, it's us with good news!" exclaimed Ingrid.

"Thank God," said Dad, as he slumped back on the bed.

Steve took the phone. "Rolf just came out of surgery. He's not totally out of the woods yet, but Peskin says everything went well in the operating room. He needed three blood transfusions, but he's doing okay."

"Did they have to do an ileostomy?"

"Yes. It ended up being what we thought. He's going to be one sore guy when he comes around, which should be in an hour or so. He's been in post-op for ten minutes now."

"That's good news," said Dad. "I'm leaving for the airport in a few hours, and if all goes well, I'll be back about 7 o'clock tomorrow night. I'll call Mom with the update. Now that Rolf has survived the operation and I'm coming home early, I'll tell her to stay in Tutzing until she's ready to leave."

In the recovery room, I slept quietly on my back as the anesthesia slowly wore off. A total of nine devices were attached to my body. Besides the usual IV lines and Foley catheter to my bladder, two rubber catheters called "Red Robinsons" had been inserted next to my incision to irrigate the abdominal cavity. Near the bottom of the incision, two larger rubber catheters, called Chaffin-Pratt drains, were removing excess fluids.

I was moved to the Trauma Unit just after 11 p.m., about the same time television and radio stations around San Diego were leading their newscasts with information about my emergency surgery. I was listed in "critical condition," the reports said, but neither the hospital nor the family were releasing further details.

Nurse Sheana Funkhauser greeted me as the gurney was

rolled into the Trauma Unit.

"It's great to see you. We prayed that you would be brought back to us safely," she said. "Seeing you is God's answer to prayer."

I managed to say her name—"Sheana"—before several pairs of hands carefully slid me off the cart and onto my bed. I soon fell asleep, unaware that my life would never be the same.

Saturday, October 27
7:30 a.m.

Drs. Peskin, Griffith and Mowery were all back early, as was Steve. They examined the long ugly wound that started just under my sternum and traveled past my belly button to just above the pubic bone. The large wire sutures added a sur-real Frankenstein look.

At this point, I was far too drowsy to know or care what was going on.

"Can you hear me, Rolf?" asked Dr. Peskin.

I muttered something, but it was apparent I was a million miles away.

"Hang in there, buddy," said Steve, clutching my hand.

Not until the early afternoon did I finally awake from my drug-induced stupor. When my eyes focused, I saw Ingrid smiling at me.

"Hi there, good looking," she chirped. "Dad is on his way home."

"That's great," I said, my lips cracking. "It seems like a long time since I've seen him or Mom."

"Well, Mom is going to stay a while longer with Opa. I know it seems a lot longer to you, but they only left on Wednesday."

"And today is. . . ."

"Saturday. That's four days ago."

Steve joined Ingrid at the side of my bed.

"Hey, Rolf. You're looking a heckuva lot better now than you did this morning."

"But I feel awful. It's like I'm burning up inside. It hurts more than it did yesterday or the day before. And I can't believe they sewed me up with wire! How are they going to get them out?"

Steve smiled. "Don't worry about that now. It won't be easy, but they'll come out okay. Actually, those wire sutures will be the least of your problems."

"What do you mean?" I asked, fearing the worst.

"Rolf, they had to give you an ostomy last night to save your life."

I stared at Steve and Ingrid, a thousand thoughts careening around my brain. *This can't be happening. He must be joking. There's some mistake. Not me.* I could feel my breathing quicken and my face flush. I stared at my hands resting on the covers. I couldn't lift them and face the truth.

You mean I'll never sit on the toilet again to go to the bathroom? You mean for the rest of my life I'll be crapping into these bags hanging on the side of my body?

Steve broke the silence for me.

"They didn't tell you before the surgery because they didn't know for sure you would need one. In all honesty, Rolf, they should have done an ostomy nine days ago during the first surgery. I think they made a poor decision, one that unfortunately caused you to go through a lot of suffering and put your life at risk."

I continued to stare at my hands.

"I'm sure Peskin didn't know exactly what he was going to do until he opened you up again yesterday," continued Steve. "Then he did what he *had* to do."

The reality was slowly sinking in.

Steve and Ingrid left at 10 p.m. to go pick up Dad at Lindbergh Field. My father hadn't slept for more than twenty-four hours when my brother and sister greeted him at the airport.

"It's so good to be back," he said, hurrying toward the baggage claim. "So how is Rolf?"

"It's obvious that the second surgery, so soon after the first one, has been awfully tough on his system," said Steve.

Dad asked how my spirits were.

"He's really down," said Ingrid. "He keeps talking about how hopeless it all is."

"That's not unexpected for what he's gone through," said Dad. "Remember, Rolf's been fighting this disease for more than a year. I don't think any of us realize how difficult the past twelve months have been for him. He's tried his best to deal with this all by himself and not let us know how much it hurt. And now, after all this surgery and the assault on his dignity and pride, we're going to have to really try to lift his spirits. None of us can possibly know what it's like to live with an ileostomy. But right now, he's still in a day-to-day struggle to live."

Dad's words fell on Steve and Ingrid like a wet blanket. They hopped in the car for the short drive to the hospital so Dad could make a quick check on his sleeping son.

"Hello, Dr. Benirschke," said the night nurse at the desk. "Rolf's sleeping. It's the first time he's really slept all day."

"Let him be. I just want to see him for myself." Dad lingered for a moment in the darkened ICU, fighting back tears. It had killed him to be away, and now that he saw his son hooked up to all the different machines, the enormity of the situation hit him hard.

Sunday, October 28
8 a.m.

It was like music to my ears to hear that authoritative, full-of-energy voice greet the nurse on duty. "Where's my son?" asked Dad, and in a moment, my father pulled back the curtain partition.

"Hi, Dad. It's so good to see you," I whispered through the discomfort of the NG tube in my nose and throat.

"The feeling is mutual, Rolf." He wore a gauze mask to protect me from the cold he had caught while riding airplanes for sixteen hours.

Dad squeezed my leg, and our eyes met. Within seconds, tears welled up in his eyes. I could count the number of times that I'd seen Dad cry before. As if a bit ashamed for this emotional display, he turned away from the bed.

"It's okay, Dad."

"I know. Your mother feels very badly that she's not here, too, but I told her you're getting better, and that she needed to be with Opa."

"How is Opa?"

"Not well, but stable. In any event, Mom will be back Thursday."

Dad had brought his work with him, and after scanning my chart and talking briefly about his trip, he settled down in the chair beside my bed and began reading.

"Dad?" I said, interrupting his concentration.

"Yes, Rolf."

"I've missed you. I feel like this place is for the dying, not the living. And the nurses here—except for Sheana and Carla—are too busy or too businesslike. They don't seem to really care."

"Rolf, it's hard for them. They're exposed to so much that they almost need to detach themselves just to get by. But don't worry. I'm going to stick around here all day, not only to make up for lost time, but to see for myself what your care is like."

Dad changed the subject. "Steve is returning to Cleveland tonight. He has to get back to medical school. Ingrid is home cleaning and doing laundry, but she will stop by soon."

I recoiled on the bed as another wave of pain hit me like a hard punch to the stomach. "Oh, God!" I cried out, as I twisted the bed sheet in my hands.

Drs. Peskin and Griffith, both wearing masks, arrived on rounds shortly before noon. They shook hands with Dad and spent a few minutes examining my chart. When they moved closer to my bed, Dad spoke in a concerned voice:

"He's in a lot of pain. It ebbs and flows, but when it's there, it's very powerful."

"We'll get him another shot of morphine," said Dr. Peskin.

"Not more morphine," I moaned. While morphine cut some of the pain, it also caused anxiety and weird hallucinations for me.

"There's no need to be a hero, Rolf. Small amounts of morphine will help," said Dr. Peskin, as he made a notation on my chart.

"His lungs are clear," Dr. Griffith said, "which is a good sign. He also seems to be breathing better."

"The spiking fevers are most likely due to pockets of bacteria that are still getting released into your system," said Dr. Peskin, as he motioned Dad toward the nurses' station. Once there, he spoke softly out of earshot.

"Obviously, the next couple of days are crucial," whispered Dr. Peskin gravely. "He is not home free yet. But if we can weather the next few days without a crisis—if we can somehow keep Rolf's spirits up—the worst will be behind us."

"Gerald, he keeps talking about the poor quality of nursing care here on weekends."

"Sad to say, he's not the first to comment on that. I'll rattle some cages again to see what I can do. And you might do the same. But it's probably not going to have much of an effect unless we can prove gross negligence or improper procedure."

Dad turned my bed so that we could watch that afternoon's game between the Chargers and the Los Angeles Rams at the Coliseum.

"They're floundering without you," said Dr. Peskin, trying to raise my spirits.

"Thanks, Doc, but I don't think so. They're doing just

fine," I said, feeling sorry for myself.

Dad turned to Dr. Peskin and said, "The Chargers have won two games and lost one without Rolf. When he was with them in September, they were three and one. But they have missed him as a kicker, and they're giving a new man a try today. I can't think of his name."

"Mike Wood," I interrupted, almost smiling. "Dad, I didn't think you followed the Chargers that closely."

"I had a lot of time on the plane," he said sheepishly.

Apparently, Roy Gerela had booted his way out of a job, so the Chargers were giving free agent Mike Wood a shot. He had a good game against the Rams, kicking two field goals and four of five extra points. The Chargers also played well, crushing the Rams, 40-16.

Late in the game, I couldn't keep my eyes open.

"Get some sleep, Rolf," said Dad. "You need it . . . we all need it."

When I awoke a couple of hours later, Ingrid and Steve were talking with Dad outside the partition. When they heard me stir, they pulled back the curtain.

"Hey, buddy," said Steve. "I wanted to say goodbye before I took the red-eye to Cleveland tonight. How about one more walk before I go?"

All three of them helped me out of the bed, and we shuffled for five minutes down the length of the trauma center. After hoisting me back into bed, they assisted me with my breathing exercises.

I looked at my brother. "You being here has meant a lot to me, more than I can ever express to you, Steve. And I know you made it easier for Mom and Dad, too. I hope I didn't cause you to miss too much school."

"It's no big deal, Rolf. It was kind of like on-the-job training anyway. Besides, I would have been useless anyway trying to study and keep up with my classes while you were going through this."

I smiled and squeezed his hand again.

Dad turned to Steve and Ingrid. "Let Rolf get some more sleep. And Rolf, Ingrid and I have been invited for dinner at Flo and Wayne Kennedy's house. We'll stop by after we're done, okay?"

No sooner had they left when a nurse came to remove the dressing on my large abdominal incision. The doctor wanted the wound exposed to air to quicken the healing process. After she left, I gazed at my horribly cut-up stomach, and tears of self-pity welled up in my eyes.

As if to make matters worse, I was suddenly seized again by shaking chills. Because of my exposed chest wound, I couldn't move at all, which meant I was unable to reach the nurse call button or the telephone. I was helpless—like a turtle on its back. I tried calling for a nurse, but I didn't have the strength to raise my voice.

I became panicked, frightened that I would begin shaking and tear out all of my sutures. Fifteen minutes passed before someone finally heard my plaintive cry.

I was still shaking violently when the nurse found me.

"I called and no one came," I cried with terror in my voice. "Where were you?"

"Sorry," replied the icy voice, "but we have a lot of sick people here who need tending to. Besides, I was on dinner break."

On dinner break! What if something had happened?!

My fever had soared to 104.3, and my resting pulse was 150. The nurse became concerned and called for an orderly. They gave me some Tylenol and, together, lifted me onto a cool water-filled blanket to try to control my temperature.

At the same time, I felt ice cold and begged for some warm blankets. My wound was hastily covered, and I lay there shaking, teeth chattering, as scared and helpless as I'd ever been in my life.

"Please call Dr. Peskin," I pleaded. "And please try to

reach my father."

"It's Sunday night," she said coldly. "I hate to call a doctor on Sunday night. The Tylenol will help."

"Okay, call my father then!"

"We tried, but there's no one home."

Where did he say he and Ingrid were eating dinner?

"Keep trying, please!" I was getting frantic. This was the most frightened I had been since entering the hospital.

She left to attend to another patient, but matters got worse. I began another bout of shaking chills, and suddenly something exploded off one of the machines above my head, sounding like a gun had gone off.

I didn't know what had happened, but in my anxious state I figured it had to be serious. I frantically tried getting the nurse's attention, but once again I was unsuccessful. When she finally dropped by twenty minutes later, she offered no explanation or words of sympathy.

I implored her to try to reach Dad once more, but it was almost an hour later before they found him. He had just gotten home from dinner.

When my father and sister finally arrived at 9 p.m., they found me in a state of virtual panic. I broke down with relief when they walked in.

"It was horrible!" I sobbed uncontrollably. "These people don't care! Dad, don't leave me alone again, please!"

"Easy, Rolf, easy. Things will be better now, we're here."

Dad went to the nurses' desk and called Dr. Peskin at home.

"He's not doing well, Gerald. Something has scared him terribly, and his fever is up again. It's like he's seen a ghost!"

"I'll come right away," the surgeon assured him. "I don't like the sound of this."

When Dad came back, I was still upset.

"Dad, I was terrified and helpless. I couldn't get anyone to help me! I still feel frightened to be alone."

"I know, Rolf. It shouldn't be like that. I guess they're a little shortstaffed on the weekends. But from now on, we'll be sure that one of us is here—twenty-four hours a day—whenever Carla or Sheana are off duty. We'll put a rotating `watch team' together so this can't happen again."

Dr. Peskin arrived at the Trauma Unit at 9:30. He examined the chart, asked a few questions, and quickly ordered two more units of blood. After a quick check and irrigation of the surgical opening, he announced. "The good news is that the ileostomy is working. The bad news is we still haven't gotten the bacteria in your system under control." He called the head of the infectious disease team at home, and together they decided to be more aggressive with their use of different antibiotics.

Carla Van Hooten arrived for the 10 p.m. shift.

"Oh, Carla," said Ingrid, "Thank God, you're here. Rolf almost came unglued tonight when we were gone. He's so frightened and needs to have someone here that he has confidence in. You're one of the few people."

"Poor guy," Carla responded. "He's going through a lot right now."

"Yes, he sure is."

Monday, October 29
5:30 a.m.

The phone rang at the nurses' station.

"Hello, Carla, this is Dr. Benirschke. I've been up half the night, worrying about Rolf."

"I'm afraid Rolf had a ghastly night, Dr. Benirschke. He hardly slept, and when he did, he was hallucinating and having terrible nightmares. Probably a reaction to the morphine. I've already notified Dr. Peskin, but we're all very concerned."

"I'll be right there."

When my father arrived, I was having another terrible chill, but my temperature was a boiling 104 degrees. Although

I was well-covered by blankets, I felt cold as ice.

"I can't stop shaking, Dad. I can't stop no matter how hard I try. Is this what it's like before you die?"

My father looked into the distance. I could tell he was weighing his words.

"I'm dying, Dad. I know it. You know it. They *all* know it."

"Rolf, stop talking like that," Dad interrupted. "You are *not* dying. Your fever should break shortly. It has to."

But an hour later, the chills were still persisting. "Dad, this is unbelievably awful," I mumbled, hardly coherent. "It's like something is tearing me up inside." My hands were clenched tightly, my teeth were chattering, and my body was shaking visibly.

"Dad?"

"Yes, son?"

"I'm really scared."

I paused and squeezed my eyes shut, then opened them and looked at my father.

"Will you promise me one thing, Dad?"

"Yes. Whatever you want."

"Promise me that you won't let them keep me alive if there is no hope."

A long, agonizing pause came between us.

"I promise . . . no, I won't let them keep you alive."

"Thanks, Dad."

My father blinked away a couple of tears, but he didn't want me to see him cry again.

Ingrid arrived at noon, and Dad left my side for the first time in nearly six hours. In the hallway outside the Trauma Unit, he found Bob Ortman, a longtime sportswriter for the *San Diego Evening Tribune*.

Ortman, who had covered the Chargers since they began playing in San Diego in 1961, had been stopping by University Hospital nearly every day since my first surgery. He was never allowed into the Trauma Unit to see me, but he none-theless picked up information about my condition from a passing nurse or my father. He also wrote me little notes of encouragement, but on this day, the look on my Dad's face told him it was my father who needed the support.

"I hear he's in rough shape," offered Ortman.

Dad couldn't answer. All the pressure of the last two weeks finally got the best of him, and he began to sob big, heaving cries. The sportswriter wrapped his arms around Dad and let him cry. It was several minutes before Dad could speak.

"He just made me promise that I wouldn't keep him alive if it came down to artificial means, or if I thought he was ter-minal," said Dad. "I'm afraid he's losing his will to live."

Ortman continued to console Dad, and over the next few hours, Dr. Peskin visited me several times. He switched anti-biotics again, changed my dressing, and irrigated the surgical wound. Then some good news: My fever finally broke in mid-afternoon, dropping to 100.2, and for the first time in twenty-four hours, my body relaxed. The ordeal, however, had left me exhausted.

Dad, who had regrouped, took the opportunity to bolster my spirits. "I don't know if you are aware of it, Rolf, but a whole bunch of people are donating blood for you through a small blood drive organized by your good friend, John Grantham."

(None of us anticipated that this "small blood drive" would become the largest single-day blood drive in the coun-try. Now known as the San Diego Chargers Blood Drive, the event continues to draw more than 2,000 donors each year.)

"There are a lot of people pulling for you, Rolf," added Ingrid. "Everyone I run into asks me about you and how you're doing. It's got to make you feel great to have so many people behind you."

Before I could answer, Dr. Peskin arrived on his rounds. He motioned for Dad and Ingrid to join him in the hallway outside the ICU.

"I know it's always dangerous to speculate on these things," he said, "but I have good feelings about what has happened here this afternoon."

"That *would* be wonderful," said Dad, his face drawn and sunken from too many days with too little sleep.

"I know it's been a rough couple of weeks," said the surgeon, "but I think we've finally found the right combination of antibiotics. His white blood cell count is beginning to drop noticeably, and it appears the healing process is finally kicking in."

My father and sister went home that night, emotionally whipped after a roller coaster day. But they also felt upbeat, and for the first time in days, they actually got a good night's sleep.

CHAPTER 10

Return to Sender

Tuesday, October 30
9:10 a.m.

I was just waking up after a groggy night of sleep when Jim Adkins stopped in. He lifted my spirits immediately. He wasn't there ten minutes, however, when we were interrupted by an officious hospital administrator in his early thirties. He held a clipboard in his hands.

"Mr. Benirschke?"

"Yes," I replied.

"Mr. Benirschke, if you have a moment, I need to go over some things with you."

"Go ahead."

"It seems that your insurance company has not been responsive, so we've had to turn your account over to a collection agency. The amount is in excess of $20,000."

"What are you talking about?" I asked in utter disbelief. "Look at me. I just had surgery a few days ago. I'm fighting for my life, and you're coming in here asking for money! Forgive me for being a little rude, but just for your information, my dad *does* work here. It's not like I'm going to skip out of the country." My patience was gone.

"Ah, no, I wasn't aware of that," fumbled the administrator. "There must be some mistake here. Perhaps I can go back to my office to straighten it out. . . ."

With that, he turned on his heels and left the ICU.

"Can you believe that, Jim? It's like I'm not a person at all—just a bill to be collected on."

"Now calm down, Rolf. There has to be some kind of explanation."

Just then Dad and Ingrid walked in, and Jim replayed what had just taken place.

"It really was unbelievable," said Jim. "I can't understand what they were thinking."

Dad looked bewildered. He was embarrassed for the behavior of the hospital he was proud to work for, and to have that incident happen to a family member caused his anger to boil. "I'll get to the bottom of this, Rolf. Don't worry about it one minute more."

With that, Dad strode over to the nurses' station and called downstairs to University Hospital's administrative offices.

"This is Dr. Benirschke," he said, his right hand cupped over the receiver. "You will have to excuse me for being a little upset, but rather astonishingly, my son, who is in the Trauma Unit, who is recovering from a second major surgery four days ago, has just been told that his hospital bill has been turned over to a collection agency!"

The excuse—that it was the bill for the anesthesia from my first surgery and that the departments bill separately—didn't hold water. I could almost hear the backpedaling, and when Dad came back to my bed, I knew that was the last time we would be bothered.

"They recognize things should have been handled differently, and that it was an extremely insensitive thing to do under any circumstances," said Dad. But he couldn't hide a faint smile as he spoke. To a doctor, he knew my righteous anger was indicative of one thing: I was getting better.

Wednesday, October 31
8:45 a.m.

I awoke with Dad's secretary, Mary Byrd, sitting in a chair at the foot of my bed. Mary was one of a half-dozen friends who had volunteered to maintain an around-the-clock vigil after my bad night five days earlier. Waking up to her pleasant smile bolstered my spirits, and it was the best I'd felt in weeks. When Dad dropped by after breakfast, he noticed the difference right away.

"That secretary of yours is really special," I grinned.

"I know," he replied. "After what happened, we're just not going to take any chances anymore. I'm afraid the nursing service is just understaffed."

Until now, my preoccupation had been on surviving, but now I knew I needed to begin dealing with the outcome of my surgery. On this morning, I would receive my first ileostomy lesson. Melba Conner, an enterostomal therapy nurse, was scheduled to come in and teach me how it all worked.

Naturally, I felt apprehensive and skeptical. But Melba had an ileostomy of her own, and out of that experience she had become one of the first ET nurses in the country. When she told me she had helped more stoma patients than anyone, she quickly gained my trust. She talked openly about living with an appliance, what I could expect, and how little it would change my life-style.

I still wasn't convinced that I could lead a normal life. "I don't know, Melba. I'm not sure I can handle all of this," I blithely said.

"It's not a question of whether or not you can handle it," she stated firmly. "There is simply no option. Besides, if it weren't for the surgery, you'd be six feet under right now, and you wouldn't have any choice at all."

I stared at her. She had my attention now.

"I know this is a huge change for anybody," she continued, "and maybe more so for someone as athletic as you.

Listen, I don't follow football much, but I've never before heard the nurses talk about a patient getting so much mail. You must have a lot of support out there, so if I were you, I'd be thankful for my blessings."

Melba touched my stoma with her index finger. "Now, let's get to the basics. It's going to seem overwhelming at first, but for now, just watch what I do."

I shook my head and closed my eyes. *If only those bags would disappear.*

"Look, Rolf," she said, as if she was reading my mind. "These appliances are not going away, and you must learn how they work. For the rest of your life, you're going to have to do this. If you learn well, they shouldn't interfere with anything you do."

Melba took my hand and had me touch my left stoma. It was shiny, a bit wet-looking, and dark pink—not unlike the lining of the mouth. The one-inch round stoma protruded from my side about half an inch.

Melba explained that there were no nerve endings in the stoma, so touching it couldn't hurt. The stoma's redness meant it was well vascularized, she continued, adding that I may notice a little blood—perfectly natural and no cause for alarm—when changing the appliance.

"You're lucky to have had your surgery now," she said. "Modern appliances allow you to go five or six days before changing pouches. It wasn't so long ago that virtually nothing was available. Patients would have to fashion their own, using pasted-on water bottles or jerry-built devices. They would leak and smell, and the corrosion on their skin was absolutely horrendous."

"Maybe I am fortunate," I said with a little optimism. . . the first positive thought I'd had in a while.

"You are," she replied. "Now let's change those appliances of yours."

Melba gently removed my old appliances and cleaned the

stomas with soap and water. She was careful not to snag any-thing on my protruding wire sutures or touch my painful incision. Then she patted them dry with a towel and used an alcohol swab to completely clean the area. Next, she cut two stoma-sized holes out of a pair of faceplate barriers that would snugly fit around the stomas to protect my skin from the burn-ing digestive enzymes. Before she attached them, however, she spread a whitish paste around my stomas and waited several minutes for the glue to get tacky.

With the gentleness of someone who had done this thou-sands of times, she carefully fitted the face plates over my stomas one at a time. After adding some paper tape around the face plate borders, she attached the new pouches, which snapped into a secure position. *Voila!* I had new appliances, and the whole process took only ten minutes.

Melba checked the clip on the bag collecting the waste. "When you're up and around, you're going to need to empty your pouch six or seven times a day," she said. "You'll learn very quickly how your digestive system works and when your bag is full."

"How am I going to empty it?" I asked.

Melba led me over to the bathroom and asked me to sit on the toilet. "What you do is take the pouch and drop it between your legs."

I did as she ordered.

"Then undo the clip, and drain the contents right into the bowl. When you're done, take some tissue and clean the end, fold it and clip it, and you're on your way."

"Okay" I replied, "but what about the odor?"

"Not a problem. The new appliances prevent that. The odor is only there when you empty your pouch in the privacy of your own bathroom. That's no different than any normal bowel movement."

We walked back to my bed. Melba had made it all look so effortless. I lay there and wondered whether I'd ever be able to do it so easily.

"Any more questions?" she asked.

"No. The toughest part is accepting this. It's not a pretty sight."

A firm look returned to Melba's face, but then it softened. "Don't worry," she soothed. "You're going to do just fine. There may even be a day when you will look back at all of this and count your blessings. Life has a funny way of getting our attention and teaching us what is really important when we least expect it."

No Resistance

The wire sutures in my abdomen were hurting, and I felt like a pin cushion. For the last few weeks, my body had been poked and pushed and squeezed and shaken in more ways than I thought possible. Doctors and nurses came in and did whatever they wanted . . . and I could offer no resistance.

That afternoon, I was helped out of bed twice for walks around the room. Despite the activity, my fever did not rise. Finally, a good sign. Until now, I had come to associate walks with immediate rising fevers and shaking chills.

Five days after the surgery, the Infectious Disease Department was beginning to win the battle with my massive infection, and there was a noticeable change in my outlook. Dr. Peskin said I could begin taking food orally for the first time since my second surgery, as long as I felt up to it. In the meantime, the get-well cards continued to be delivered by the bagful. The thought of so many Charger fans taking the time to sit down and write me a letter of encouragement really humbled me. I felt undeserving of the attention, but I certainly appreciated the get-well sentiments. I knew that most people suffering from these diseases struggle alone, or have just a few close family members or friends aware of what they are going through.

Meanwhile, Ingrid had been reading through some of the

letters the nurse had just delivered.

"Rolf, you've got to listen to this," she said.

I'm twenty years old, and I had the same surgery you did. In a period of just two months, I went from seemingly perfect health to having a disease and a type of surgery that I had never even heard of before.

The experience made me realize just how fragile life can be. But it also made me aware of how resilient and adaptable the human body is. While feeling sorry for myself after surgery, my father sympathetically pointed out that there were a lot of people worse off than me, and all I had to do was look around at other patients in the hospital. I soon knew he was absolutely right.

My condition suddenly seemed minor compared to others I saw. I treat life and health with much more respect now than before my illness, but the desire to experience life to the fullest is stronger than it's ever been. I know you're probably going through a rough time right now, but I just want you to know that my thoughts are with you. I thought maybe hearing my story might help.

"Wow!" I said. "What a neat guy."

"Here's another," said Ingrid.

You're not alone. I have suffered with IBD for more than ten years. The worst came seven years ago when my small bowel perforated, requiring three operations within two weeks. Rather than reconnect my intestines, my doctor decided on an ostomy.

Those next sixty-one days in bed were very difficult. I'll never forget the first step I took on that sixty-first day, just before passing out. My strength comes from my music. The nurses would help me to the hospital piano—wheelchair, tubes, and all—where I could play with whatever energy I had left. Slowly, each day, I noticed I could play a little longer. At that point, I knew my recovery was certain, even though I was only 120 pounds.

Since then, my wife and I have had two beautiful children, and I have a good job. I have always liked the challenge of mountain climbing and thought I might not be able to do it again. But that's not the case. During my many climbs, I have had to face storms, cold, darkness, mountain walls, ice, snow, getting lost, and running out of water at 14,000 feet. But my confidence has never been better. It means more to me now than ever.

"Is that remarkable or what?" asked Ingrid incredulously.

I tried my best to gulp down the lump in my throat. "It's pretty amazing," I agreed. "How could he do that?"

My ostomy surgery had not yet been publicly announced, but the newspapers and local TV news were busy reporting that I had Crohn's disease. From the letters I was receiving, it was clear that people familiar with the illness recognized that I had probably undergone ostomy surgery as well. I would later discover that there was a network of people, thousands of them, who were out there ready to help.

I closed my eyes and thought of the many walks I had taken around the hospital corridors. I remembered the woman in 11D with the spinal-cord injury; she would never walk again. I remembered seeing the man without arms and legs in 11J, and next door were several patients in oxygen tents with their mouths open and their eyes shut.

Melba was right: I had been feeling sorry for myself. There were people right around me, right on this floor, who were much worse off.

Ingrid interrupted my thoughts. "The entire mail sack is filled with encouraging letters like this. And this is only the start of it. The Chargers are going to bring a couple more bags of mail over to the house tomorrow."

"Ingrid, how am I going to answer all of these people?"

Ingrid smiled. She knew that none of these people expected an answer; they just wanted me to know they cared.

Simply, that they were thinking of me. That was all. I was deeply, deeply moved and humbled by all the attention.

Thursday, November 1
6:30 a.m.

I awoke early to find Mary Byrd reading a book under a small lamp. She had been their all night again.

"Mary, it's so great to have you here," I said.

She smiled. "It's nice to see you finally get some sleep. Besides, now I can say I spent the night with a handsome Charger hero."

I laughed, but then I realized that it had been a long time since I thought about the opposite sex. I had been dating my college girlfriend, Kris, fairly steadily since my sophomore year. But our relationship had been a little rocky for more than a year, partly because she lived in Los Angeles, and partly because we were both still growing up. Although we had begun to go separate ways, Kris had called Mom and Dad to find out how I was on several occasions.

The hospital dietician came by at 8 o'clock and interrupted my thoughts. "Dr. Peskin says you can start eating some regular foods," she said. "Any special requests?"

"Yeah. Scrambled eggs and toast for breakfast. And how about a hamburger and fries for lunch?" I licked my lips with anticipation.

"C'mon, now. Within reason."

"Well, actually, I have this terrible craving for cherry popsicles. Do you think I'm pregnant?" I felt good enough to make a joke.

"I don't know about the pregnant part, but cherry popsicles we can handle. More importantly, that's something you can handle. I also think you'd like some good ol' chicken noodle soup."

"To tell you the truth, it's been so long since I've even thought about food, I've almost forgotten what it tastes like."

Mary Byrd was smiling. "I know how you feel about pepperoni pizzas. When you're ready, I promise I'll bring you one."

At noon, Dad and Carla helped me out of bed for a walk around the room. But the effort exhausted me, and I needed to rest in a nearby chair. As I sat, I was suddenly overcome by the enormity of my situation. I was so weak and frail.

"That was nothing more than a simple walk around the room. So why did it wipe me out?"

Dad looked at me, and I could see his shoulders sag.

"Obviously, your body is still going through it," he answered. "We just have to learn to be a little more patient, Rolf, and not expect too much too soon," he added encouragingly.

Dr. Peskin arrived and announced he was going to start pulling the drains in my abdomen. "Not all the way out, but part way to see how your body handles it."

Dr. Peskin had told me the day before that he was going to move the drains, but he promised it wouldn't hurt. They always tell you that when you're in the hospital.

My four drains, which had been placed around the incision, were about six inches long. They were like flat balloons, about half-an-inch wide. They needed to be pulled out an inch a day. There was only a moment of real pain as each drain was tugged, but the apprehension was always murder!

Encouragingly, there appeared to be no pus or other signs of infection. But ten minutes later, after Dr. Peskin had left the room to continue his rounds, I had a fever spike to 103.5.

"Oh, Rolf," comforted Ingrid. "Let me see if I can find a doctor."

Dr. Peskin quickly answered his pager and came racing back to the Trauma Unit. "I don't believe there's any reason to panic," he said. "Moving the drains has probably seeded some bacteria into your bloodstream, but I anticipate it'll return to normal quickly enough."

The doctor was calm and reassuring and, as always, I felt better after he visited. Dr. Peskin sensed that, and he continued to visit me frequently.

He ordered Valium and Tylenol for me, and then he told Dr. Griffith that the Foley catheter could also be removed after I settled down a bit.

The fever broke about forty-five minutes later.

The "Rolf Watch" continued with Dad succeeding Ingrid and Jim Adkins succeeding Dad. At midnight, when Nurse Carla came on duty, my temperature was a stable 99, my pulse 88. I slept through the night.

When Cammy Mowery came on her rounds early Friday morning, she had me try the blow bottle.

"Excellent," the intern pronounced. "Your lungs are clearing, and, except for the one fever spike yesterday when Dr. Peskin moved the drains, we've kept your fever under control for more than forty-eight hours."

"Is that really that big a deal?" I asked hopefully.

"It may not sound like much to the outside world, but in your situation, it's very significant. We still need you to get out of bed three or four times today. You've got to keep pushing yourself."

I was taking four walks during the day, including two with Ingrid and Sheana. Although there were no more fever spikes that day, I lay tensely in bed after each walk, expecting the worst.

The only discouraging sign was my white blood count, which had risen to 21,300, indicating the infection still wasn't under control. All we could do was wait.

To help distract me, Ingrid opened more mail.

I was humbled to learn that a church had put my name in the Sunday bulletin asking for prayer; another congregation was circulating my name in their prayer chain.

Ingrid read two more letters aloud before noticing that I was nodding off. She put the notes down and said, "Get some sleep. Mom gets back tonight, and I know she'll be anxious to see you. Save some energy for her."

I nodded before dozing off. I thought my most difficult days were behind me, but none of us could have been prepared for what was to happen next.

CHAPTER 11

Not a Third Time

Thursday, November 1
6 p.m.

Dad dropped by my room in time to watch the Chargers on a rare Thursday night edition of "Monday Night Football." After examining my charts, he settled into his now-familiar chair for a relaxed evening of football.

Just before the opening kickoff, the announcers were discussing the key matchups when the camera suddenly panned the Charger's bench. There, holding a homemade sign, was equipment manager Doc Brooks and several Charger players.

The camera zoomed in, and as I made out the words, goose bumps came over me. The sign read:

Get Well Soon, Rolf
We Need You!!

The sign completely surprised us, and my father and I watched in silence as Howard Cosell, the enigmatic ABC announcer, provided the verbal caption to the touching scene. "He's an exemplary young man," said Cosell in his purposeful tone of voice, "and all of us here at ABC join in wishing him a rapid and complete recovery." By this time Dad and I both had tears in our eyes, and we couldn't look at each other. It took several minutes before we could finally speak again.

Sitting in my bed, I understood in a real way that I would probably never kick a football again on the national stage. I had no idea what Cosell's comments meant to the tens of millions of football fans watching the game that evening, but to an emaciated patient lying on his back in San Diego's University Hospital, they will never be forgotten.

After the game, Dad prepared to leave for the airport to pick up Mom.

"Wow, what an evening," he said. "I'm sorry Mom wasn't here to see it, but I'll fill her in. Actually, maybe it's better she missed it. You know how she cries at these things. By the time I pick her up at the airport, it'll be too late to bring her by, but I'm sure she'll want to see you first thing in the morning."

I nodded in agreement. I was already fading from the emotional evening and looking forward to a good night of sleep. Things had been going so well that we had decided to forego the all-night bedside vigils carried out by those on the "Rolf Watch." It would be my first night alone in days, but it felt good not to be a burden on everybody.

Shortly after Dad left, two nurses arrived to get me out of bed for a brief walk.

"Do I have to?" I asked plaintively. "It's late, and I'm really tired."

Secretly, I still feared the fever and shaking chills that had followed so many of my previous laps around the hospital halls.

"The doctors say you should be getting up four to six times a day now," one of the nurses explained. "They also say it's important for you to walk just before bedtime."

Flanked by the two nurses, I trudged to the end of the Trauma Unit and back. They helped me back into bed, where I turned on the television set again, this time to watch a rerun of one of my favorite shows, "M*A*S*H." This had become my routine: walk, climb back into bed at 11 p.m., and turn on "M*A*S*H." On this evening, I knew that the nurse would be coming in with a thermometer to record my rising temperature and check to see if I would again have a shaking chill.

Tonight, it was Carla.

"It's happening again, Carla!" I moaned. "The evening nurses insisted I get out of bed, and now I've got the shakes. When are they going to stop?"

Coupled with a soaring temperature, my body was trembling from the indescribable chill. Even though I knew better, I blamed the nurses for insisting that I walk.

I huddled under the covers, trying to stay warm. Carla gave me Tylenol, applied cold compresses to my forehead, and sat with me for almost an hour until the fever finally broke.

Sheana relieved Carla in the morning, and when she brought my breakfast—oatmeal, milk, and canned peaches— I refused to eat. I couldn't! I nibbled on a piece of dry bread and a few saltines. Although I had begun eating solid foods several days earlier, it was still a struggle.

When Mom and Dad arrived just after 8 a.m., they expected to see a happy, much-improved son.

"Rolfie! How are you?" Mom gently hugged me and stroked my head. "I missed you so much."

When she cupped my face in her hands and pulled away to take her first good look at her youngest son, she saw tears in my eyes.

"Honey," she cried. "What's the matter?"

"It's not getting any better, Mom. They got me out of bed last night after Dad left, and my temperature went crazy again. I can't fight it anymore. It's so discouraging. I was hoping to be doing better when you got back."

"Now, Rolf," Dad interrupted. "You are getting better. Everything is pointing in the right direction. It's just that there will be setbacks. You've got to keep hanging in there."

Out of the Blue

Later that morning, after catching up with Mom and hearing how Opa was doing, I began experiencing cramps in the lower left quadrant of my abdomen. This pain felt different from the other ones, and that worried me.

Sheana called Dr. Peskin. After pondering the problem and reviewing the charts, Dr. Peskin felt there was a strong possibility that a fairly sizable abscess had formed, which would also explain the fever spikes.

Dr. Peskin ordered an ultrasound to see if an abscess could be located. Sure enough, the ultrasound revealed what appeared to be a walled-off pocket of pus.

Dr. Griffith came to see me before noon. He had been given the unpleasant task of informing his sick patient about the finding.

Dr. Griffith wasn't quite sure how to begin, so he went for the direct approach. He had learned that the best way to handle me was to be upfront and honest.

"After reviewing the ultrasound results, Rolf," he began, "it looks as if we've located an abscess. It needs to be drained. The only way we can drain it is to take you back to surgery one more time. We've scheduled you for 3 o'clock this afternoon."

As those last words hung in the air, Dr. Griffith saw me close my eyes, clench my teeth, and turn away. *Not again.*

I couldn't handle another operation. I was on empty. I was done—through. There was nothing left in reserve. Eighteen months of fighting the disease had taken its toll. The countless number of painful tests, the two major surgeries, multiple IVs, needle sticks, blow bottles—I was running on fumes. I didn't want to give up, but I didn't think there was any way I could get up for another operation.

Mom got out of her chair and gently squeezed my hand. What a horrible homecoming for her. She stroked my forehead while deep sobs shook my body.

Having made his announcement, Dr. Griffith walked out of the room quietly, leaving Mom and me to process what had been said. A full five minutes passed before I could even try to speak.

"I can't go through it again, Mom. I just can't. I won't be able to survive another surgery. I just know it."

Mom's response was to squeeze my hands even tighter. If I had looked at her, I would have seen tears in her eyes, too. Her voice, however, never wavered. "Rolf, if another operation is what it's going to take, we'll get through it, too."

I lay there, staring at the clock as the nurses prepped me for one more trip to the operating room. I found myself praying, not with my mind, but from deep within my soul. I explained to God that I had done all I could, and if now was the time to die, I was ready to die. *I know I can't survive the coming surgery*, I prayed. *Lord, if now is the time, okay. It's all in your hands, and I'm ready.* A great peace settled over me as I handed my future over to Him.

Before I was wheeled down to the operating bay, Dr. Griffith manually examined my abdomen again. Strangely, the extreme tenderness had lessened. As he probed further, he wondered if he had missed something, or if the spot he had seen on the film wasn't an abscess after all.

Dr. Griffith decided to order another ultrasound. Using a pen, he marked the spot on my abdomen where the tenderness had been earlier that morning. If he was correct, the X-rays would show the abscess and confirm where he would make the incision.

On the way to Radiology, I showed little or no emotion. I felt like I was out of my body looking down on what was happening. What I was going through was completely out of my control, and I felt content, almost peaceful.

I recognized the Radiology nurse, who tried to act cheerful as she and an orderly gently assisted me onto the table. She applied the cold sonography gel to my abdomen and then began to roll the transducer across my midsection. Strangely, nothing appeared on the monitor. The more she looked, the more curious she became.

"Dr. Griffith," said the nurse, "we are looking for an abscess, right?"

"Yes, I felt one this morning, and we both saw it on the last ultrasound."

"It was on the left side wasn't it?"

"Yes, that's why I marked it."

The nurse continued to explore my abdomen, but she found nothing. After fifteen minutes, Dr. Griffith asked the nurse if they could talk for a minute.

They walked over to a corner of the room.

"There doesn't appear to be anything there," she whispered uncertainly.

"You're right," said Dr. Griffith. "According to the sonography from this morning, there should have been a mass showing. But whatever was there before is gone. I don't understand this at all."

After several more minutes of hushed discussion, Dr. Griffith turned to me, somewhat embarrassed, and said, "Rolf, it looks as if we've made a mistake. You don't appear to have an abscess after all. We're going to cancel surgery."

Was I dreaming? No surgery! Relief like I've never experienced before flooded my body. I closed my eyes and uttered a silent prayer of thanksgiving. I believe God had answered my plea and spared me.

Dr. Peskin arrived a few moments after I was brought back to my room. "The only thing we can figure," he explained, "was that there must have been a gas pocket rather than a fluid mass. When Dr. Griffith examined you manually, the intestine could have shifted and caused you to expel the gas."

That statement didn't sound plausible to me. Perhaps the doctors needed an explanation, but I was convinced that God had divinely intervened. He *knew* I wasn't capable of surviving another surgery.

Dr. Peskin paused. "Now for some more good news. Since your blood gases have been stabilizing, we won't need to do any more arterial blood draws. I'm also going to have the hyperalimentation discontinued, which will make it a lot easier for you to take your walks. The fact is, your ileostomy is functioning beautifully with the solid foods you've been getting. Some bacteria in your system may slip into your bloodstream when you exercise, but it should be downhill from here. Believe me, Rolf, we want to get you out of the ICU and into your private room as soon as possible."

Spirits Improving

I made slow but steady progress over the next two days. My temperature had gotten no higher than 100.9 on Friday, and it remained unchanged on Saturday.

After Dr. Mowery visited me Saturday, she wrote on my chart: "Appetite is improving, along with spirits and attitude. Lungs clear."

Mom and I watched some college football games on TV as she read more mail to me. "I must tell you, Rolfie, you look 100 percent better tonight than when I first saw you yesterday morning."

"I feel better," I said. "Or at least I do until I look down and see those bags. Can you imagine?"

"Rolf, we can't worry about those now. We need to be concentrating on leaving the hospital and getting you back on your feet. Once we're home, we'll worry about the bags. Remember, it takes lots of little steps to climb a mountain, but before you know it, you're right back where you were. For the moment though, we still need to take it one day at a time."

Mom was really something. I knew that with all that had been going on with Ingrid, Opa, and me, it had to be almost too much for anyone to handle. But she was there for me when I needed it most.

Drs. Peskin and Mowery made the rounds together on Sunday morning.

"I'm impressed by your diligence in exercising," Dr. Peskin said smoothly. "The nurses tell me you're becoming a regular in the halls out there."

"I want to get out of this place, if for no other reason than to regain my sanity. I mean, I've been here... how many days?"

"Almost a month," Dr. Mowery answered.

Dr. Peskin had a question. "How'd you like to get out of intensive care and back to the sixth floor?"

"You're kidding!" I bubbled. "Back to a private room? I'd love it. Do you think I'm ready?"

Mom, Dad, and Ingrid arrived at lunch time as an entourage of nurses and orderlies readied me for the move from the Trauma Unit to the sixth floor. One of the nurses was Helen Del Gado.

"You're getting your old room back," she grinned. "And you're not the only one who feels great about that. We're all excited that you're back with us and one step closer to going home."

The whole family watched a pro football game on TV that afternoon, and then it was time for Ingrid to leave for the airport. She was finally returning to New York and her job with a publishing company.

Mom and Dad sensed that we wanted to be alone, so they quietly stepped into the hallway. Ingrid walked to my bed and sat down next to me. "It looks like you're going to be all right, Rolf," she started, not really knowing how to begin.

"I hope so," I said as I squeezed her hands.

This was a tender moment for both of us. "It's hard to imagine after all you've been through that you're going to walk out of this place in a few days," she said.

"It sure didn't look like that a week ago, did it?"

"No, but you made it. I really think you're going to show them what can be done with a second chance."

At that moment, I felt a deep love for Ingrid. Although she had been through a big ordeal herself, she was more concerned about me. We had always understood each other well and gotten along better than most siblings, but I sensed our relationship deepening. Now she was leaving and I was going to miss her. I knew I was lucky to have such a special sister.

After Dad and Ingrid departed, Mom gave me some time to collect my feelings before taking me on another walk around the sixth-floor corridor. By this time, I had set my mind to walking six times daily, adding a lap each day. It was slow going at first, but as each goal was set and accomplished, I felt my confidence build.

I must have looked like a man possessed as I doggedly pushed my IV pole with bags and bottles rattling. Each time I shuffled along the halls in slippers and hospital gown, I counted the laps. The exercise reminded me of many workouts I had put myself through in the past, but this time the stakes were a lot higher.

Learning of Others

On Monday afternoon, Dad walked with me around the corridor. Then he said something that would have a profound effect on my life.

"I'm going to attend a meeting of the National Foundation for Ileitis and Colitis tonight at Scripps Hospital. They're organizing a local chapter."

"No kidding?" I said with real interest. "A lot of the cards and letters I've received have mentioned that organization. It seems like they've done a lot of good for people."

"Yes, they have. I've been talking to a woman named Suzanne Rosenthal, who's here from New York. She can tell you that the publicity you've created is causing their phones to ring off the hook. Your illness has brought the whole subject out of the closet. The NFIC is willing to help you with anything you need during your recovery."

On Tuesday, the last of the abdominal drains was removed, and I was given permission to take my first shower in nearly four weeks.

As I was wheeled to the shower unit, Carla warned me that I might feel light-headed if I stood too long under the hot water. I was a little apprehensive about getting my incision wet, but she assured me the water would be good for it. As I carefully slipped my hospital gown off and eased under the shower, I turned my back to the nozzle. The warm water rolled over my back and onto my abdomen. Once I was satisfied that the water wasn't hurting the open wound, I turned around and let the stream hit my face and chest.

The bloody incision and the two appliances hanging from my body were not a pretty sight—but it didn't matter. I stood there for fifteen minutes and let the warmth of the water penetrate every pore on my body. It was marvelous!

The joy I felt, however, disappeared as quickly as the water that ran down the drain. Back in my room, Mom looked puzzled and alarmed. "What's the matter, Rolf?" she asked.

"I don't know . . . I just feel very down. All of a sudden, I don't know how I'm going to handle all of this." Standing in the shower with my appliances was like—well, a cold shower of reality.

"But things are going so great right now."

"Maybe it's the ostomies. Maybe it's the uncertainty about my future. Maybe it's because Kris hasn't called," referring to my on-again, off-again girlfriend. Although I was improving physically, I continued to brood on the dark side, and I became more and more depressed.

I had become an All-Pro worrier. I worried when my temperature made a relatively insignificant jump from 99.2 to 100.1 following a walk. I worried when a nurse I didn't know drew blood for a lab test. I worried about what I ate. I worried that I wasn't improving fast enough.

I realized later that these sudden fits of depression were natural reactions to the heavy medications and the emotional impact of the surgery. Nearly everyone who has undergone ostomy surgery goes through them.

At home Friday morning, Dad and Mom talked about me over breakfast.

"It's terrible to see how depressed he is, Marion. He looks and appears to feel better every day, but he continues to anticipate the worst, even though his temperature rarely tops 100 degrees anymore."

"I know, Kurt. Yesterday was the first time he has had to be pushed out of bed to exercise."

"The bags," said Dad. "It must be those damned bags."

"It's a lot of things, I think. He even grew bored with my reading cards and letters to him yesterday. He told me he didn't want to hear any more."

Back at the hospital, Dad sought out Dr. Peskin to discuss my mental state.

"Kurt, I don't think I have to tell you that this kind of operation is major and has many potential consequences. Ostomy surgery is especially difficult for young people because it can be extremely damaging to their self-image," said the surgeon. "We had a rough start, but once we got the infection under control, the healing has progressed beautifully. Despite that, he's been through a lot, and this is not unexpected. I do have some good news, however, which might really help. It looks like Rolf can go home Monday."

My father looked relieved. "That will help," he said. "What's peculiar to us, though, is that Rolf seems to be cordial and friendly with casual visitors, but when Marion and I come around, he dumps everything on us."

"That's normal, Kurt. It's because you and Marion are safe to talk to. You're his parents. Getting counseling for him might be a good idea. I know that he has resisted seeing Dr. Ward, the staff psychologist, but it may be time to revisit that option."

Dr. Peskin cut the number of antibiotics to one, which would be administered until my projected discharge on Monday, November 5. I was getting out!

Another Lesson

A daily calorie count showed that I had taken in 3,428 calories Thursday, most of them from rich milkshakes bolstered with protein supplements. I need to put some weight on my frame, since I weighed only 123 pounds.

Besides trying to gain weight, I was also learning how to deal with my ostomy.

"Oh, I hate this," I said during another demonstration from Melba.

Practice was starting to make perfect, however, and when I gave my first good return demonstration, Melba said, "Excellent! Now you're getting the idea."

I was beginning to understand the digestive rhythms of my body. I was learning that it was best to change my appliances before breakfast. Melba taught me how to cut a new face plate to the correct size for my stoma, position the appliance, and properly "window tape" it. The process wasn't so overwhelming anymore, but it certainly wasn't routine either.

Just then Phil Tyne, the Chargers' strength and conditioning coach, stopped by to check on me.

"I talked with your doctor, and he said that as soon as the sutures have been removed and your soreness is gone, we can begin the rehab process."

"Great, Phil," I said sarcastically. "Where do we start? The two-mile run? How about some wind sprints? Look at this body, will ya? It looks like I've been in a concentration camp. This isn't going to be easy."

"Yeah, but when was it ever easy? As I recall, you never did have much of a chest." I looked up to see a toothy grin on Phil's friendly face.

I would need Phil a lot in the coming months. He would

be the key to my recovery and would become the person I would rely on more than anyone. We would develop a very special friendship.

New Sights and Sounds

It was a glorious Indian summer day in San Diego later in the afternoon when Mom walked into my room. Like Phil, she had a grin on her face. "I just talked to Dr. Peskin, and he said if you feel up to it, I can take you outside for half an hour."

"Are you kidding? Let's go!"

Mom quickly grabbed an extra blanket, and together with Carla, they arranged all of my IV bottles and a wheelchair. The next thing I knew we were heading down the corridor I had already walked hundreds of times. Only this time, I was headed for the elevator and my first chance to breathe fresh air in over five weeks.

The halls were bustling with nurses and doctors, and I saw new patients lined up at the admitting desk. As we headed toward the front door, my eyes adjusted to the brilliant sunshine, and I imagined what it would be like to leave this place for good.

Outside, we found a lawn already occupied by several other patients. Mom stopped pushing the wheelchair, and together we soaked up the warmth of the sunshine and delighted in the fresh air. I drank in the sights and sounds like a man who thought he would never taste again.

"This is nice, Mom, really nice."

"Isn't it, Rolf? You know, it won't be long now."

Back in my room, things suddenly didn't seem quite so hopeless. "Mom, I'm beginning to feel better now . . . like I'll be able to deal with everything, no matter what it is."

The unexpected improvement in my mental attitude accelerated my already rapid physical improvement.

On Sunday morning, Dad arrived at University Hospital at 9 o'clock. By that time, I had already gone for three walks around the corridors.

In the afternoon, we watched the Chargers earn a hard-fought 20-14 victory in Kansas City. Mike Wood, my replacement, kicked two field goals that proved to be the margin of difference. I slept seven hours that night, and I was up walking the halls with Helen at 6:45 a.m. the next morning.

"Helen, I'm so excited. I can hardly believe it's finally happening. You've been such a help. It'll be fun to come back and visit you and Colleen when I've regained my weight and I'm in shape again. You won't even recognize me!"

"Having you here has been a real pleasure," said Helen.

"Oh, c'mon, I've been a monster patient. I know that and you know that. I wouldn't have wanted to take care of me for anything."

"You haven't been that bad Rolf, really. Besides, we knew what you were going through."

Monday, November 5

Discharge day was an emotional one. I was leaving a hospital and the doctors and nurses who had saved my life—but a life that had changed forever. I knew I was a different person. In a sense, when the doctors removed part of my colon, they also removed any of the youthful innocence that remained. At the time, I felt they may have also robbed me of my future. Only time would tell.

After Mom and Dad packed up the remaining letters and the things I had accumulated over the weeks, they pushed me down the hall in my wheelchair. I felt like I knew every square inch of linoleum between my room and the elevator.

As I waited outside for Dad to go get the car, I basked in the sun and felt like a man who had just been released from prison.

When Dad pulled up to the curb. I carefully got out of the wheelchair and shuffled over to the car. The wire sutures made getting in uncomfortable, but I reminded my parents that the pain wasn't anything like what I'd been through.

I said very little on the ride home, choosing to stare at the familiar landmarks passing by. Life was going on as usual, and it seemed I had been gone for only a little while.

Although I was excited to finally get back to the house, the trip had exhausted me. I needed to lie down, so my parents led me straight up to my old bedroom. Dad had tied a rope at the end of the bed so I could pull myself up and get out of bed without assistance.

I wouldn't need the rope that day, however. I wasn't going to be getting up. I was tired and happy to finally be back home, in a room without the beeps and clicks of monitors, and where nurses weren't going to interrupt me every few hours. Sleep would come easily.

CHAPTER 12

Home Sweet Home

For the first time in five long weeks, I felt at peace. All night long, there wasn't a single interruption from nurses, residents, interns . . . or anyone else.

I probably would have slept until noon if Mom hadn't been told how important it was to monitor my temperature. She finally woke me up—very gently—at 8 a.m.

"You know something, Mom? After the second surgery, I was really down. I would dream of being home in my old room, of you and Dad, and it seemed like I'd never get here. It was like when we were kids back in New Hampshire in the middle of a hot and humid summer imagining snow on the ground."

Speaking of temperatures, mine was normal, and it remained that way even after Mom joined me for a walk around the house. As we passed my parents' bedroom, I paused for a moment. I knew they had a scale in their bathroom.

What the heck, I thought. *I might as well know where ground zero is.* With a little trepidation, I shuffled into their room and stepped on the scale. One hundred and twenty-six pounds—more than fifty pounds below what I was listed at in the Chargers' media guide!

I turned to my mother and smirked, "My new playing weight." We had a good laugh together.

On that first afternoon home, we drove together to downtown La Jolla, ten minutes away. I stayed in the car while she did a few errands, but I was thrilled to see some familiar stores and watch shoppers stride down Girard Avenue.

The outing didn't last long, but it exhausted me nonetheless, and I quickly fell asleep after we returned to the house. I woke up when Dad came home. He had done some shopping and had purchased a present: a pair of oversized white bib overalls that fit loosely over my wire sutures. The overalls would enable me to move around easier.

I stood in front of the full-length mirror on the bathroom door. "A real fashion statement," I exclaimed, studying my spindly arms sticking out from under the shoulder straps.

The Phone Call

Fittingly, it was a gray and wet Wednesday morning—ten days after my release from the hospital—when Mom received the sad telephone call from Omi in West Germany. Opa had died in his sleep, succumbing peacefully after a long illness. Mom took the news stoically on the phone, but after she hung up, she began to sob deeply.

I pushed aside my protein shake and took her hand. "Oh Mom. You've been through so much this past month."

"I felt so terrible, so guilty, when I was there," she admitted as she dabbed at the tears running down her cheeks. "All the time I was in Germany, I kept thinking I should have been back here with you and Ingrid. But now that he's gone, I'm so thankful I was there and able to see him alive one last time."

We talked for a while about Opa and what Mom's life was like growing up. It was good medicine for her. Mom's stories fascinated me, but our discussion was cut short by the need to change my ileostomy bag. This time, however, we didn't have Melba. We were on our own, and that prospect frightened us.

Carefully, we arranged all the supplies in front of us. We began the procedure by cutting the face plates. No sooner had we removed one of the worn-out appliances when the stoma began to ooze. Caught unprepared, all we could do was watch in horror as the waste matter leaked on my stomach and slid slowly onto my clothes. Of course, the foul smell was not pleasant for either of us.

We quickly wiped up and continued.

"We've got to clean the skin around the stoma before we apply the adhesive paste," instructed Mom. Sensing urgency, Mom began to wipe me, but as if on cue, the stoma began to ooze once again. In the fumbling, Mom managed to drop the paste tube on the floor.

"Not again!" Mom said in a frustrated voice.

We were living Murphy's Law: Anything that could go wrong did go wrong.

We made four or five attempts at cleaning around the stoma, prepping the skin, and applying the paste before we were finally able to properly position the stupid bag. A procedure that should have taken not much longer than the time it takes to kick a game-winning field goal took us forty-five long, agonizing minutes.

"This is ridiculous," I declared in anger. "Is the rest of my life going to be like this?"

"Well, you better get used to it," Mom snapped. She was every bit as frustrated as me, and we had lost patience with each other. We were not handling this well.

I was twenty-four years old, used to being self-reliant and in charge of my own destiny. But after two major operations and one huge incision, I could barely move around. What was worse, however, was having to rely on my mother to go to the bathroom. That was humiliating.

What's it going to be like when Mom isn't around to help? I thought. *And what about all this talk about resuming a normal life? That's a crock. This isn't going to be as easy as all those ET nurses made it out to be. Is it going to be like this every time I have to change these stupid bags?*

I was really upset when the phone rang. By coincidence, a stoma nurse was on the line. "Yes," Mom said, "we could use some help. Good, I'm glad to hear that you can drop by tomorrow. We'll look forward to seeing you ... and we do have some questions."

Eating Alone

Dinner that evening was at 6 o'clock sharp, as it always was in my parents' house. Depending on the night of the week, the menu was often the same: spaghetti and meatballs, Cornish game hens, cold cuts, or soup and salad. For a special treat every now and then, Mom would cook my favorite meal—Wienerschnitzel.

I joined them at the table, sitting in my customary seat at one end. Dad, as always, sat at the head, with Mom between us. While sipping on a protein shake mixed with an egg and banana, I watched them eat spaghetti and meatballs.

"Are you sure you don't want some of this?" asked Mom. She twisted my arm.

"Okay, but just one meatball."

Dad turned to Mom. "Then you've decided for sure that you're not going back for the funeral?"

"Yes, I think so. My brother said he'd fly to Germany to take care of the arrangements. There wouldn't be that much I could do. I was there to say goodbye to him, thank God, and that's what gives me solace now."

On Thursday morning Robert Honsik, a longtime friend, visited the house. We had known each other for nine years and played sports together at La Jolla High.

I was sitting on the patio, enjoying the sunshine and trying to read a book when Mom brought Robert through the house into the back yard.

"Hey, buddy," I said, slowly getting to my feet. We embraced awkwardly.

We hadn't seen each other since I went into the hospital,

but it was obvious that Robert was shocked at my appearance. Although he tried his best to hide it, he wasn't prepared for what he saw.

"You look like you've gone through hell," he remarked.

"I feel like I have," I agreed.

Robert couldn't stop staring. "I knew you were going to be skinny, but this is ridiculous!"

"Yeah, but I'll be back. You'll be able to run me all over the tennis court for a while, but don't get used to it because it's not going to last."

I could tell Robert didn't believe me. I knew he was wondering if I'd ever be able to play tennis again, much less beat him.

Still, I found myself marveling at our conversation. Two weeks ago, I was fighting for my life, unsure if I would live, and all of a sudden, I was talking to a good friend about hitting tennis balls. Things were changing in a hurry.

"I tried to visit you in the hospital," Robert began, "but they wouldn't let me in. I talked to your parents a few times, but I didn't really want to bother them, so I listened to the radio and read the newspaper, just like everyone else. Wow, you've had a rough time."

"Don't feel badly, Robert. I knew you would have come if you could have. The fact is they wouldn't let anyone visit. I'll never forget all the cards and flowers though, and all the prayers said for me. It really made a difference."

Before we could continue the conversation, Mom came out. "Someone else is here to see you," she said as Dr. Peskin followed her onto the patio. He smiled in approval of what he saw.

"Home cooking is obviously doing you good, Rolf. You look like you're beginning to put on some weight."

I glanced at Robert, who no doubt could hardly believe what he had just heard.

"Dr. Peskin, this is my buddy Robert. He wants to know

when he'll be able to start whipping me in tennis again."

"Well, that won't be for a while," laughed Dr. Peskin, "but I have a hunch we'll all be amazed at how quickly our star patient will come around. And now, Robert, if you'll excuse us for a couple of minutes, I need to examine Rolf."

"No, Doctor," I jumped in. "If you don't mind, I'd like Robert to see this. He's a great friend, and I'm going to have to lean on him during the next few months. I'd prefer that he know exactly what's going on, if he doesn't mind."

Robert nodded yes, a little unsure of what he was about to see.

"Okay, then let's take a look," Dr. Peskin said, as he opened the front of my oversized bathrobe.

The robe fell away, revealing my hideous midsection: thirteen wire sutures holding together a black, crusted-over surgical incision that looked like it might never close.

The sight was almost more than Robert could stand. He inhaled sharply and his face flushed in shock, but he gathered himself quickly. Dr. Peskin proceeded with his examination.

"Rolf, you're coming along just fine. Everything is healing beautifully, and in ten days or so we should be able to start taking the sutures out."

"You really think so?" I asked hopefully. The wires were a painful nuisance, and they kept getting snagged on my clothes. I would be relieved to have them gone.

"I do. You've gone five days now with normal-range temperature. Your blood pressure has stabilized, and your mother tells me you weighed in at 128 pounds this morning; up two pounds since you left the hospital. Things are certainly looking up," said my surgeon optimistically.

I believed him, but Robert must have thought we were both crazy. He stood in the background, trying to recover from what he had just witnessed. Neither of us knew at the time, however, how important he would be to my recovery.

CHAPTER 13

One Mailbox at a Time

Friday, November 9

The next afternoon, I had another visitor, Gordon Jennings, who lived next door to my condo. He had heard on the radio that I was recuperating with my parents, so he stopped by to say hello.

It was a beautiful afternoon, and Gordon must have sensed my desire to get out of the house. "We could drive up the coast," he offered. "We can go anywhere you want. You must be going nuts after being cooped up for so long."

"Hey, Gordon, that'd be neat. You can't believe how many times I've dreamed about seeing the beach again."

With his help, I gingerly climbed into the front seat of his little sports car, and we headed north on old Highway 101 past the Torrey Pines bluffs and through Del Mar, Solana Beach, and Encinitas. The scenery was breathtaking! The sun shined brilliantly, and we rolled down the windows to experience the full sensation.

"Gordon, this is unbelievable! It's just like I imagined it would be. As long as I live, I'll never take life for granted again."

Gordon and I were gone for almost two hours. When we returned to the house, I was concerned that the little excursion might have caused my temperature to rise. But it was satisfying to see the thermometer stop at 99.2, the highest it had been since my discharge, but still comfortably within normal range.

"Hallelujah!" smiled Mom. "That's wonderful." She was always taking my temperature and cheered each time it was normal.

The good feelings didn't last very long, however. That night, while sitting at the dinner table with my parents, my abdomen began to ache painfully around the wire sutures. I tried to keep it to myself, but. . . .

"Rolf, what's wrong. What is it?" asked Mom.

"Nothing, really."

"C'mon, Rolf," Dad piped in. "Your face is a dead give-away. What is it?"

"It feels as though there's a tiny knife pricking each one of the wires every time I move."

Dad knew exactly what was happening.

"Well, your skin *is* getting cut," he explained. "As you gain weight and your stomach stretches, the wire sutures can't expand. They're actually cutting into your abdomen. It's nothing serious, but you're going to have to bite the bullet for a while until they're out."

I slept sporadically that night. Since the ache of the wires persisted, I put a call into Dr. Peskin the next morning and outlined my symptoms.

"Nothing to be alarmed about, Rolf," said Dr. Peskin. "As long as your temperature remains normal and you feel good, there's no problem. Your father is right; experiencing pain in the sutures area is part of the healing process."

"After all the things that happened to me in the hospital, I was just worried that something else might be going wrong," I explained.

"I can understand that," Dr. Peskin said in a calming voice. "The worst is over for you. You're well on the road to recovery. I'll bring some pain pills over later today, and we'll take another look at the sutures."

Dad came home for lunch just as Mom and I were coming back from my morning walk.

"Weigh-in time," he announced. I stepped up on the bathroom scale and watched the dial spin to 128 1/2—up a half pound from two days earlier. A good sign.

Surrounded by bathroom mirrors, I was fascinated by my gaunt frame. I raised my right arm and tried to flex a muscle. Not much happened. The sight made me laugh, and Dad joined in.

Then he had an idea. He walked over to the hall closet and pulled out his trusty 35mm camera. "I want to take some pictures of you so that when you're healthy, you'll remember how sick you were. You know, before-and-after shots."

Dad took photographs of me in my shorts. "Look at this body," I said. "Have you ever seen anything so pathetic?"

"Not much muscle, that's for sure," he said with a smile.

"And this scar. Did you ever see anything so ugly?"

He responded by taking a close-up of the incision that split my abdomen in two.

The next morning, Sunday, November 11, I weighed 130 pounds, up nearly five pounds in the six days since my discharge from the hospital. My old appetite had returned, so Mom decided to prepare my favorite meal as we all sat down to watch the Chargers play the Cincinnati Bengals. In a game the Chargers were supposed to win, San Diego had to rally late to defeat the Bengals, 26-24. The Chargers scored ten points in the fourth quarter, including a game-winning field goal by my replacement, Mike Wood, his fourth of the day.

"Remarkable!" I said to Dad. "This team is 8-3, and if they can beat the defending Super Bowl champion Steelers next Sunday, there's no telling how far they can go."

I, too, was excited for them, but also felt an overwhelming wave of regret that I was no longer a part of the team.

Back in Training

The next day, Mom and I began a walking program that was measured by the mailboxes on our street. In training, every athlete needs a goal. Mine was adding at least one mailbox to my walk each day. That doesn't sound like a lot, particularly in California, where the houses are usually close to each other, but I needed to start somewhere. My goal was to get strong enough to walk up and down Prestwick Drive without stopping.

We began with two mailboxes. On Tuesday, we added two more. By Wednesday we were up to eight, and I was actually walking alone. Friends and neighbors, driving by in their cars, slowed down to wave encouragement as they watched me shuffle along in my sweatsuit. Those walks were great times to reflect on what I had been through. I was still really unsure of the future, still needing to take things one day at a time.

On Thursday morning, after a glorious walk in the sun, I sat down at the breakfast table and downed a glass of orange juice.

"Mom, I really think I'm going to be able to handle it. It's going to be okay."

She sat down next to me and smiled. "I know you are, Rolf. We just have to remember that it takes little steps. . . . "

". . . To climb a mountain," I interrupted. "And, boy, are you right about that."

That night I got a surprise visit from Doc Brooks.

"Hey, man, how ya doin'?" asked our popular equipment manager.

"Doc, a couple of weeks ago I couldn't make it across this room. Now I'm starting to take short walks by myself. I'm still not ready for much more than that, but it's a start."

"That's great, Rolf. Me and a bunch of the guys were talking, and we were wondering if you were feeling well enough to come out to the stadium this Sunday for the Steelers game."

"Well, I don't know," I hesitated. "I haven't thought about doing anything like that. Where would I sit?"

"Don't worry, Rolf. You and your parents just be at the player's gate an hour or so before game time. Come down to the locker room if you can."

I had to get approval from Dr. Peskin. On Saturday, he stopped by to begin removing the thirteen wire sutures. He came armed with wire cutters and a pair of pliers that he could have bought at a local hardware store. I looked at those tools and felt like the Tin Man in "The Wizard of Oz."

"I'm not going to kid you," the surgeon began, "but this is going to hurt like hell for a minute or two. That's why I'm going to do it in stages over the next week—three or four sutures at a time."

Dr. Peskin walked back into the house and called for my mother. "Marion, we may need your help for a moment. This is going to hurt Rolf, and I need someone to distract him."

Wanting to get this over with as soon as possible, I took off my shirt and positioned myself on the patio lawn chair, gripping the armrests as tight as possible. "Okay," I said bravely, "let's get going."

"The procedure is simple," said Dr. Peskin. "I'm going to snip the wire sutures—that part won't hurt. But then I'm going to have to twist and pull the wire out . . . and that will hurt. Are you ready?"

I nodded, perhaps a bit unconvincingly.

With Mom talking to distract me, I tried not to watch. Then Dr. Peskin snipped the first wire, and it sounded like a wire wrapped around a bundle of newspapers being cut. Dr. Peskin was right; that didn't hurt. The pain started when he began to pull the wire out.

He grunted as he tugged and twisted the wire. *Would this ever end?*

"Hold on, Rolf, we're almost there," said Dr. Peskin. "Just a little bit more . . . and that's it." He straightened up, took a deep breath himself, and held a three-inch piece of wire triumphantly in the air. I relaxed my grip on the arms of the lawn chair as beads of sweat formed on my forehead.

Then I remembered he wanted to do a couple more sutures.

"One down. Let's keep going," I said.

Dr. Peskin grasped hold of the next wire with his pliers. The pain was bad, but truthfully, it lasted only a moment. Before I knew it, he had two more sutures out. When he finished, Mom brought some refreshments out for a little celebration.

"Three more visits to get the last ten out," said Peskin. "Monday and Tuesday . . . and maybe Thursday, Thanksgiving Day, for the last session. Would that be okay?"

"Fine with me," I replied. "Actually, the sooner the better. But Doc, before you go I have to ask you something. I have been invited by the team to watch the Chargers game tomorrow at the stadium. Do you think I can go?"

Dr. Peskin looked at me as he carefully considered his answer. He saw the anticipation in my eyes and heard it in my voice.

"Rolf, if you feel up to it, you can go. Just remember that you're still very weak, and this outing will be quite strenuous. If you have some place to sit and relax and someone there to assist you, I think it might be really good for you."

"Thanks, Doc. I'm really looking forward to seeing the guys again."

Cheers and Tears

I walked into the kitchen as Dad was marking another day off on the wall calendar. I didn't know it then, but the new date—Sunday, November 18, 1979—would be a day I'd remember forever.

I was going to watch the Chargers play the Pittsburgh Steelers in a crucial football game for both teams. I was almost as nervous as if I was going to play myself. I found it hard to believe it had been only eight weeks since I had last set foot in an NFL stadium. Had it really been only two months since I had collapsed on the team plane coming back from New England?

But I didn't have time to dwell on those thoughts. Right now, I needed to get ready for the game. I put on my "uniform"—the big white painter overalls and a sweatshirt.

My parents and I arrived at San Diego Stadium ninety minutes before kickoff, and were ushered to seats in the private box of General Manager Johnny Sanders.

I sat there for a few minutes, soaking in the familiar sights and sounds that are found nowhere else but in a big league stadium. The band was warming up in the corner as players, coaches, and referees strolled the neatly lined stadium grass, preparing for the upcoming battle.

I was anxious to get down to the locker room before things got too hectic. Sensing this, Rick Smith, the Chargers' public relations director, led me to the elevator. On the way, we passed several sportswriters—who almost didn't recognize me in my emaciated condition. We exchanged pleasantries, but I was looking forward to getting downstairs.

When we arrived at the locker room, the first guy I ran into was Doc Brooks. He was sporting an ear-to-ear grin as he stuck out his hand to shake mine. He quickly sized me up, and like a good equipment manager, said, "That uniform will never do."

"Doc, I don't need anything else. I just came down to say hello to the guys and to wish everyone good luck."

Doc and Rick led me through the doorway into the players' private world. Suddenly, everything came back to me. The stereo was going full blast, and the guys were in various stages of getting dressed. On a couple of cushioned tables, several teammates were getting stretched by the training staff.

Phil Tyne, our strength coach, noticed me first. He literally dropped the leg of the defensive back he was working on to come over and greet me. "Wow, Rolf, what a surprise!" he said. "It's great to see you. You look a helluva lot better than when I last saw you in the hospital."

A gruff voice called out from behind me. "Hey, Benirschke! Where'd you get those designer overalls?" It was our leader, quarterback Dan Fouts, irreverent as usual.

Before I could respond, Louis Kelcher, our big, gentle All-Pro defensive tackle, came up and carefully wrapped his six-foot-five-inch frame around me. I grinned as I remembered the time he came to visit me in the intensive care unit but was told that visits were strictly limited to immediate family.

"But I am a family member," he had told the nurse indignantly. "I'm his big brother, Louie Benirschke."

Since Louie weighed 325 pounds and was a good half-foot taller than me, the nurse had good reason to be skeptical. But she allowed this "big brother" to see me—a memory I still smile about.

After we exchanged pleasantries, Louie, unbeknownst to me, stepped away and sought out Coach Don Coryell.

"What do you think if we made Rolf honorary captain for the day?" asked Louie, who, along with tackle Russ Washington, were co-captains, although Louie was still recovering from a knee injury sustained in training camp.

"Sounds fine to me," said Coryell. "I think it would be good for the team."

Kelcher came back a few moments later with a big surprise. "I just spoke with Coach Coryell, and you, good buddy, are one of our co-captains for today's game. You'll have to come out on the field with me and Russ for the coin toss before the opening kickoff."

I tried to object. I honestly didn't know if I'd have the strength to walk that far. But Louie insisted. "Don't worry, Rolf, if you can't walk all the way, I'll just have to carry you!"

Doc Brooks emerged from his office with my number 6

jersey and handed it to me with a wink. I reminded Louie and Russ that I'd have to walk slowly—very slowly—because of the wire sutures still in my abdomen.

While I was collecting my thoughts, the players were returning from pre-game warm-ups. We were about ten minutes from kickoff, and I could feel the tension mounting as I sat quietly in a corner of the locker room.

With about four minutes to kickoff, Coach Coryell, a master motivator, began charging up the troops with another special pre-game oration. I always felt that Coryell didn't miss very much, and he proved it that afternoon. "Listen up, everybody," he said. "We have a special visitor today. Rolf came down to check up on us. I'm happy to tell you he's going to be one of our co-captains today."

The players exploded in cheers and applause. I must have been quite a sight sitting there next to all those giant men with my skinny frame draped by my oversized Charger jersey. I felt rather sheepish and just wanted to get out of the way. I didn't feel like I belonged. My teammates had a big game to play, and they didn't need any distractions.

I watched the players file out of the locker room, and I waited until everyone had left before I followed. Just before stepping onto the playing field, I paused and looked back at the messy dressing room. I sadly wondered if this would be the last time I'd see a locker room on game day.

As I slowly shuffled to the Charger bench, the offense was being introduced to the year's largest home crowd. I looked up into the stands and wondered what my parents were thinking. I had been gone more than forty-five minutes.

When the Marine Corps band began to play the National Anthem, I lined up with the rest of the players on the sidelines. It felt so good! Most athletes experience overpowering feelings of pride, excitement, and a little nervousness as they stand listening to the "Star Spangled Banner." Those same feelings rippled through me with even greater intensity at that moment.

When the National Anthem was finished, I turned to find Louie. I was worried I would take too long to walk to midfield. The voice of the public address announcer snapped me back to reality. "And now, ladies and gentlemen, the team captains for today's game. . . ."

After introducing the Pittsburgh captains, my heart began pounding. The crowd watched expectantly as Louie, Russ, and I began walking slowly to midfield. I could sense a low buzzing from the crowd, but it changed dramatically when the PA announcer blared, "And now, ladies and gentlemen, San Diego Charger captains Russ Washington, Louie Kelcher, and, returning for the first time in many weeks, Rolf Benirschke!"

As if in unison, the 52,000-plus fans rose to their feet and began applauding and cheering. The noise grew louder and louder and by the time we reached midfield, I could feel tears starting to form. I was overwhelmed by this spontaneous demonstration of encouragement.

At that moment I didn't know if I would ever walk on another football field again, but it didn't matter . . . I was just happy to be alive. The emotions that I had tried to hold in check over the past few months came gushing out. Like a dam that had broken, tears flowed freely down my cheeks.

Well, at least Mom and Dad know where I am, I thought. When we reached midfield, the Pittsburgh co-captains greeted me with warm smiles and handshakes. "Mean Joe" Greene, one of the greatest Steelers of all-time, yelled above the din of the crowd, "These people must really care for you." Then Jack Lambert, another hard-nosed Pittsburgh standout, shouted, "Hey, Rolf! Welcome back."

The officials, caught up in the emotion, allowed the cheering to go on for several minutes before making the coin flip. "Mean Joe" made the call, but I couldn't hear a thing. The moment was magic for me.

Apparently, it was a memorable occasion for others as

well. A few years later, Chargers owner Gene Klein described this scene in his autobiography, *First Down and a Billion*:

> In the two decades I owned the team, that was the most heart-wrenching moment I experienced. We all knew Rolf's football career was over. We just wondered if this was the last time we were going to see him alive!

We won the coin toss, and Louie escorted me back to the bench, holding my left hand in his giant paw. All the time, the huge crowd never stopped cheering and applauding.

By the time the game started, I was exhausted and completely wiped out, emotionally and physically. I knew I had to get back to the security of the box. Always thinking ahead, Rick Smith was right there to help me off the field.

We happened to leave in the middle of a play, but as the fans near the exit tunnel saw us approaching, they stood up again and cheered once more. The rest of the Charger fans throughout the stadium picked up on what was going on, and they followed suit. An impromptu stadium wave developed, and, for the second time in ten minutes, I was completely overcome with emotion.

I can honestly say those few minutes were the most thrilling of my life. The crowd's response had taken me totally by surprise, but what I didn't realize was that moment would play a very important part in my eventual recovery.

The heavily favored Steelers may have been the defending Super Bowl champions—and on their way to another NFL crown—but that day my inspired teammates went out and destroyed Pittsburgh, 35-7.

That night, I enjoyed my best sleep in two years.

CHAPTER 14

It Takes Little Steps

November 22
Thanksgiving Day

One of my problems—and it was a nice one to have—was my weight. Since my release, I had gained seven or eight pounds, but when I moved around, the wire sutures cut deeper into my skin. I knew I would be gaining *more* weight today, especially after smelling the mouthwatering aroma of Mom's baking turkey. I couldn't wait to dig in!

I also couldn't wait for the last wires to come out of my stomach, even though I knew that would be painful. Late Thanksgiving morning, Dr. Peskin stopped by, as promised, to complete the task. These sutures would be the most difficult because they were deeply embedded next to my belly button. Dr. Peskin thought it would be a good idea to inject the area with Novocaine before he went to work. I told him that sounded like a great idea, but even then, the experience was a miserable ordeal.

Once the final wire suture was out, it was like my appetite was unleashed. All I could think about was eating a plateful of gravy-covered turkey and stuffing, and that's what I did—twice. I ate more food that day than I had in ages, and I remembered thanking God for all my blessings—especially the gift of life.

A week later, Robert Honsik dropped by to visit. After chitchatting for a while, my longtime friend asked me what I was thinking for myself down the road. Until then, I really hadn't had a chance to give my long-term future much of a thought.

"I'm not sure," I reflected. For the last couple of months, I had been caught up in the moment because that was the only way I could deal with it. But now, without warning, a buddy was asking me about my future—a question I had avoided asking myself.

"Well, do you think you'll ever kick again?" probed my friend.

"I don't know, Robert. The thought of playing pro football with an ostomy seems rather farfetched, doesn't it? No one has ever done it before."

Then the memory of walking into the Charger locker room just before the Pittsburgh game returned to me. I had felt completely comfortable amidst the raucous atmosphere. The more I reflected, the more I thought, *That is really where I want to be, but can I do it?*

For the next few days, as I walked past mailboxes on Prestwick Drive, I contemplated a comeback. I wondered if I *could* come back. Kicking field goals, I knew, wasn't supposed to involve much contact, but it was still football. The more I wondered about it, though, the more I decided to test what so many ET nurses had told me: *Your ostomy bags shouldn't keep you from doing anything you want to do*. If I could just figure a way to protect my stomas, the Chargers might give me an opportunity to kick again.

For weeks, I had been receiving the most encouraging and heartfelt letters from people with ostomies. As the letters poured in, I was amazed at what so many others had to endure. Here is one such letter:

I am writing to you about my wife, Darlene. It all started nearly four years ago shortly after the birth of our second daughter, Kristen. It seemed like everything that Darlene ate or drank gave her such pain and terrible bowel movements that it was almost unbearable. We couldn't go out to dinner, see a show, or go dancing without knowing first exactly where the ladies' rooms were located.

We went to a specialist, but after all kinds of tests he sent my wife to a psychiatrist to make sure the pain she was experiencing was not just mental. We knew it was not. The pain grew worse, and Darlene practically stopped eating because of the aggravation it caused.

It was at that point that she was finally diagnosed as having an early form of colitis. She was put on Prednisone, and doctors limited her work and outside activities. She got better for a while, but within a year, Darlene needed two surgeries to remove most of her large and part of her small intestines. But her condition did not improve, so more surgery was required.

Darlene has now had a total of thirteen operations. She could have given up very easily, but she insisted that she would beat this disease before it beat her.

Between everything, Darlene has still found time to raise our two daughters, run a household, and hold down a steady job. Oh yes, she also bowls in three leagues, goes camping, and is a wonderful wife, friend and lover to her husband.

I've read that you've had two surgeries, and that you've gone through a lot. You may have thought at one time that you would be better off dead. Don't think that!

Darlene's only real wish is that a cure for colitis is found, and found soon so that other people, young or old, do not have to go through what she has gone through.

After pondering this inspiring letter and many others like it, I finally screwed up enough courage to ask Dr. Peskin if he thought there was a chance I might play again. His answer emboldened me: "You can do it if you want, Rolf. Nothing that's happened—the illness, the surgery, the ostomy, having to wear appliances—can stop you if you really want to try it. I must tell you, however, that it's never been done."

As we neared Christmas, I made an early New Year's resolution: I would get into the best shape possible in time for Chargers' training camp in July and then see if I could win my job back.

Getting in Shape

For the better part of a year, I had lost all desire for most foods. When I first became ill it didn't take long to figure out that eating food started a chain reaction of bad things. The first effect was often nausea. This was followed by severe intestinal pain and abdominal cramping. Lastly, and sometimes the most difficult to deal with, was the uncontrollable diarrhea.

For some people with IBD, eating is not an option—they must receive their nutrition intravenously. Fortunately, I had to experience hyperalimentation only once during my hospitalization, but I know many people who get their nutrition exclusively by hooking themselves up to an IV line in their neck or chest.

Imagine never experiencing the pleasure of eating real food of any kind . . . no chicken fajitas, no lasagna, no strawberries, no Häagen Dazs! People do, and this proves once again that the human spirit can cope with almost anything when the alternative is not being alive.

But all of that was left behind following my ileostomy surgery. As 1979 came to a close, food was once again a pleasure. I couldn't get enough of all the things I had missed, and the results were showing on the bathroom scale almost daily. You can't imagine how great it was to see my weight begin to climb to 132 . . . 133 . . . 134. They were small steps to be sure, but I knew that those were the kind I needed to get to the top of the mountain. At first I was cautious about what I ate. I learned to avoid certain stringy vegetables, nuts, and fruits with skins. Too much popcorn was a problem, and I learned that certain foods caused more gas than others. Nevertheless, I had few limitations and none could take away the joy of eating again.

In early December, Phil Tyne, our strength coach, surprised me by giving me a set of one and two-pound dumbbells.

"Here," he said, "work with these while you're reading or watching television. We won't miss them in the Charger weight room," he smiled.

I looked at my skinny arms and realized I had a long way to go. The weights Phil had given me were for young kids or senior citizens, but for me, these light dumbbells were all I could lift. It was a starting point.

Although Phil was just doing for me what he would do for any other player, his dedication was instrumental to my comeback. I would come to rely on him for encouragement and inspiration over the hard months of conditioning.

"Now don't push yourself too hard," cautioned Phil. "We can't afford to rush things and get you injured when you're just starting out."

I had just moved back to my condominium, but I was becoming bored with taking walks on my own. Phil sensed that, so he suggested I start coming down to the Charger practices at the stadium. I was delighted. The team was in a playoff drive, and there was excitement in the air.

Invigorated by the atmosphere, I wanted to get at it. Phil knew I had to take it easy, so the first day we started by taking a slow jog down the length of the football field. We then walked the width of the field and jogged back down the other sideline. The exercise was strange and scary and exciting and tiring all at once. In itself, that could have been overwhelming, but Phil wouldn't let me dwell on it.

Next, Phil took me into the weight room and announced, "The place to begin is at the core of the body—the abdominal muscles." We did a handful of painful sit-ups. Well, they weren't really sit-ups, more like lean-ups.

We then proceeded to the weight machines, where it didn't take long before I was whipped. My muscles—whatever I had left of them—quivered as I walked out of the weight room.

The Chargers had a great year, finishing with a 12-4 record, matched in the AFC only by the defending Super Bowl champion Steelers. But since we had crushed Pittsburgh on that memorable afternoon, the Chargers would have home-field advantage right up to Super Bowl XIV, if necessary.

Unfortunately, the Chargers' season came to an abrupt and disappointing end, losing to the wild-card Houston Oilers in the first round of the playoffs. Houston had come into San Diego racked by injuries and decided underdogs, but they shocked everyone with a 17-14 upset win. It was time to start thinking about next year.

CHAPTER 15

Larger Than Me

Following the devastating loss to the Houston Oilers, the Charger organization made a commitment to get back to the playoffs. I got caught up in that excitement, so in late January I stepped up my workouts. Phil Tyne urged caution until my weight was a bit higher. "You just don't have any stamina yet," he counseled.

I discovered he was absolutely right when I was finally cleared to play tennis again. I was amazed at how slowly I moved around the court; it seemed like I was running in combat boots. The good news was that I was able to hit the ball without pain, although my timing was way off. The best news, however, was that my ostomy bags stayed on just fine during thirty minutes of running around the court.

I was getting used to the feeling of wearing the appliances during physical exercise and more confident that they would stay on. As I grew stronger and stronger, I began to appreciate how quickly my body began to recover.

My mind was a different story. Here I was, working my tail off, not knowing for sure if the Chargers were even going to allow me a chance to compete for my job. It began to gnaw at me, but I was too afraid to bring up the question with the coaches . . . afraid of what they might say.

I continued to eat well and put on weight. By late March,

I weighed just over 150—hardly anything to write home about when it comes to pro football, but excellent progress nonetheless. I had become increasingly concerned, however, about what I might do if football didn't work out. Self-doubt crept into my thoughts more and more, and I fought hard to counteract it by counting my blessings. I was alive and had my health back. I had great friends and a family that had just demonstrated that they would do anything for me.

Then out of nowhere, I was offered a job as a radio and TV commentator for the San Diego Sockers, a pro team in the now-defunct North American Soccer League. Since I loved the game and had played soccer in high school and college, I was intrigued by the opportunity.

Besides learning what it took to be a broadcaster, it turned out to be a wonderful way to keep up my rehab program. Since most of the games were in the evenings or on weekends, I could continue my daily workouts with Phil. And as I traveled with the team and developed friendships with the players, I was included in their team practices.

The Sockers often needed another player to round out teams in their "small-side" practice games. The focus was on conditioning, with an extra emphasis on starting, stopping, and making short passes. My legs gained strength during these intense sessions, and my stamina slowly returned.

In addition, the broadcasting job gave me the confidence to realize that if I didn't make it back into football, there were other stimulating things to do. (As it turned out, I wound up broadcasting for the Sockers for three happy years, 1980-82, and I developed speaking skills that I continue to use today.)

Big Bertha

Phil Tyne was my shadow throughout the spring. Except for an occasional Sunday, there was hardly a day in which we didn't lift weights, run, or do something physical. We did nearly all our running in San Diego Stadium, developing what we called "The Course." The Course was a torturous twenty-five-minute run that consisted of running up and down virtually every step, ramp, and escalator in the cavernous stadium.

One particularly long escalator that rose from the ground floor to the upper deck we dubbed "Big Bertha." She shot up nearly six stories and had eighty-eight steps. I know it was eighty-eight because I counted each step every time we sweated our way to the top.

My body was rounding into tip-top shape, and Phil remembers the day when it all came together:

> It was late May, and we were out for our usual tour of "The Course." We ran up Big Bertha and then down the stadium stairs at a good clip. We were really pushing it.
>
> Until this day, Rolf had always run behind me, letting me set the pace. But on this morning, Rolf moved ahead and said, "It's your turn to follow." I was already exhausted, but I couldn't show it. We pushed on, further and faster. It was amazing to watch him. I had witnessed his spirit and the strength of his will for months, and now I recognized that his body had recovered and finally caught up. From that moment, I was sure that Rolf would make it all the way back.

By June, I was back to my old self, feeling great—all the time. That's something most people take for granted, but when you have IBD, you feel miserable and rotten—all the time! With training camp less than a month away, I started kicking a football for the first time in nearly nine months. I was careful not to overextend myself, but from the first kicks, I knew I could play again in the NFL . . . if I was just given a chance.

A Happy Camper

The Chargers opened training camp on July 15th at UC San Diego, and I weighed in at 172 pounds, just a few clicks under my playing weight from two years earlier. But because I had been working out so intensely, I knew I was stronger than ever. From the first days in camp, I was excited to feel the ball jump off my foot and to discover my range was just as good—if not better—than before my illness.

Special teams coach Wayne Sevier, however, was determined to bring me along slowly. Experience had taught him that it wasn't a good idea to allow any kicker—especially one who's stamina was still suspect—to kick too much in camp. With Sevier carefully monitoring my on-the-field progress, I was left with several other concerns:

(1) Would my ostomy appliances stay on during the rigorous two-a-day practices?

(2) Would the Stomahesive melt in the summer heat and cause the appliances to leak or fall off?

(3) Could I find a way to protect my stomas from a hit?

(4) Could I find football pants to fit over the appliances?

The last two questions turned out to be no problem. Our equipment manager, Doc Brooks, worked with our trainers to develop two small pads that fit over my stomas. The pads were held in place by an Ace bandage that wrapped around my waist. My pants fit fine without any extra tailoring, and nothing showed. Although I didn't relish the thought of getting hit, I was now well-prepared for anything.

Competition Heats Up

My placekicking competition in camp was Mike Wood, a big, muscular guy who looked more like a middle linebacker than a kicker. Mike, of course, had replaced me the season before and had done a great job in relief, going eleven-for-fifteen and hitting every field goal inside 50 yards.

Mike did, however, have a crucial kick blocked in the 17-14 playoff loss to Houston that the Oilers returned for a touchdown. Although the blocked kick wasn't all his fault, coaches have a way of remembering those things, and they began to question whether he got the ball up quickly enough.

Shortly after the start of camp, I asked for a private audience with Charger owner Gene Klein. It's unusual for a player to make such a request, but I needed to discuss something that had been bothering me.

When I walked into his spacious office at San Diego Stadium, Mr. Klein motioned for me to have a seat. I got right to the point. "I really appreciate all you've done for me," I said respectfully. "I particularly want to thank you for the chance you've given me to compete again for my job."

Mr. Klein nodded and leaned back in his chair.

I pressed on. "As you know, there has been a lot of public sentiment expressed on my behalf. It has been very gratifying, but it has left me a little uncomfortable. I don't want the kicking job handed to me. I want to compete heads-up and earn it back. If we don't do it that way, it wouldn't be fair to Mike or the team. I think we both know the Chargers have a great chance to make it back to the playoffs, and you're going to need a reliable kicker. . . the best kicker."

"Fair enough," replied Mr. Klein. "We wouldn't want it any other way either, but I appreciate you coming in. I'll meet with Coach Coryell and inform him about our conversation."

With that, I thanked Mr. Klein and left his office.

Normally, NFL teams have four preseason games, but the Chargers had been picked to play in the Hall of Fame game in Canton, Ohio, the week before the start of the regular exhibition season. Having an extra game to prove myself was quite a break.

We traveled to Canton in mid-July, and on the morning of our game, the NFL inducted its new Hall of Fame members. We were scheduled to play the Green Bay Packers in the afternoon at an adjoining high school field. Since the locker rooms were too small to accommodate the 100 players on each team, we dressed en masse in the basketball gymnasium.

When we left the relative comfort of the air-conditioned building and made the short walk to the field, I could tell it was going to be a hot one. The mid-summer temperature topped 95 degrees, and the hot air was as humid as a greenhouse. During warm-ups, I was worried my appliances might not hold up in the sweltering conditions.

Coach Sevier told me that Mike and I would alternate kicks, with me leading off. In the first quarter, I trotted out for a routine 35-yarder. But this was my first kick in almost a year, and I felt like a rookie all over again. In my nervousness, I rushed the kick and watched the ball hit the upright and bounce back onto the field. I was disappointed, but I was becoming more concerned with what might be happening to my appliances in the stifling heat.

At halftime, while the team toweled off in the cool gymnasium, I slipped away to the bathroom. My uniform was drenched in sweat, and I knew that if the appliances were ever going to come off, this would be the time. I unwound the Ace bandage and cautiously checked for leaks. Nothing! Everything was still in place.

With that concern behind me, I began to concentrate on football. The second half proved uneventful until the last two minutes. With the score tied 7-7 and the Chargers deep in Packer territory, it looked like I would have an opportunity to kick a game-winning field goal.

The hot sun had given way to thunderclouds, however, with sprinkles on and off all afternoon. When the Charger drive stalled, the ominous black clouds suddenly opened up and tremendous claps of thunder shook the earth. Just beyond the stadium, sharp stabs of lightening struck the ground.

"Field-goal unit!" screamed Coach Sevier over the din. The field-goal team slogged onto the field, but as we were lining up on the ball, I noticed out of the corner of my eye that both benches were sprinting off the field.

"Hey, what's going on?" I yelled at my holder, Ed Luther.

Before Ed could answer, another loud clap of thunder reverberated through the stadium. The booming sound was quickly followed by a streak of lightning *very* close to the stadium. Immediately, the referee blew his whistle and called time-out. Then another bolt of lightning struck nearby, and the fans began stampeding for the exits.

Now everyone was in a full sprint for the locker rooms. Meanwhile, I just stood there.

"What's going on? Where are you going?" I yelled. But when I saw the referees hightailing it for the exits, I knew this pre-season game was coming to an early end. A kick that might have helped my comeback would just have to wait.

What a let-down! At least I knew my appliances weren't going to come apart on me.

Beyond My Range?

My kicking improved throughout training camp, but I missed some kicks that I should have made. I was working hard on the timing with the snapper and holder, and the pressure of kicking head-to-head with Mike was intense.

The competition was finally decided in the second-to-last preseason game against the Los Angeles Rams in Anaheim. In the first quarter, I got off on the right foot with a well-kicked 37-yarder that had plenty of distance.

Just as the first half was about to end, the Chargers faced third-and-long at midfield, and the punting team was getting set to go in. That made sense, since a field-goal attempt looked to be about 55 yards—not a kick Coach Coryell would usually try.

But Coach Sevier had a different idea. "What do you think, Rolf? Do you want to give it a try?"

I didn't hesitate. "Coach, I can make this."

When the third-down play ended with an incomplete pass, Sevier didn't hesitate. "Field-goal unit! Field-goal unit!"

Coach Coryell couldn't believe his ears. "What did he say?" he asked another coach.

But it was too late. The field-goal team was on the field, and time was running down. Ed Luther found a good spot, gave me a great set, and I nailed the kick, sending it 55 yards through the goalpost. It was my longest kick ever in a game.

As I jogged over to the sidelines grinning from ear to ear, I was mobbed by my teammates. They seemed almost as excited as I was. I caught Phil Tyne's eyes, and when we looked at each other, we both knew that all the hard work, all the Big Bertha's, and all those early morning runs had been worth it. I had made it all the way back.

I was a Charger once again.

To the Showers

Once I made the team, I had to jump over another hurdle: showering. All throughout training camp, I had kept the exact details of my surgery hidden. Although we had a large locker room, I could use individual shower stalls and maintain relative privacy. But when we broke camp and started practicing at San Diego Stadium, things were different. We had the same locker room layout, but showering was done in one community shower room.

Following the first workout at the stadium, I was uncertain what to do. *Do I shower with the guys?* I wondered. Well, of course I do. I couldn't drive home sweaty and dirty after each practice. And how would I shower following road games?

I looked around. All the players were hustling to get cleaned up and head home. Meanwhile, I struggled with what to do. Should I wait for everyone to leave? Then Phil passed by and noticed I wasn't undressing.

"Rolf, what's the matter?"

"Phil, I don't know how to take a shower."

"What do you mean, Rolf?" asked Phil.

"What I mean is that nobody has ever seen. . . ."

"Oh, that's what you're worried about. Rolf, people aren't judging you by the bags on your side, but by who you are, and, in this case, how you can help the team. In fact, I'll bet after these players realize all you've been through, they will appreciate your comeback that much more."

"Well, you may be right," I conceded. "In any event, I guess I don't have much choice. I figured this day was coming sooner or later, and now it's finally here."

With that, I pealed off my uniform, wrapped a towel around my waist, took a deep breath, and headed to the community showers. Acting as if nothing was different, I threw my towel over a hook and walked to an open nozzle. As the warm water cascaded over my head and down my body, I glanced down at the two appliances, hanging in all their glory. I guess there's no hiding them now.

Eight or nine guys were in the showers, and I held my breath, waiting for someone to say something. Amazingly, nobody noticed—or they chose to keep their comments to themselves. I washed my hair and rinsed off, grabbed my towel and ambled back to my locker. I was drying off when one of the biggest defensive linemen on the team came over and smiled at me. "Man, I didn't know you had ostomy surgery. My grandmother had an ostomy ten years ago. I know what you're dealing with."

"Thanks, man."

That seemed to break the ice, and a couple of other players approached me, curious about what they had just seen in the showers.

"What are those?"

"How do they work?"

"Does it hurt?"

After giving a full explanation, one of the players whistled. "Man, you got guts," he said.

"Actually, I'm wearing these because I don't have as many guts as I used to," I joked.

Word got around the locker room that it was show-and-tell time. As more players crowded around my dressing stall, team jokester Hank Bauer quipped, "Hey Rolf, do you have shoes to match those bags?"

There's always one in the bunch.

Season-Opener

We opened the season against Seattle, and the Chargers decided to keep Mike Wood around as insurance. Mike did the kickoffs while I was given the placement duties. I kicked two field goals, and we got off to a fast start. Mike unfortunately pulled a groin muscle the next week and was put on injured reserve, leaving me to handle all the kicking.

Although I was strong enough physically and had the range to kick off, the Chargers were worried that I might take a hit during a kickoff return. Coach Coryell issued strict orders for me to make a beeline for the sideline after every kickoff. Under no circumstances was I allowed to stay on the field and try to tackle the return man. In fact, Coryell half-seriously suggested that he would cut me from the team if I disobeyed.

Initially, that edict was tough for me to follow. A kicker's job is not over until the return man is down, and you don't want to leave your team a man short. Each time I ran to the sidelines, I felt frustrated that I was leaving the field while the ball was still in play.

I never knew what our opponents thought of my "L-pattern," but I did learn from a friend on another team that his coach had said, "Under no circumstances are you to hit or tackle number 6. If Benirschke is going to beat us, he's going to beat us with his leg. We're not going to deliberately try to take him out." That wasn't ordinary talk in the win-at-any-cost world of NFL football, but no one was complaining, especially me.

There was one time, however, that I "forgot" what Coach Coryell had said. We were playing the Kansas City Chiefs, and I booted a deep kickoff and began running off the field. Just before I reached the bench, the Chiefs' return man broke free and headed up our sideline. There was nothing between him and the end zone except for me.

Without thinking about the consequences, I closed my eyes and hurled my body in his way. We collided and were both sent sprawling to the turf. The impact felt like I had been hit by a runaway freight train, but I had saved a touchdown. The mystified return man couldn't figure out where I had come from.

"He came off the bench!" he screamed at the referees. "He came off the bench!" Meanwhile, my teammates were putting me back together like the scarecrow in the "Wizard of Oz." After a quick check, I found I was still in one piece—although a little dazed. I hadn't been hit in the abdomen, but my bell had been rung. Happily, that was the worst mishap during my comeback season.

Won't Get Fooled Again

My comeback piqued the interest of the media, and "NFL Today," a Sunday pregame show on NBC, asked to do a feature story about my return. Arrangements were made, and one afternoon a producer and a camera crew showed up at practice.

Before we started the interview, I explained off-camera to the producer that while I appreciated the opportunity to talk about my illness, I was still uncomfortable discussing my ostomies. "I'm still learning to live with them," I explained.

"Understood," said the producer. "We'll do whatever you wish." With that, we started the interview.

After thanking everyone for their support and the thousands of cards and letters I had received, I described my ordeal over the last eighteen months and how I had nearly died after surgery. I explained the differences between Crohn's disease and ulcerative colitis, but added that we still didn't know the cause—or have a cure for either affliction. I mentioned that the Crohn's & Colitis Foundation of America (formerly the NFIC) was doing heroic work, and if anyone out there was battling IBD, they should call the 800-number for more information. I then encouraged people to write me in care of the Chargers if I could help in any way.

"Okay, I think we have enough," said the producer, signaling the end of the interview. The producer walked over and thanked me for my time. As we talked, he began asking me about the specifics of my operation. Thinking he was genuinely interested, I shared the graphic details of my ostomy surgery. Little did I know the cameraman, who had taken his camera off his shoulder, was continuing to film me from his hip!

The next Sunday was a home game. As was our custom, the team stayed at a local hotel near the stadium the night before the game. After our team breakfast on game day, my roommate, punter Jeff West, and I went back to our room to relax for a moment and pack up to leave for he stadium. We flipped on the TV and caught the beginning of "NFL Today."

"And we'll be right back with the remarkable story of San Diego kicker Rolf Benirschke," I heard the announcer say.

"Hey, Jeff, you've got to watch this," I said, curious to see how it would turn out. After the commercial break, the feature began with a summary of my short career and illness.

Suddenly, the camera angle changed and I saw myself explicitly describing the intimate details of my ostomy surgery and appliances! I had been snookered! All the things I was trying to work through privately were now literally broadcast across the nation. I was stunned and shocked, and feelings of betrayal welled up inside me. I continued to stare at the TV screen in disbelief.

"How could they do this?" I asked Jeff. "They knew all that stuff was off the record!"

"Amazing, but I guess that's life in the public eye," he consoled.

I was still fuming when I arrived at the stadium. Phil Tyne dropped by my locker.

"Nice interview, Rolf. Way to go."

When I didn't return the comment, he asked, "What's the matter?"

"Phil, that was supposed to be off the record. All that

With Arusha the cheetah. "Kicks for Critters" helped raise
more than $1.5 million for the San Diego Zoo's Center for
Reproduction of Endangered Species.

Dad, Louie Kelcher, and me, reliving the time Louie posed as my brother during a hospital visit.

Coach Coryell was never comfortable in a suit, but at this fund raiser he was joined by (from left to right); Sid "Doc" Brooks, Jim Laslavic, Kellen Winslow, Charlie Joiner, Willie McCovey, Dan Fouts, and me.

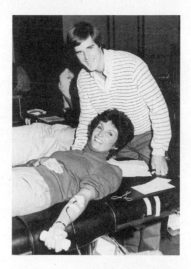

My need for blood started an annual Chargers' blood drive.
Here, Joyce Klein, the wife of the late former Chargers'
owner, is a willing donor. (November 1982)

My glimpse into Hollywood as the host of Wheel of Fortune
with Vanna White. (1989)

In the Oval Office with President George Bush and ConvaTec "Great Comeback" winner Irene Fine of Russia.

My illness allowed me to meet some very special people. Here I pose with Barbara Bush, and her youngest son, Marvin, who has an ileostomy, and his wife, Margaret.

The greatest day of my life (February 24, 1990)

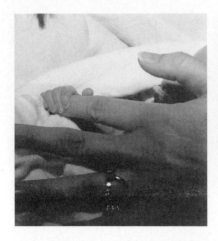
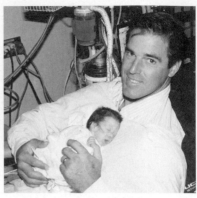

Above, right: Proud Dad. (November, 1992)

Above, left: Our daughter, Kari, holding Mary's finger two days after she was born. She weighed just over two pounds.

As Chairman of the United Way campaign in San Diego, I'm pictured here with Mary and our daughter, Kari, born 13 weeks prematurely. (April, 1994)

Enjoying a sunset with Mary and Kari on a scuba diving trip.

My ostomy didn't keep me from doing anything,
even ski racing.

The newest additions to our family. We adopted brothers,
Erik and Timmy, ages four and two, from a
Russian orphanage. (August, 1996)

The Benirschke children: Erik, Kari, and Timmy.

wasn't supposed to be part of the interview."

"What are you talking about?"

"I'm talking about the part where I explained about my ostomy, Phil. I wasn't ready. . . ."

"So, what's the big deal?" asked Phil. "So people know. That doesn't change who you are. Look at the inspiration you can be for every person with an ostomy. Didn't you tell me there are 60,000 to 70,000 ostomy surgeries performed every year? Imagine how those people are going to feel every time they watch you kick a field goal. Imagine how much easier your recovery would have been if you had known someone else who had gone through this before you."

Two days after the broadcast, I received over fifty letters, and the mail kept flowing for weeks. Almost without exception, each letter started: *I'm writing because you're the only other person I know who has gone through what I have.*

That blew me away. Phil was right: I had been given an opportunity to jump-start a national discussion about Crohn's disease and ulcerative colitis, two diseases that affect 2 million people across the country. In addition, I was able to educate many more about what it's like to live with an ostomy and extend needed encouragement.

After Phil's pep talk, the "NFL Today" feature gave me a whole new reason for playing. From that point forward, I wasn't just playing for myself. No, there was a bigger purpose here, a responsibility that I didn't fully grasp at the time. From now on, I would be playing for everyone struggling with inflammatory bowel disease or ostomy surgery.

CHAPTER 16

Getting the Word Out

As the press began asking me more questions and my story reached the public, I discovered that everything about IBD and ostomy surgery was misunderstood by nearly everyone. The very nature of its symptoms—fever, nausea, and uncontrollable diarrhea—made it difficult to talk about, especially with strangers. Let's face it, nobody is standing up in the lunchroom and announcing, "Do you know how many times I have to go to the bathroom every day?" It is a real closet disease, seemingly not fit for discussion at the dinner table or in the media.

But the "NFL Today" ambush turned out to be a blessing in disguise. After that, I figured the word was out, so I began sharing my story as openly and as often as I could. One of the people who heard about me was Suzanne Rosenthal, the co-founder and president of the Crohn's & Colitis Foundation of America, headquartered in New York City.

Originally named the National Foundation for Ileitis and Colitis (NFIC), the organization was formed in 1967 by Suzanne and her husband, Irwin, along with another couple, Bill and Shelby Modell. At the time, Suzanne was battling Crohn's disease and the Modells had a son also stricken with the illness.

The impetus for starting the CCFA began when Irwin

Rosenthal asked his wife's doctors for the names of organizations doing research on IBD. He was told there were none. Zippo! Zilch! A sympathetic doctor put Irwin in touch with the Modells, who were asking the same questions on behalf of their son. As the Rosenthal and Modell families met in the New York City area to discuss their mutual desire to do something for those with IBD, they decided to form a nonprofit organization.

Their first fund-raising event in Manhattan drew less than a hundred participants, but from that modest beginning some thirty years ago, the CCFA has grown to eighty chapters around the country. In 1995, the organization raised over $16 million to fund research and educate the public about Crohn's disease and ulcerative colitis. The CCFA has become the organization that all of us who have suffered from IBD lean on, all because two courageous families wanted to make a difference.

When I mentioned the CCFA's toll-free number on "NFL Today," the New York office was flooded with inquiries. It didn't take long for the CCFA to figure out who prompted those calls. Not long after we began teaming up to help the organization increase the public's awareness and raise funds for research.

To accomplish those twin goals, we developed a Sports Council and speaker's bureau, where notables and celebrities participate in CCFA fundraising events and speak before groups on behalf of the organization.

The Sports Council has a roster of more than twenty athletes and celebrities, including: actor Gary Collins and his wife, former Miss America Mary Ann Mobley; senior golfer Al Geiberger; Marvin Bush, the youngest son of President Bush; actor Patrick Swayze of "Ghost"; NFL hockey star Kevin Dineen; and a host of others. These folks either have the disease or have been personally touched by someone close to them who has IBD.

Kicking for More Than Me

What I remember most about my comeback season is the way my "Kicks for Critters" program took off. When I first started playing professional football, I recognized the importance of players putting something back *into* the community. Athletes are given platforms, and I always felt we should use it wisely. I discussed these feelings one afternoon with my attorney, Leigh Steinberg, and together we came up with "Kicks for Critters."

For every successful field goal I kicked, I promised to donate $50 to the San Diego Zoo's Center for Reproduction of Endangered Species (CRES). I had studied zoology at UC Davis and had spent my collegiate summers working at the San Diego Zoo. I was keenly aware of the zoo's endangered species research projects. When I announced the "Kicks for Critters" program during my rookie season, I urged others who cared about wildlife to make "matching pledges" for every field goal.

I had no idea how "Kicks for Critters" would be received, since it was the first program of its kind. Leigh and I realized that such a public program could leave me vulnerable to criticism from the media and the fans—particularly if I shanked a few field goals. Did I really need the extra pressure?

"Listen, Rolf," explained Leigh. "There are always going to be critics—people who are quick to judge and will find something negative to say. But that's okay. What you need to ask yourself is whether your motivation is pure and if you believe in what you're trying to accomplish for the zoo."

It didn't take long for me to understand what Leigh was talking about. After a particularly bad game against the Kansas City Chiefs in which I missed several kicks, the headline in the *San Diego Union* the next day read: "There Were No Kicks for Critters!" I couldn't help laughing myself, even though I was struggling at the time.

"Kicks for Critters" raised $76,000 during my comeback

season—the bulk of the money coming from Charger fans also interested in the plight of wildlife. As a result of all the publicity, I had the opportunity to visit classrooms all over San Diego and talk about endangered species and "Kicks for Critters."

Many of the students I spoke to were becoming environmentally conscious, and they wanted to help in any way they could. As a result, we developed "Cans for Critters," a program in which youngsters could collect aluminum cans, recycle them, and donate the money to the zoo.

We offered the students incentives: 750 cans collected earned a pizza lunch, and lesser amounts won pencils, notepads, and bumper stickers. With the help of Leigh Childs, a dedicated teacher, we developed a curriculum for the teachers and energized thousands of kids to scour their neighborhoods in search of cans.

Perhaps the most satisfying result, however, were the dinner table conversations that ensued when these elementary school children asked their parents to assist them with their collection efforts and to become more environmentally responsible in the process.

I'm happy to report that "Cans for Critters" endures today with approximately 100 San Diego schools still participating. Since the program started more than fifteen years ago, "Kicks for Critters" and "Cans for Critters" have raised more than $2 million for research at the San Diego Zoo. I must confess I have a special appreciation for where the money is being spent because it was my father who had started the Zoo's Center for Reproduction of Endangered Species.

Déjà Vu All Over Again

All season long, the Chargers were atop the AFC West division. Our final regular season game in 1980 was a Monday Night contest—at home against the Pittsburgh Steelers. That was also the night in which San Diego Mayor Pete

Wilson announced that the stadium would be renamed San Diego Jack Murphy Stadium in honor of the late sports editor of the *San Diego Union*.

It was a big rematch, and I was symbolically named honorary captain for the game. Incredibly, one of the Steelers' captains that night was running back Rocky Bleier.

As I walked to midfield for the coin toss, I couldn't help but remember reading *The Rocky Bleier Story* a year earlier in my hospital bed. I had drawn a lot of encouragement from his gripping story. He had been drafted into the Vietnam war and gotten shot in the foot. Doctors said he'd never play football again. But a tortuous recovery program, hours of painful rehabilitation, and a great faith and determination had brought him back.

Somewhere along the line, a coach had given Rocky a chance, and he became a special running back on one of the best pro football teams of all-time. Our Monday Night contest was Bleier's final game, and the knowledgeable Charger fans knew it. When he was introduced, the sold-out stadium honored him with a standing ovation.

At midfield, while the cheers rained down on us, I stuck out my hand to Bleier.

"Congratulations, Rocky, for your great career," I said. "Thanks for being an inspiration to me and so many others."

We didn't have time to talk further, but after the coin flip, I jogged to the sideline, reflecting on what the past year had brought: *Has it really been only twelve months since that painful walk to midfield with Louie Kelcher?* What a difference a year made! I was psyched to kick well, and as it turned out, we needed four field goals to secure a huge 26-17 victory.

We finished the season at 11-5, and I had my most productive season ever. We beat the Buffalo Bills in the first round of the playoffs, but in the AFC championship game—with the winner advancing to the Super Bowl—we didn't play well and lost a heartbreaker to the hated Oakland Raiders.

We honestly felt we had the best team in the NFL that year, which made it doubly tough to watch the Raiders beat up on the Philadelphia Eagles in the Super Bowl in New Orleans. With the close of the season, however, I realized I had accomplished two important things: I had successfully resumed my NFL kicking career, and I had helped educate millions of football fans about inflammatory bowel disease.

I felt like the luckiest guy in the world. The season's end also brought unexpected awards and recognition. I was named "Hero of the Year" by the NFL Players Association; "Most Courageous Athlete" by the Philadelphia Sports Writers' Association; "Headliner of the Year" by the San Diego Press Club; "NFL Comeback Player of the Year" by *Football Digest*; and "Chargers Most Inspirational Player" by my teammates. The Associated Press also named me to its All-Pro second team. Later, when network TV decided to bring back "This Is Your Life," the surprised guest on the first show was a grateful young man—me.

Each time I received an award, however, I couldn't help but think of the many brave people who were battling IBD without a national audience cheering them on. They were the ones with real courage.

New Swing of Things

Almost a year to the day after my surgery, Al Geiberger, one of the best golfers of all time, was lying in a hospital bed, recovering from ileostomy surgery for ulcerative colitis. He had earned the nickname "Mister 59" when he became the first person ever to break 60 in a PGA tournament, but on this particular Sunday, he was down and feeling sorry for himself. He was wondering if he would live to *see* another golf tournament, let alone *play* in one.

Al was not a model patient. As he was bemoaning his fate to his nurse, the TV set in his room just happened to be tuned to the Chargers game. I had just kicked an extra point when the nurse responded to Al.

"You see that young fellow," said the nurse, pointing to the TV. "He has an ostomy, and if he can kick in the National Football League, less than a year after being in the hospital, you ought to be able to live and play golf again!"

"You're kidding! What's his name?" asked Geiberger.

"Rolf Benirschke, and when the Chargers were here in Denver last week, he kicked three field goals to beat my Broncos."

As Al watched the football game, he began to believe that maybe there was life after ostomy surgery. Perhaps he, too, could return to a sport he loved.

It was a short time after Al was released from the hospital that he tracked me down. We arranged to meet in San Diego during the San Diego Open, held every February at the Torrey Pines Golf Course in La Jolla. This would be Al's first visit to a PGA Tour event since his surgery, and he was looking forward to seeing his friends and meeting me.

We decided to rendezvous at the Torrey Pines restaurant for breakfast, with the idea of walking the course for a few holes afterward—depending on how he was feeling, of course. When he shuffled into the restaurant, I had no trouble recognizing the hunched-over gait of someone still trying to recover from abdominal surgery. His face was gaunt, and he appeared to have lost quite a bit of weight. Seeing him was like going back in time and seeing myself.

We started off our conversation just getting to know one another. Al was convinced he'd never play professional golf again, and he wondered how I could play football. I assured him with a twinkle in my eye that anything was possible.

After breakfast, we left the privacy of our corner booth and stepped onto the verandah next to the practice putting green. This was Al's world, and he was recognized instantly by fans and tournament officials. They knew all about his surgery, and dozens walked up to shake his hand and tell him they were glad to see him again. "Great to have you back, Mister 59! Can't wait to see that beautiful swing of yours again!"

We slipped into the player's locker room, where I witnessed the kind of impact this man has had on his peers. His fellow pros—just like the fans outside—were delighted to see him. They welcomed him with warm, genuine expressions of love and concern. It was interesting to watch these tender exchanges between men who competed against each other week after week. These were men that Al had spent a profitable career beating.

When Al suggested we walk a few holes, I was elated. I was not much of a golfer, but I certainly respected the skills of Tom Watson, Jack Nicklaus, Lee Trevino, Tom Kite, and the rest of the PGA pros.

As we walked, we reveled in the sunshine and the camaraderie of his friends and fans. It didn't take long for Al to get tired, however, so we headed back to the locker room and talked about several issues that were still troubling him.

"Will I be able to play eighteen holes without going to the bathroom?" he asked.

"No problem," I assured him.

"Will the gallery be able to see my appliance through my shirt and pants?"

"Nope," I said. "The gallery will never see it."

"What appliance do you use?"

"I'm a big believer in ConvaTec," I replied. "Their product is easy to put on and great for people as active as we are. The company is very responsive to the needs of patients. I played twenty-two games last year, including the preseason and playoffs, and I never once had a problem or a leak."

"Really? I've never heard of ConvaTec," said Al.

"Well, you have now, and you really ought to give them a try."

I put Al in touch with the company, and he quickly became a ConvaTec convert. It wasn't long before he got himself back into playing shape and made a triumphant return to the PGA tour. Al's comeback generated the same kind of media attention that I had received.

Al and I kept in regular phone contact, and one evening, during one of our long conversations, we came up with the idea of asking ConvaTec to use us in testimonial ads to encourage others who were facing ostomy surgery. We jokingly agreed that this would be one of the most honest endorsements in sports.

At the time, ConvaTec was a young company in the ostomy appliance business. A division of E.R. Squibb & Sons, Inc., the company had recently developed Stomahesive, a new product that served as a skin barrier and revolutionized ostomy appliances.

Our testimonials were much appreciated, and they helped ConvaTec develop an instant identity. Today, ConvaTec is a division of Bristol-Meyers Squibb and the largest manufacturer and distributor of ostomy products in the world.

As time passed, Al and I became increasingly concerned that some people might not be able to relate to a couple of professional athletes, and that when our careers were over, ostomy discussions would again return to the closet. This concern became the impetus for a program called Great Comebacks®

Our idea was to find and recognize a new person every year who had successfully overcome ostomy surgery and/or inflammatory bowel disease. We would select a winner through an application process and honor that person at the annual Crohn's & Colitis Foundation of America banquet held every June in New York City. The winner would receive a Steuben Crystal Eagle and a three-day, all-expenses-paid trip to the Big Apple. More importantly, a brochure describing their story would educate and encourage others in similar situations.

During the fifteen years of the program, we've honored some remarkable people from a variety of backgrounds. One year we saluted George Vogt, an Air Force fighter pilot, who was facing a forced medical discharge following his total colectomy. But after working closely with the CCFA, George appealed his case through the entire chain of command, right up to the Secretary of the Air Force. He was granted another flight physical–which he passed with flying colors-allowing him to become the first pilot in Air Force history to return to active flight duty following an ostomy. A year later George was named Air Force Pilot of the Year!

Then there was Bill O'Donnell, a U.S. Park Service volunteer who dreamed of becoming a Park Ranger when he began experiencing symptoms of IBD. He reluctantly saw a doctor, and ultimately needed several operations, including an ileostomy. Despite health setbacks and people advising him to stop considering such a strenuous career, Bill never lost his determination and eventually became a Park Ranger. He has since worked in several remote and demanding parks, including Yellowstone National Park and the Florida Everglades.

Another winner was Dr. Kent Cullen, a colon and rectal surgeon who nearly died when his ulcerative colitis began hemorrhaging. He needed multiple blood transfusions to save his life just prior to ostomy surgery. These days, when his patients ask, "What can I expect after surgery?" or "How can you understand what I'm going through?", Dr. Cullen can matter-of-factly reply, "I do know what you're going through, because I've had an ostomy myself for over twenty years... and look at all the things I can do!"

But my favorite Great Comebacks® story belongs to Irene Fine. I first met Irene through a letter she sent, dated December 5, 1989. It began:

Dear Rolf,

Perhaps you are surprised to receive a letter from someone in the Soviet Union. My name is Irene Fine, and let me tell you my story.

And what a story! Irene was a twenty-year-old engineering student in Moscow who had developed ulcerative colitis. After seven surgeries, her doctors basically threw up their hands and said there was nothing more they could do for her. She was declared an "invalid of the state" and left to live out life as best she could, confined to a tiny apartment with her mother and grandmother.

It wasn't much of a life. The Russian appliances were so bad that Irene was forced to improvise with diapers, cotton balls, and tufts of wool. Her stomas leaked all the time, and the stench was awful. She had to quit her engineering studies. "I was not living, I was just existing," she wrote.

One day, Irene happened to be visited by an American nurse. She was so moved by Irene's plight that when she returned to the U.S., the nurse sent her a box of ConvaTec appliances. The appliances dramatically changed her life, allowing her to return to university and socialize again.

ConvaTec was made aware of her situation, and the company continued to send her supplies. One of the boxes happened to contain a Great Comebacks® application; hence the letter to me.

When I read her story, I was blown away by her courage and perseverance. If there was anyone who deserved special recognition, it was Irene Fine. Suzanne Rosenthal and Terry Jennings at the CCFA agreed, and together with Liz Doyle, Scott Gillis, and Joe Solari at ConvaTec, we arranged for her to come to the U.S.

The highlight of her trip occurred when we flew her to Washington, D.C., to meet President Bush in the Oval Office. Just three days earlier, Soviet President Mikhail Gorbachev had participated in a summit meeting at the White House, and now the President was going to entertain Irene! We arrived in Washington for our appointment, all quite nervous and excited. After a brief wait, we were ushered into that famous office, where immediately the President bounced up from his chair and greeted us warmly. "So great to meet you," he said to Irene, whose eyes were as big as White House china saucers.

"And Rolf, glad you could join us, too. Have a seat." He motioned to two chairs on either end of his desk. I had met the President a few years earlier when his youngest son, Marvin, was struck with IBD and needed surgery. President Bush's kindness and concern were genuine, and he gave us twenty memorable minutes of his precious time.

As we were leaving, I couldn't help but notice the tears glistening in the corners of Irene's eyes. Perhaps it was the realization she had just been talking to the President of the United States, or perhaps it was the feeling Cinderella must have had when the Prince picked her out of all the girls in the land. But for Irene, her dream wasn't going to be over at midnight.

From Washington, we flew to New York, where Irene received a special International Great Comeback award at the spring CCFA banquet. We also arranged for her to meet with several physicians, including Dr. Irwin Gelernt at Mt. Sinai Hospital. Dr. Gelernt quickly determined that she needed surgery to fix an incorrectly created stoma. He and several others donated all their medical care, and the hospital waived their costs as well.

After surgery, Irene stayed in the houses of several CCFA volunteers during her three-week recovery. When Irene finally boarded a plane for Moscow, she was returning to Russia as a healed woman with a whole new appreciation for the kindness of people. I was never so proud to be an American.

I've kept in touch with Irene over the years. She emigrated to Israel where she applied her considerable intellect to learning Hebrew and completing her engineering studies. In the summer of 1995, she married Vladislav Tsirkin, and the carriage never did turn back into a pumpkin.

CHAPTER 17

Checking It Out

Although I had become well-adjusted to my ileostomy and was prepared to live with an appliance for the rest of my life, I began to investigate several surgical options that were being developed. These new procedures created an internal pouch and eliminated the need for an appliance. I had adapted well to my bags and was doing everything I had done prior to my surgery, but in the violent world of professional football, I was more at risk of injury with an external stoma. The idea of having an internal pouch was appealing.

One of these, the Kock pouch, sounded like the best alternative for me. I had read as much as I could about the procedure and discovered that it was only available for people with ulcerative colitis. The Kock pouch wasn't recommended for those with Crohn's disease because of the strong likelihood that the disease could come back at any time in the walls of the pouch. If this were to happen, the pouch would have to be removed, compounding the patient's troubles. The patient would have to return to a conventional ileostomy and risk developing "short bowel syndrome," in which too little intestine would be left to properly absorb nutrients.

Ever since my first operation, when my father looked into the microscope at my diseased colon, he had believed that I was suffering from ulcerative colitis, not Crohn's disease.

Although Dad was regarded as one the world's best patholo-
gists, he wanted other opinions, so he sent slides of my diseased colon to specialists around the country. We found it
interesting that each doctor came back with a diagnosis
"strongly in favor" of ulcerative colitis.

Despite their suspicions, no doctor was willing to say they
were 100 percent sure. A few specialists claimed the symp-
tomatic and radiological evidence were inconclusive. I have
since learned that doctors have difficulty making an exact
diagnosis in about 10 percent of patients with inflammatory
bowel disease.

Still, I felt I might be in the other 90 percent, so I decided
right after the season that I would find out if I was a candidate
for a Kock pouch. One of the leading hospitals for continent
ileostomies was the famed Mayo Clinic in Rochester, Minnesota. When the Charger season ended in January 1981, I flew
to the Mayo Clinic in the dead of winter to undergo a week of
extensive tests to determine if I had ulcerative colitis or Crohn's
disease. If I had the former, a Mayo Clinic surgeon had agreed
to operate and give me an internal pouch immediately. That
way, I would have time to get back in shape for training camp
in July.

I must admit that I wasn't looking forward to another
round of medical tests, but the thought of waving goodbye to
two poorly placed stomas brightened my attitude.

Unfortunately, the trip turned into a bad nightmare when
my tests left the wary doctors still unsure of what disease I
was actually suffering from. Because of their reluctance to commit to a diagnosis of ulcerative colitis, they were unwilling to
perform the Kock pouch surgery.

Heading East

Following the Mayo Clinic debacle, I regrouped and discussed my options with Mom and Dad. We decided that I
should play another season and, in the meantime, continue to

examine my options. One of the names that kept coming up was that of Dr. Irwin Gelernt. Our inquiries confirmed that he was an experienced colon-rectal surgeon based at Mt. Sinai Hospital in New York City. He headed a group that had performed more successful ostomy surgeries than any other in the country. Dr. Gelernt also had the reputation of being one of the best Kock pouch surgeons in the world, having trained in Sweden under Dr. Nils Kock himself.

I didn't waste any time. I called Dr. Gelernt and brought him up to speed on my complicated medical history. I added that in recent months I had seen increasing amounts of blood in one of my appliances. "What do you think it means, Dr. Gelernt?"

"It's clear to me that active disease has returned to your colon," he replied.

"Which means. . . ."

"You should have the colon removed."

We discussed the possibility of a Kock pouch, but Dr. Gelernt said he wanted to review my medical records and examine me in person. Since the Mayo Clinic tests had been inconclusive, he was cautious about raising my hopes.

"When will we know?" I asked.

"I can't tell you for sure. We'll have to do a biopsy and see what the results tell us. If we are able to do the pouch, you should plan on staying in New York for approximately one month—three weeks in the hospital and one week as an outpatient."

"Whatever it takes," I said, "but we'll have to wait until the end of the football season."

"That's fine," said Dr. Gelernt.

Check-In Time

Shortly after the 1981-82 season ended in January with the Ice Bowl loss in Cincinnati, I flew to New York for my scheduled colectomy surgery to take care of my bleeding colon. At the same time, Dr. Gelernt would determine if I was a Kock pouch candidate.

My first day in New York was spent with some friends from the CCFA. I had been doing volunteer work for the foundation for more than a year now, and the meeting was good medicine. It also gave me a chance to see Suzanne Rosenthal again. She had also been operated on by Dr. Gelernt, and she reassured me I was being treated by one of the very best. After the meeting, Suzanne offered to help check me into Mt. Sinai, so we grabbed a cab and headed for the hospital, located on the upper east side of New York City on 99th and Fifth Avenue. Mt. Sinai was certainly different from any hospital I had been in before. The place was a huge maze of corridors, but what struck me most was the number of blue-uniformed policemen in the lobby. Ah, New York.

An orderly escorted me to the tenth-floor wing, where I would spend the next several weeks. While striding down the linoleum-floored hall, I was assaulted by the smells . . . the frantic pace . . . the people in wheelchairs . . . patients on gurneys . . . dozens of medical personnel in white coats and white dresses.

I was relieved to reach my room in the Klingenstein Pavilion wing of the hospital. After I unpacked what few clothes and belongings I had brought along, I pulled open the curtain on the window and found I had a wonderful view overlooking Central Park—a frozen landscape dotted by barren trees, all gray in the late afternoon light. But with the view also came the sounds of the Big Apple—belching buses, honking cabs, and cars accelerating from the traffic light just up the street.

The scouting report on Mt. Sinai was that it was a great hospital with good people, but that the facility was terribly understaffed. I was tipped off that the only way to insure proper attention was to have full-time, round-the-clock private-duty nurses. Because I was facing major surgery, my parents and I decided I would need that kind of care, especially the first week after surgery.

Since my sister, Ingrid, lived in Manhattan, I knew she would visit me as much as she could, as would my new friends from the CCFA—including the Modells and Rosenthals. But the biggest comfort was knowing Mom would be flying out for my surgery.

While I was getting settled, Dr. Gelernt dropped by to introduce himself. Surgeons have a reputation for being strong-willed and sometimes difficult, but I felt immediately comfortable with this man I had heard so much about. Gentle and quick to smile, he was very comfortable with himself and a good listener. Perhaps his understanding of what I was about to go through was made easier by the fact that he had recently undergone heart-bypass surgery himself. It didn't hurt that he was a big football fan who lived and died with his New York Giants. He was doing a lot of dying in those days.

Dr. Gelernt explained that I would undergo two days of tests, followed by surgery early on the third morning. The tests went fine, and the night before the colectomy, I was visited by an anesthesiologist and given a full rundown of what would take place the following morning.

"There is one additional thing I need to tell you," explained the anesthesiologist as he was getting ready to leave. "Because this is a rather extensive surgery and involves cutting in a delicate area, there is a five percent chance you could become impotent following the surgery."

"Wait a minute," I interrupted with horror clearly etched across my face. "I'm only twenty-six, and that's five percent too high!"

He smiled knowingly. "I'm required to tell you that, but actually most of those problems occur in much older men. You should be okay."

"Easy for you to say," I said shaking my head skeptically.

When he left the room, I couldn't get my mind off that five percent. Having been raised in a physician's family, I knew only too well that bad things can happen during surgery. Life doesn't come with any guarantees. I spent quite a little time praying that night, and reliving all that I had been through. I knew I was lucky to be alive and very fortunate to be back playing football again. I reminded myself that God must have other plans for my life and would be there to help get me through this, too.

I managed to get a little sleep before being awakened at 6 a.m. by the anesthesiologist. I was give an oral tranquilizer and an injection to relax me. By the time I was wheeled into the hospital room, I was pretty woozy, but I recall telling Dr. Gelernt that I didn't want to remember any of this. I didn't. The next thing I knew, a nurse was gently shaking me and asking me in a loud voice to wake up. The lights were very bright, and as I slowly came to, I heard someone inquire, "How are you feeling?"

"Okay, but when are you going to get started?" I asked, somewhat confused. Then I heard the voice of Dr. Gelernt.

"We're done, Rolf. It's all over. Everything came out great. You're in the recovery room now."

I smiled with relief.

Any kind of abdominal surgery is very painful, and this operation was no different. I knew the week after the procedure wouldn't be easy, and it wasn't. I was receiving both Demerol and morphine for the pain, and I often hallucinated and faded in and out of consciousness. I'm glad Mom was there to get me through the worst. I was relatively coherent when I was awake, even taking phone calls and carrying on reasonably intelligent conversations. Later though, when asked about them, I couldn't remember anything I had said. Perhaps it was a combination of the medication and the mind's way of blocking out unpleasant experiences.

On the seventh day after surgery—February 7, which

happened to be my 27th birthday—the nasal gastric (or NG tube that's inserted through the nose and into the stomach) was going to be removed. I couldn't wait. The purpose of the NG tube was to continually suction out anything and everything going into the stomach.

The NG tube is taken out when the physician feels your bowels are ready to begin functioning again. Unfortunately, my NG tube was taken out prematurely. Several hours later, I began throwing up the Jell-O I had just eaten. Vomiting was excruciatingly painful, and I became worried that my heaving stomach might have reopened the incision. Fortunately, it hadn't, but the NG tube would have to be put back in again, this time while I was conscious. (Normally, the NG tube is inserted at the end of surgery while the patient is still anesthetized.) That was no fun! It was shortly after the awful reinsertion procedure that Dr. Gelernt walked in with a big smile on his face. I couldn't understand his glee, particularly after what I had just gone through. He didn't leave much time to wonder.

"Happy birthday," he said, hardly able to contain himself. "I have some very good news. Analysis of your removed colon has convinced us that you don't have Crohn's disease, you *had* ulcerative colitis. You are now cured. And if you're still interested, you are now definitely a candidate for a Kock pouch."

Was I interested? Of course I was! I closed my eyes to fight back the tears. My father's hunch had proved to be correct. For more than three years, I had lived with the uncertainty of Crohn's disease, wondering if it would come back and interrupt my life and football career again. And now it was over. That threat was gone.

Lying in my hospital bed, I couldn't help thinking that there were millions of people out there who weren't as fortunate as me. I looked around the room, filled with flowers and cards. I looked at Mom, sitting there with tears running down

her cheeks but smiling as well. At that moment, I made a conscious decision—a promise to God—that I would continue to
work with the CCFA and other groups to help find the cause
of ulcerative colitis and Crohn's disease and encourage others
who were struggling. Thankfully, that was not an idle promise, one made during a moment of great emotion. Nearly
fifteen years have elapsed since that afternoon, and my life
has been greatly enriched as a result of working with people
suffering from inflammatory bowel disease.

The next few days in the hospital were a painful struggle,
but my intestines finally began working, and the doctors
removed the NG tube again. No complications this time
around. My body was starting to recover. With my improved
condition also came thoughts of the mini camp that was just
around the corner. I needed to begin getting back into shape
and was suddenly anxious to return to San Diego.

The night before I was due to be discharged, the two
Modell boys surprised me with a very special going-away
present. They knew how much I was missing normal food
and decided to do something about it. With one of the boys
distracting the floor nurse, the other quickly snuck a piping
hot pepperoni pizza down the hall past the vacated nurses'
station into my room. We were laughing and giggling like little
kids as we shared the first real food I had eaten in fifteen days.
It was a special evening. I couldn't eat a lot, but it was a genuine New York pizza, and I loved every tasty bite. It turned out
to be a good test. My system handled the pizza without any
problems, so I knew I was getting better.

Although I had lost about twenty pounds during my
stay at Mt. Sinai, I was confident my conditioning program
with Phil Tyne would put the weight back on quickly.
Training camp was still five months away, but I was anxious
to get started. Oh, by the way, remember that five percent
chance I was worried about? It turned out to be no problem.

CHAPTER 18

A Surgery to Anticipate

The 1982 football season was one the NFL would like to forget. The players went out on an eight-week strike and threatened to end the season. Fortunately, both sides came to their senses and we played a shortened schedule. The Chargers managed to qualify for the NFL playoffs, but the Dolphins exacted a measure of revenge for our dramatic playoff victory the previous year and beat us soundly in Miami.

Personally, I had a satisfying year despite breaking my wrist just three days before the strike was resolved. I needed two pins and a cast, which was protected by a huge wraparound pad. I didn't miss a game, however, and I actually earned my first trip to the Pro Bowl in Hawaii. The recognition was the culmination of a dream every NFL player has, but in my case, it also brought trepidation. Once again, I would have to shower with a new bunch of players who had only a vague idea of what I had been through.

During our week in the Islands, the players were wined and dined and entertained by everyone from the governor of Hawaii to network and league officials. The whole experience was quite memorable, but I was glad when the Pro Bowl week was finally over. Ever since Dr. Gelernt had decided a year earlier that I was a candidate for Kock pouch surgery, I had planned on having the operation immediately following my last game. Being selected for the Pro Bowl prolonged my season by almost a month, so I was anxious to get on with things.

Following the game, I spent a couple of days on Waikiki Beach mentally preparing for what I hoped would be my final surgery. Gazing into the azure-blue Pacific, I relived the four years that I had been ill with inflammatory bowel disease. I had suffered a lot, and my once-sound body was now scarred forever. I had been forced to deal with the possibility of dying at a young age. I had learned about the uncertainty of life. I knew I must regard each day as a special gift, never to be taken for granted.

Finally, I had learned that there was nothing more important than relationships, first with God and then with family and friends. Although my family and I weren't the best at expressing our love for one another, our devotion and concern for each other came out strongly during our time of crisis. It's hard to express the depth of my feelings for my mom and dad and brother and sister, but I will never forget how they responded when it counted. I had many friends, too, who were there when I needed them—friends who wouldn't let me quit or feel sorry for myself when I didn't think I could go on.

My experiences challenged me to re-examine my life and to try and understand what it all meant. The self-examination set me on a path to discover a faith in Jesus Christ as my personal Savior and a belief that there was a purpose for my existence that was bigger than kicking footballs through a goalpost. Although I had been reluctantly thrust into speaking out for those struggling with inflammatory bowel disease or ostomy surgery, I quickly learned to appreciate the opportunity.

The Last Time

I celebrated my 28th birthday lying on the warm sands of Waikiki Beach, but knew that in a few days I would be lying on the cold steel of an operating table at Mt. Sinai

Hospital in New York City. If all went as planned, I would wake up with a Kock pouch.

Dr. Gelernt, who had done my colectomy surgery a year earlier, would be the man in charge once again. I was hoping for a Pro Bowl performance from him.

I was really psyched about this surgery, but I knew this last hurdle would be a big one. Kock pouch surgery in itself is not life-threatening, but neither is it a day at the beach.

As it turned out, Dr. Gelernt did a masterful job. Everything went just as planned, and I was home within a month, never experiencing any of the postoperative problems I had been warned about.

Over the next few months, I carefully controlled my intubating schedule as instructed, and the pouch slowly expanded to capacity. By the time training camp came around in July, I was completely healthy again and ready for the next chapter in life.

Booted Out

I continued to play football for four more years following the Kock pouch surgery, but it was increasingly clear with each season that the best days of Air Coryell were behind us. Our success spawned contract disputes and numerous trades. In the mid-1980s, the Chargers were a team in transition—and in trouble. Owner Gene Klein lost his heart for the game, and he sold the club in 1984 to Alex Spanos, a successful real estate developer from Stockton, California.

The team slipped further into disarray, and by 1986, Coach Coryell was asked to "resign" in mid-season. Al Saunders was named to replace him, and we finished the 1986 season with a 4-12 mark.

It was clear that Spanos, a businessman not accustomed to losing, wouldn't stand for things as they were and wanted to put his personal stamp on the team. For the veteran players, this was expected; after all, this was the business side of football. Change was inevitable, but the way things were changed wounded many of us in the organization.

Coach Coryell had been a marvelous coach and grown very special to not only his players, but to the city who had recognized his genius way back in the 1970s when he was coaching at San Diego State University. We all hurt when he was let go, and we felt it could have been handled much more gracefully.

With Coach Coryell gone, the excitement of Air Coryell and our high-powered offense left as well. Just as important, however, was the crumbling of friendships and unity that had been part of this team.

As the Chargers began their rebuilding program, I ached for the camaraderie of the Air Coryell years, but I found my teammates getting younger and younger. They had never had the chance to learn the lessons that were ingrained in us by Coach Coryell, and it was becoming clear that I had less and less in common with them.

As I sorted through my feelings, I recognized that I had never chosen this profession, and although life as an NFL kicker had been a thrilling ride, I knew it was time to begin thinking about life after pro football. At the same time, however, I was just like any other pro athlete who was finding it difficult to step away from the game.

From the first day of the 1987 training camp, it was apparent my relationship with the Chargers would be ending. Equally apparent was that the team wasn't sure how to get rid of me. I was still a good kicker, and over ten years, I had become a fairly popular player. If they chose to release me overnight, it would be difficult to explain to the public.

At camp, the Chargers brought in several kickers to compete for my job, including journeyman kicker Vince Abbott. This was nothing new: every incumbent kicker expects preseason competition. What was different was that no matter how well I kicked, I was never allowed to attempt a field goal during the exhibition games. As the preseason came to a close, it became clear that I wasn't being given an opportunity to compete for my job. The fans and the media knew something was up.

Finally, with the media clamoring for an answer, the Chargers orchestrated a trade to the Dallas Cowboys a week before the final preseason game. These two articles from the *San Diego Union* sum up what happened at the time. The first story, written by sportswriter T.J. Simers, appeared on the front page of the September 1, 1987 edition:

"Benirschke Traded to Cowboys"

Chargers coach Al Saunders, in making the announcement of the trade of placekicker Rolf Benirschke to Dallas for an undisclosed draft choice yesterday, said emphatically, "He did not lose his job."

Yet there was very little doubt from the outset of training camp that if upper management prevailed, Benirschke would have little opportunity to keep the job he has held with the Chargers for ten years. Although informed he would have to battle for his position, the personable and highly visible Benirschke, who nearly died of ulcerative colitis in 1979, was given no opportunity to attempt any field goals in the preseason.

"The team is in a tough situation," Benirschke said yesterday, hours before the trade was completed. "If I'm allowed to kick in the final preseason game and kick well, then what does the team do?"

The team, of course, never put itself in that position. But the conflicting explanation behind the trade announcement suggested Benirschke may never have had a chance. "There was equal competition between the two (Benirschke and free agent Vince Abbott)," Saunders said. "Rolf and Vince competed ever since the beginning of training camp, head-to-head."

"The coaching staff basically decided Vince Abbott had a strong lead in the position to be the kicker on this club," said Steve Ortmayer, the team's director of football operations. "They indicated they were prepared to play with Vince Abbott."

Ortmayer later amended his statement after being informed of Saunders' remarks, saying, "That's (Saunders' assessment) was basically true, too. It (Ortmayer's statement) was probably the incorrect thing to say."

"It was clear for a while that I wasn't going to be the kicker here," said Benirschke, 32. "I don't know anything that I could have done to keep my job. I was kicking the ball well, and I was healthy and strong. I have no idea what else I could have done."

Saunders, a friend and supporter of Benirschke, was asked if he was in complete agreement with the decision to trade Benirschke.

"It's a transaction we feel that is best for the organization at this time," Saunders said.

Ortmayer, asked if he thought Benirschke was given a fair opportunity to make the Chargers' roster, said, "Yeah, I do." Ortmayer said it was the Cowboys who made overtures about acquiring Benirschke following an early August scrimmage with the Chargers in Thousand Oaks, California. But Cowboys vice president for pro personnel Bob Ackles told the Dallas media it was the Chargers who shopped Benirschke in the last week.

The trade became a topic at training camp at UCSD yesterday long before it was announced. Both Benirschke and the media knew of it early in the day, adding to the bizarre treatment afforded Benirschke this training camp.

"I feel like a leaf blowing in the wind," said Benirschke. "It's been an awkward situation in this training camp. I've tried to understand it, but I really can't completely understand it."

That article monopolized the right hand side of the front page. In the center was a deep three-column picture, taken on November 18, 1979, showing me walking hand-in-hand to midfield with big Louie Kelcher just before the start of the game with the Pittsburgh Steelers. And to the left of that was a touching column—a life story, actually—by *San Diego Union* sports editor Barry Lorge:

To appreciate what Rolf Benirschke has meant to the Chargers and San Diego, to football fans and other critters, you only have to look back to the poignant pictures of Nov. 18, 1979.

That was the day the popular placekicker, down to 123 pounds from an intestinal illness that nearly killed him, visited his teammates before an important game against the Pittsburgh Steelers. They designated him honorary captain. Benirschke wasn't sure he could make it to the center of the field for the coin toss.

Defensive tackle Louie Kelcher—who had gone to see his buddy at University Hospital when his condition was so grave only family visits were allowed, telling nurses he was "Rolf's brother, Louie Benirschke"—reassured him again: "Don't worry. If you stumble, I'll carry you. We want you there."

Benirschke donned his jersey, No. 6, over his street clothes and slowly, shakily followed Kelcher to midfield, clutching the big lineman's hand. Well-wishers cried in the stands. The crowd rose and gave a favorite son a heartfelt welcome back that also might have been a fond farewell.

Benirschke, who nearly succumbed to complications from surgery, had lost fifty-one pounds. He never expected to play football again. He had come to say goodbye to a team that was on the rise—8-3 before a 35-7 victory that afternoon, on the way to the first of three straight AFC West championships.

But after a determined rehabilitation, Benirschke came back courageously in 1980 and hit a club record 24 of 35 field-goal attempts—one his career longest of 53 yards. The next season, he made 19 of 26 and three game-winners, including the clincher in a 41-38 playoff epic at Miami in overtime.

As of yesterday, when he was traded to the Dallas Cowboys for a conditional draft choice, Benirschke was the third-most accurate kicker in National Football League history with a .702 field-goal percentage (146-of-208). He is also the Chargers' leading career scorer (766 points), and one of its most beloved personalities.

His story is the stuff of television drama, featured on "This Is Your Life" in 1983.

The son of Dr. Kurt Benirschke, renowned pathologist and conservationist, Rolf started playing soccer at age five, as conditioning for youth skiing and hockey in Hanover, N.H. When he moved to San Diego as a high school sophomore, he became a soccer-style kicker for La Jolla High. He went to the University of California at Davis on an academic scholarship, earning a degree in zoology in 1977.

He was the next-to-last collegian drafted that year, by the Oakland Raiders, who subsequently waived him. The Chargers signed him as a free agent, beginning a memorable decade for them, and for him.

Handsome, articulate, soft-spoken, community-spirited, he was popular from the beginning. But his remarkable recovery from what was first diagnosed as Crohn's disease, and later as ulcerative colitis, made him a folk hero.

Benirschke was always thoughtful, a kind of cerebral saint in a brutal game, but his illness made him even more introspective and philosophical. His personal credo became: "It's the journey that counts, not the destination."

In a world of violent collisions and giant egos, he realized that you do nothing in this life alone. He is a humanitarian and a friend of God's other creatures. He has been involved in charities and civic causes from the Chargers' annual blood drive, which was inaugurated in 1979 to help him through his surgery, to the Crohn's & Colitis Foundation of America. His pet project, Kicks for Critters, has raised more than $1 million to help preserve endangered species.

Typically, Benirschke left the Chargers yesterday sad but not bitter . . . kicking but not screaming.

If he thought he never got a chance this training camp and preseason to demonstrate that he can still do the job, he wouldn't blame the organization.

"I don't want to bad-mouth anybody," he said softly between phone calls to his home. "I believe this is part of football, part of the good and bad of a game I love. I am excited about having a chance to continue playing. I love the Chargers, but I have to move on."

Exultation, anguish, triumphs, pitfalls—they are all part of the wondrous journey. He wants to keep experiencing them. He has enough business interests and projects going to have retired comfortably in San Diego, which always will be his home, but he thought it over and decided to report to the Cowboys. "I believe I have a lot more football left in me," he said. "I'm looking forward to the challenge."

People who have watched him in games and practice the past three seasons think he isn't the sure shot from medium-range he used to be. Maybe that will change in Dallas, where he will kick on Astroturf. Football can be a cruel business.

"There is a lot going through my mind," he sighed yesterday after learning of the trade. "Unforgettable memories of my years here, the friendships, the great games, the support I've had for so many years.

"The strongest memory, the most powerful, will always be when I went out on the field before that game in 1979, when I was hardly able to walk, and the response people gave me."

His voice started to crack. He tried to choke back the tears but couldn't. Rolf Benirschke occupies a unique place in the hearts of San Diego sports fans. Look at the pictures and you will understand.

I joined the Cowboys just before the final preseason game. I knew in my heart that I could still kick, but I felt like a pawn being moved around the NFL chessboard. Because of all I had gone through, however, I began to wonder if some of the rumors being spread were really true.

But from my first practice with the Cowboys, I kicked as well as I ever had. The team had an experienced snapper and holder, and suddenly, the goalposts seemed ridiculously wide. My confidence was sky high going into the final preseason game, where I made one field goal and hit two long kickoffs that weren't returned. I felt strong. I *was* strong.

But then it became obvious: *Dallas wasn't going to keep me.* They had already made up their minds to go with a younger— and cheaper—kicker. The deal between San Diego and Dallas was simply a graceful way for the Chargers to extricate themselves from a difficult position.

In a way, I was relieved when the news of my release came down from Coach Tom Landry. I decided my playing career was over. Besides, I couldn't wait for the next chapter in my life to begin.

CHAPTER 19

Along Came Mary

Just before the Chargers shipped me off to Dallas, something happened that August that changed my personal and spiritual life forever.

It all began at an outdoor street carnival in La Jolla, where I was walking with Jill, my girlfriend at the time. Jill and I had been dating steadily for eighteen months, but our relationship was on the ropes—and we both knew it. I have to take a lot of the blame. Although we had both enjoyed athletics and the outdoors, we came from different backgrounds, and we really weren't right for each other.

As Jill and I strolled along the streets, we ran into a group of friends. One of them introduced me to Mary Michaletz, a speech pathologist with a practice in San Diego. She worked primarily with children, she said.

I stood there transfixed by her beautiful smile, her winsome attitude, and her lithe, trim figure. But more than that, I was intrigued by her kindness. As we made small talk, we discovered that I knew one of her patients.

In one of those twists of fate, Jill excused herself to find a restroom, leaving me with my friends and new acquaintance, Mary. As the minutes passed, I became more taken with the way Mary interacted with everybody and how comfortable she appeared to be with herself.

When Jill returned, our conversation ended and our two groups went our separate ways. I *really* went a different way; the following week I was traded to Dallas . . . and was soon out of football.

Being released from the Cowboys turned my life absolutely upside down. I had a lot of things to think about, but strangely my thoughts kept coming back to Mary, a young woman I had talked to for only a few minutes.

On a whim, I decided to see if I could find her in the phone book. I remembered that she was a speech pathologist, and figured there couldn't be that many in San Diego. Sure enough, I found her listed in the Yellow Pages. It took me several days, however, to muster up the courage to call her. When I finally did, I asked her out to dinner.

She was hesitant to accept at first; after all, I was almost a total stranger, and it had been more than a month since we had first met. But after talking for a while, she decided to take a chance and see what this goofy guy was all about.

We decided to drive up the coast to a quiet dinner spot overlooking the Dana Point harbor. The fifty-minute drive could have been awkward, but we found that conversation came easily. The meal was wonderful, and it wasn't long before it seemed like we were the only two people in the world.

The ride back was different, however. I realized I was falling in love, and I knew I would have to tell her about my ostomy. Mary sensed something was wrong.

"What is it?" she asked cautiously. "Just a few minutes ago we were having a great time, and now it's like you're afraid to talk to me."

"I guess I am," I replied tentatively. "You see, I have to tell you something. I was very sick a few years ago, and I needed several major surgeries to save my life. The surgeries left me different than most people."

"What happened?" Mary asked curiously. "As far as I can tell, you seem pretty normal to me."

"Well, I'm not exactly normal anymore." I struggled with what to say next. This was it. The moment of truth. The moment I had worried about ever since my first operation.

By now, however, I had learned that most people took their cues from me. If I was comfortable with the situation, then they would be comfortable as well. Besides, I had no choice. I had to be absolutely honest. There was no bluffing or hiding this. I decided it might as well be sooner than later. That way, if she decided she couldn't deal with it, I could at least get on with my life.

With these thoughts in mind, I began to tell Mary my story. The whole story. I talked about waking up with two ostomy appliances. About wondering if I would live, and, if I did, whether or not life would be worth living. When I finished, I glanced over and saw she was crying. Big tears were rolling down her cheeks, and she gently touched my arm.

"You're okay now, aren't you?" she whispered. "Does it still hurt? Can I touch you?"

"I'm doing fine," I smiled, glad that the truth was out.

We talked the rest of the way home about what I had gone through and by the time we arrived back in San Diego and said goodnight, we both knew something special was going on.

Mary and I did fall quickly in love, and we began seeing each other quite often. But I was still sorting things out, wondering what life would be like after football. What was I going to do? I received lots of interesting opportunities, including hosting "The Wheel of Fortune" with Vanna White (see the next chapter). But all this turmoil and change were tough on our relationship, and after eighteen months of dating, we broke up.

Again, a lot of the blame could be placed on my shoulders. The thought of getting married frightened me to death. I didn't feel capable of being a good husband, and I didn't want to fail at marriage.

We had other hurdles to overcome. One was Mary's

rebellious streak. She was raised in a good Catholic family, attended parochial schools (back in the days when nuns were nuns), but when she became an adult, she wanted to do things her way. I, of course, had my own ideas, and when we realized that we held opposite political views, we struggled even more.

In addition to these obstacles, Mary was more prepared for marriage than me. She was ready to get on with her life, but I was too immature—spiritually and emotionally—for matrimony. So we parted ways.

Yet like many other times in my life, something good was going to come out of this extremely painful situation. I just didn't know it at the time.

In the midst of our struggles, I was wrestling with my own personal issues. I had just finished reading Pat Morley's *Man in the Mirror* and been particularly challenged by the trap he describes as the rat race of life.

At the same time all of this was going on, a friend called from out of the blue and invited me to church. Unfortunately, I hadn't been to church for several years, but for some strange reason, I accepted. Wouldn't you know it, the sermon that first Sunday was on marriage.

For the next month, the pastor expanded on the marriage topic and explained that, by far, the essential ingredient in a healthy marriage was placing God at the center. I didn't really understand what that meant, but as I attended several Sundays in a row, the sermons started to make sense.

Over the next five months, I became involved with some special men in a Bible study and, for the first time in my life, really began to wrestle with some private beliefs. This was a very difficult time, but as I became honest with myself, I realized I couldn't continue living as I had been. After spending hours reading the Bible and really understanding what Christ's dying on the cross meant, I made a commitment to accept Him as Lord and Savior of my life.

Meanwhile, nearly six months had passed since I had last spoken to Mary. Ending our relationship was especially painful for her. She insisted that I not call or write, and she even asked me not to run into her at the gym or the restaurants we used to frequent.

One afternoon, after giving a luncheon talk, a close friend of Mary's came up to say hello. I felt awkward chatting with her, but suddenly I had an overwhelming desire to find out how Mary was doing. Finally, I couldn't help myself anymore.

"How is Mary?" I asked hesitantly.

"She's fine," responded the friend. "I know she was really hurt when you two broke up, but she's moved on with her life. She's back to dating now."

When we said goodbye, I couldn't get Mary out of my mind. Literally every night for the next week I found myself waking up at 2 a.m., thinking about Mary. I tried everything to fall back asleep, but nothing worked. Instead, I would just lie there, tossing and turning until daylight when I could finally get dressed and go to work. Looking back, it's clear the Holy Spirit was prompting me, but back then, I didn't understand what was happening.

Finally, unable to stop thinking about Mary and rapidly losing the ability to function in my sleep-deprived condition, I called her friend.

"Is Mary in love with anyone?" I needed to know.

"I'm not sure," came the answer, "but she is seeing someone."

Buoyed by this ray of hope, I tried to reach Mary at her office. She wasn't in, but her secretary explained she would be back at noon and wouldn't have another patient until 1:30.

The time was 11:30, so I jumped in my car and drove to her office, knowing the whole way that we were right for each other. The idea of marrying her suddenly seemed like the most natural next step to take. I just hoped she would recognize my change of heart and feel the same way.

When Mary stepped into her office and found me sitting there, she was absolutely stunned. Her face began to flush and she began to get angry, but before she had a chance to say anything, I got on my knees and apologized for what I had done.

"Mary, I'm sorry for the hurt I've caused you," I said with tears in my eyes. "I know it's been hard on you. I know I haven't been easy to be around. But Mary, I've taken the last six months to grow up a lot, and I really miss you. I'm ready to get on with my life—to make a commitment to you. Will you marry me?"

"Rolf, don't do this to me," she replied, still in shock. "I'm just getting over you. Why should things be any different?"

"Mary, I know that the time we dated was difficult, but I also know that we had something special."

"I know, Rolf, but what about the things we've struggled with?"

"We can work those things out. You know a lot of that was caused by my selfishness and immaturity."

Mary was beginning to see that I *had* changed. I *was* different, thanks to Christ working in my life. Although she could tell I was absolutely serious, Mary still wasn't willing to go along with my proposal. How could she say yes after not having seen me for six months?

"Rolf, would you be willing to go see a marriage counselor? Would you be willing to see if we can work out some of our issues?" she asked bluntly.

"Absolutely!" I responded, sensing I was getting somewhere. "Whatever it takes. How about if we talk about this over dinner tonight?"

"I can't."

"Why not?"

"Because I have a date."

"A date? Can you break it?"

"Rolf, I'm not going to, and I don't want you telling

anybody that we've even talked. I still don't know you're for real, and I'm not willing to go through the pain and embarrassment of trying to explain it to everyone again."

We soon began our counseling sessions, and after a few visits we knew our love for each other was real. We followed up our counseling times with an emotional Marriage Encounter weekend in which we discovered that Mary had also returned to her faith during our time apart.

We began attending church together, and for the first time, our relationship was grounded in Christ. That made all the difference. Our on-again, off-again romance was on for keeps, and in November 1989, we became officially engaged.

Mary's younger sister Joni—one of five sisters—was already engaged and planning an April 1990 marriage. Since we didn't want to wait until June or July, we asked Joni if she would mind if we got married in February. Both she and her fiancé, Earl, bless their hearts, gave us their blessings, and we rushed to get started.

With only three months to plan the wedding, we found a pastor, a church, and a reception area . . . and exchanged "I do's" on February 24, 1990.

The Questions of Life

Being married to Mary has been everything I hoped it would be—and much more. I finally understand now what the Bible means when it talks about a husband and wife "becoming one flesh."

We are one flesh, and our faith in Christ is the common denominator. The development of my faith, however, has been a journey, like it has been for many other people. God was my anchor when I was at my lowest point during the 1979 surgeries. When I stood at the edge of the cliff, staring into the dark abyss, I asked some tough questions: *What happens when I die? Is that it? Is there any hope? Is this all there is to life?*

My faith allowed me to come to grips with dying, and as

a result, a feeling of extraordinary calm came over me. I felt at peace with the Lord. I meant it when I told my father not to let the doctors keep me artificially alive if it meant being on life support. I was prepared to die and meet my Creator.

But looking back over the years, I can see where I had more of an "intellectual faith" during those dark days in the ICU. I believed because it was comforting—not because I had a relationship with Christ. Instead, I had an instinctual faith that things were going to work out, and if they didn't . . . well, that was okay, too.

But once I got back on my feet, like so many others, I put God back in His box. *I appreciate You getting me through this, but I've got a great life as an NFL kicker going now. See You later.* I resumed taking charge of my life and went back to doing things that I knew were inappropriate. I wasn't a bad person, but I was living a hypocritical life. My guilt kept me from going back to church, and the more I stayed away from Christian fellowship, the easier it was to rationalize my behavior.

Perhaps that was because my faith was a mile wide and only an inch deep. Perhaps it was because I didn't have strong friends to hold me accountable. Or, perhaps it was because I was just unwilling to turn everything over to God.

When Steve, Ingrid, and I were kids back in New Hampshire, we went to Sunday Mass and catechism class during the week. We took communion regularly and were confirmed in the Catholic faith, but in the winter, when the snow was good, skiing at the Dartmouth Skiway often took precedence over the Sabbath.

Not until my rookie season with the Chargers did I encounter a group of Christians for the first time. Included in that group was Mike Fuller, a special guy who also happened to be my holder.

For a kicker, there are no more valuable people on the team than his holder and his snapper. I absolutely relied on Mike Fuller. But Mike Fuller absolutely relied on Jesus Christ.

No matter how the season was going, Mike was always the same. Oh, Mike was just as competitive as everyone else, but there was a calm about him that was hard to put your finger on. Whether we were going out to kick a game-winning field goal or a meaningless extra point with a thirty-point lead, Mike was always the same. I didn't understand it, but I knew I wanted it.

When Mike encouraged me to attend team chapel, I gladly accepted. He was the first to introduce me to the writings and radio ministries of Dr. James Dobson and Chuck Swindoll. Mike planted the seeds of faith inside me, but it wasn't until I became sick with IBD a year later that I began moving closer to Christ.

During my battle with ulcerative colitis, I discovered the fellowship of Christian friends and the comfort that reading the Bible brings. So when I lay there in the hospital in the fall of '79, I honestly felt I had nothing to fear . . . no matter what happened.

I believed I had done everything I could do. I had excellent medical resources, talented doctors, attentive nurses, a loving family, and faithful friends. Although I trusted that God was providing, it was still sad to see the pain on my parents' faces. I knew that if I died my death would send them into deep grief. Still, God was in control, I told myself, and I rested in that thought.

The regular visits I was getting from my minister friend, Jim Adkins, were a tremendous source of strength. He was kind, gentle, sensitive, and giving. He read comforting Scriptures and fed my soul. That helped a great deal. One of my nurses, Sheana Funkhauser, regularly prayed with me. I liked that.

But all those years I never knew that believing in Jesus Christ is not a religion—it's a relationship. All Christ was asking me was to believe in Him, and I would have eternal salvation. You see, I had always believed that I had to do something to earn my salvation—attending team chapels, having the right person pray for me, giving money to charitable organizations. I always thought that I had to "be good"—or at least better than my teammates—to go to heaven. But no, all I had to do was accept His free gift by saying, "I believe in You, and I humbly turn my life over to you, asking that you forgive my sins and take control of today and tomorrow."

In the end, that's all Christ wanted, and when I made that commitment, everything changed—including my relationship with Mary.

Our lives haven't been the same since.

CHAPTER 20

Wanna Buy a Vowel?

One morning in 1987, my life took another unexpected turn. I had been invited to appear on a well-watched Southern California morning television show called "A.M. Los Angeles" to talk about life with IBD. I had done this often on shows like "The Today Show," "Good Morning America," "The CBS Morning Show" and a half-dozen talk shows, including "Sally Jessy Raphael." I always found the experiences rewarding because my appearances usually prompted hundreds of people to write or call the Crohn's and Colitis Foundation of America to request information.

But "A.M. Los Angeles" would be different. Do you know how people in show business say you should never work with kids or animals or risk getting upstaged in a big way? Well, I learned first hand on both counts! The first segment of this morning program was devoted to two talented and precocious child stars of the "Les Miserables" stage production which was running in Los Angeles at the time. They sang beautifully, clowned around with the host, and were just adorable. As I watched the closed-circuit feed in the green room, I thought, *Boy, how do you follow this and talk seriously about anything, let alone a difficult disease?* But I didn't follow the kids.

The next segment featured what the host introduced as the "Pet of the Nineties." I watched in disbelief as thirty rabbits were brought out in cages. There was every size and shape of rabbit imaginable: lop-eared rabbits, little tiny rabbits, big cottontail rabbits.

As the trainer talked about each kind of rabbit, he would take it out of its cage and let the little furry thing loose on the stage. Before you could say "Hide the kids!" several of the rabbits began doing what rabbits do best right there on live TV.

Not wanting to miss an opportunity to embarrass the hosts, the cameramen quickly zoomed in on the hare-raising activities. Suddenly, the whole group was going at it. Meanwhile, the host and hostess were trying their best to keep the program's PG rating by pulling the little guys off the little gals as quickly as they could. They were losing the battle, however, and the hysterical studio audience only added to the pandemonium. Finally, the exasperated host, realizing that he had lost complete control, stuck his face in front of the camera and said, "We have to go to commercial, but we'll be right back with former football star Rolf Benirschke."

My worst nightmare! How do you follow that?! We managed somehow and as fate would have it, one of the TV viewers that day was Merv Griffin. Besides being a famous TV personality, he was also the producer of such successful game shows as "Jeopardy" and "Wheel of Fortune." Griffin, who was in the midst of putting together another game show, was looking for a host. He must have liked what he saw that morning because he tracked me down and asked if I would like to audition. Griffin told me that "Wheel of Fortune" host Pat Sajak had just been picked to begin a late-night talk show opposite Johnny Carson and "The Tonight Show." This would necessitate Sajak relinquishing his role as the network daytime host of "Wheel of Fortune," although he would still continue hosting the nighttime syndicated version of the same show.

His offer took me by surprise as I never had aspirations for television, let alone hosting a game show. Of course, I had never thought about playing professional football until I was drafted either. The parallels were not lost on me, so I decided to view my tryout as an opportunity to get a glimpse into an industry I didn't know much about.

The search for a new "Wheel of Fortune" host generated lots of publicity. All kinds of experienced game-show hosts and TV personalities from around the country were trying out—plus some unlikely folks like tennis star Jimmy Connors.

My audition was nervewracking, and I felt overwhelmed by the studio's size and all the stage hands, makeup artists, cue card holders, cameramen, producers, and stage directors. Of course, there was also Vanna White. It was like being a rookie all over again. Somehow I got through that first introduction to Hollywood and was invited back for several more auditions. On the set, I learned that "Wheel of Fortune" was the most-successful game show ever produced, generating hundreds of millions of dollars. The program was broadcast in the mornings by NBC and syndicated at night in most markets across the country. This show was huge!

After my auditions, I had pretty much decided there were many more talented people than me seeking the job and that I had better get back to real life. I was scheduled to fly to New York to do a speaking engagement and to visit with my sister, Ingrid. We had a great time together over dinner and a good laugh at me even trying out as a "game show host."

"What would Dad think?" Ingrid giggled. You can imagine my surprise when, upon my return, I found a message on my answering machine explaining that I had been selected as the next daytime host of "Wheel of Fortune." I couldn't believe it! Me? With Vanna White? I had never done anything like this before. Sure, I had been on TV a bunch of times, but never where it was my job!

The next morning I was awakened by a phone call from the show's producer. After congratulating me, she explained that we would be begin taping three shows on Thursday and then five more on Friday. "Thursday?" I said. "You mean in two or three weeks?"

"No," she replied. "Thursday this week."

Thursday was in three days! Didn't they know that this was all completely new to me ? What about practice? Didn't they realize that I had no idea what I was doing? I couldn't admit to the producer that I had never even seen an entire show of "Wheel of Fortune." I had no clue how to segue in and out of commercials, read the producer's hand signals, or "follow" one of the four cameras. I felt overwhelmed. I had this urge to practice, to train . . . like when I was a rookie trying to earn a spot on the team.

The next few days were crazy. I was besieged by the entertainment media, curious about who I was and why I had been selected. It became such a circus that it reminded me of the locker room at playoff time. Some of the questions were just ridiculous. In an interview with David Friedman of *Newsday*, I was asked quite seriously if "Wheel of Fortune" was part of my "five-year career plan."

"Are you serious?" I replied. "But it does feel a little strange. My father is an internationally known professor of pathology, a physician, an author—and his son will be standing fifteen feet away from Vanna White and asking people if they want to buy a vowel!"

When Thursday arrived, I drove up to L.A. feeling nervous and unprepared. As I pulled into the studio parking lot, I found my parking spot next to ones reserved for Johnny Carson and Ed McMahon. Now I *knew* I was in over my head! Inside the studio, I was introduced again to Vanna White. She was very kind and gracious and tried to help ease my nervousness. We were just getting to talk about how this had all come about when the producer dropped in and said it was time for a dry run. I was amazed at the number of people coordinating the show. I counted at least fifty people doing the sound, lights, and cameras and other things I didn't know much about. During the rehearsal, I made all kinds of rookie mistakes, but I tried to absorb as much as I could. Before I knew what was going on, we began taping shows for real in front of a live audience.

Thus began my six-month stint on "Wheel of Fortune" and my Andy Warhol-like fifteen minutes of fame. The media made a big deal about my new career as a game-show host. Predictably, I became fodder for the *National Enquirer* and other supermarket tabloids. In fact, it didn't take long before I was romantically linked with Vanna. One story gushed that we had an "intimate candlelight dinner" when all we actually did was sit next to each other at the catered meal brought in between shows. The story neglected to mention that the rest of the production crew was there as well! These ridiculous stories were written while I was dating Mary. Fortunately, she was intelligent enough to recognize them as Hollywood gossip, but it was still tough when Mary's friends and relatives would call and share the articles with her.

I felt especially sorry for Vanna White. Something was always being written about her. Virtually every time we'd tape the show, someone would bring in the latest tabloid with another far-out exposé. No matter what gossip had been written, however, she always came bouncing on the set, cheery as can be, seemingly unaffected. Once the klieg lights were off, however, she became very private. I didn't blame her. She was recognized everywhere she went, and people were always wanting something from her. She needed walls just to survive.

I quickly learned that much of the television industry was driven by fear, not unlike the NFL. Instead of the fear of being waived, it was the fear of being canceled, or the fear of being too old, or the fear of not having the right "look." I found it interesting that some of the biggest celebrities and entertainers were also the most insecure. They had built their entire self-image on what others thought or wrote about them—or on their overnight ratings.

For me, I had already experienced my sport's "worst fear"—being released from pro football. In the process, I had discovered that it wasn't the end of the world. As a result, my attitude about this whole new experience was to make sure I enjoyed it. If "Wheel of Fortune" went away tomorrow, I knew I would survive just fine.

And that's exactly what happened. After six months of doing the show and getting more comfortable with each taping, NBC sold the show to CBS. Although I was told that Merv Griffin still wanted me, the new network said they had plans to change the show a little and bring in their own host. Looking back, I have no regrets. Hosting "Wheel of Fortune" was an interesting experience, kind of like a quick detour down a little-traveled side street along the highway of life. Besides, I'm now an answer to a trivia question!

CHAPTER 21

Two-Minute Warning

It's funny how NFL football games and field goals can seem so important at the time, but now that I've been out of pro football for a decade, I have a different perspective.

My football career was a lot of fun, and I was fortunate to play on some great teams with some fabulous players. But when I came down with IBD, I was forced to learn that there was more to life than Sunday afternoon football games. I'm glad I did.

After my surgeries, I became particularly sensitive to youngsters who seemed so vulnerable at such a young age. I sat in countless hospital rooms, holding their hands and stroking their foreheads, and I saw these young kids forced to deal with a horrible disease at an age when they should be worrying about their first date. It all seemed so unfair.

But through all this, I have learned that life is not always fair, and we *must* play out the hand we have been dealt. I am even more convinced that *life is always worth fighting for.* You've got to hang in there, no matter how difficult it seems at the time.

During my NFL career, I came to them as a football player, someone they may have seen play on television. Now that I'm out of the game, I'm off whatever pedestal people may have put me on. I like that.

During my hospital visits, it's easier now to establish that

I'm just like them. We often compare scars or swap embarrassing stories and how ostomy surgery has impacted our lives. A special kinship usually develops. Peering into the eyes of these young kids, I often see their anguish and self-pity turn to hope and understanding. We sometimes laugh and often cry, but the experience invariably helps both of us.

Before my illness, I remember volunteering to help out at the Special Olympics. I would spend three or four hours with these courageous youngsters, and then return to my normal life. They, on the other hand, had to continue a twenty-four-hour-a-day struggle with their challenges. I often went home feeling convicted, like I was somehow patronizing them, not really understanding what their lives were like.

Since my illness, however, I have a different outlook. I know handicapped people genuinely appreciate the encouragement they receive, and I now have no problem looking them in the eye and discussing whatever issue they may be facing.

It's particularly true when I meet kids in wheelchairs. I feel like one of the few people who can relate to their isolation, self-doubt and feelings of being different. These kids appreciate the straight talk. They know many adults try not to see them, or if they do, feel uncomfortable in their presence.

My experiences with handicapped children has helped me minister to those with ostomies, especially teens riding the roller coaster of adolescence. I can remember talking to a group of young people late one afternoon when the sun was setting into the Pacific Ocean. I asked everyone to pause for a moment and look at the red ball of fire slowly dipping below the horizon.

"You see that beautiful sunset?" I asked quietly. "It's gorgeous isn't it? Stop and enjoy it. Remember, there was a time when many of us wondered if we would ever get out of the hospital to experience a moment like this again."

I watched the teens gaze toward the horizon. "When you

think about it," I continued, "each of us has been given a second chance at life. We have been given the kind of wisdom that people ordinarily don't receive until they've lived sixty-five or seventy years, and we have an opportunity to do something special with it. You know, at an early age, that life offers no guarantees and that each day is truly precious. You need never lament that you'd do things differently if only you had another chance."

I could see the kids nodding in understanding. "I can tell you from my own experiences that I wouldn't trade the scars on my stomach for what this illness has taught me about what is important in life."

The Point After

A few years ago, I was asked to give the commencement address at the University of California-San Diego (UCSD) graduation ceremonies. I was unsure what words of wisdom I could possibly share with these bright minds, but I decided to tell a story that took place during my last season in the NFL. The year was 1986, during one of the worst seasons in Charger history. By the end of October, we were 1-6, so our popular coach Don Coryell was fired.

Our receivers coach, Al Saunders, was named the new captain of our rapidly sinking ship. Thrust into the job without any head coaching experience, Saunders' first game was against the Dallas Cowboys—and we had to play without injured quarterback Dan Fouts. Predictably, we were soundly beaten, and our backup quarterback threw *five* interceptions! We emerged from the game with the worst record in the league at 1-7.

Next up were the Denver Broncos, a team with a mirror record of ours at 7-1, the *best* in the league. Worse yet, we had to play them at Mile High Stadium, where the Broncos win over 90 percent of the time. Fouts still wasn't healthy, and we were such underdogs that Las Vegas oddsmakers took the game off the board!

We were all feeling the pressure, especially new coach Al Saunders. What happened next I'll never forget.

We were finishing our pregame meal at the team hotel when Coach Saunders stood up to address the players.

"Men," he began, pulling a newspaper clipping out of his jacket pocket, "I want to tell you about someone who just ran the slowest marathon in history." He paused for a moment.

The players looked bewildered. "What's this have to do with us?" one player whispered at our table. "Has Coach lost it?"

"Yeah," piped in another, "I know we don't have much team speed, but where's he going with this?"

Saunders took his time. He held up the clipping. "It says here that Bob Wieland just ran the New York Marathon in two days, two hours and twenty-seven minutes."

Again, you could see the players looking around at each other. "What's he doing, man?" asked one. "I mean, I could *walk* a marathon in six or seven hours."

Coach Saunders continued. "But this man ran the New York Marathon without any legs. You see, he'd been in Vietnam and was in a fox hole when a grenade landed nearby. He jumped on it to save a buddy, but both his legs were blown off."

Saunders let that news sink in for a moment. "See this picture?" he asked. "It shows Bob Wieland crossing the finish line. He ran the marathon on the stumps of his legs by swinging his legless torso—a yard at a time—with his arms. And when he finally finished, after more than two days, the race director came up to him, 'I thought you dropped out days ago. Why did you finish?'

"Wieland answered, 'Well, for two reasons. First, I've always wanted to run the New York Marathon, the greatest marathon in the world. And second, I always *believed* I could do it. Once I took those first few steps, I *knew* I was going to finish—even if it took two days, two hours and twenty-seven minutes.'"

As Coach Saunders looked around the room, you could have heard a pin drop. He folded the clipping and put it back into his coat. Then he caught a player's eye.

"Do you believe we can win today?" he asked.

But before the player could answer, he looked at another player. "What about you? Do you think we can win?" He looked at a third player. "You've heard the story. Do you think we can win?"

Saunders drove his point home. "I believe we can win, and if *you* and *you* and *you*"—he was pointing to the players now—"think we can win, then we'll beat the Denver Broncos today. That's all I have to say. Buses leave in five minutes."

It became *really* quiet in that hotel conference room. But as the players began to get up and head to the exits, I could hear them whispering to each other.

"Do you think we can win?"

"I think we can."

"Yeah, I do too," replied another. "What about you?"

"Absolutely. We can beat the Broncos even if nobody in the stands thinks we have a snowball's chance in hell!"

With that, we boarded the bus for the ride to Mile High Stadium. It was the quietest bus I had ever been on in ten years of playing in the league.

When we pulled into the parking lot, I could tell the Denver fans were really up for this game. The tailgate parties were in full swing, and everyone was dressed in orange and blue. They smelled a massacre and had come early to celebrate.

To get from our buses to the locker room, we had to walk through a gauntlet of rabid fans and endure their insults. "You guys suck!" they screamed. "You're going to get your @#$% whipped today!"

With their taunts ringing in our ears, we quietly dressed for the game. I don't know what our inexperienced quarterback Tom Flick was thinking. His disastrous performance the week before had been replayed in the media all week, and he knew he had to go back out and play again.

With Coach Saunders' inspirational words still in our minds, we took the field and played with a dogged determination that hadn't been evident in our previous eight games. Tom Flick didn't throw an interception, getting us into field-goal position three times, so we nursed a 9-3 lead late into the fourth quarter. As John Elway marched the Broncos down the field, it looked like we were destined to lose once again. But then a little-used defensive back stepped in front of a sure touchdown pass and intercepted the ball in the end zone. Our victory was preserved!

The Denver fans couldn't believe what they had just witnessed. They booed their Broncos mercilessly, flinging garbage as well as insults at their players. Meanwhile, our guys were jumping up and down, high-fiving and hugging each other like we had just won the Super Bowl instead of only our second game of the season.

Once the bedlam had calmed down in the locker room, Coach Saunders stood up and asked for quiet.

"Great job men!" he began proudly. "Today you've done something that nobody thought you could do except for yourselves. It's an awesome feeling, and I want you all to think for a moment about how it happened. You won today because you believed you could, and you relied on each other to get it done. Congratulations!"

That unexpected victory in Denver taught me a powerful lesson—a lesson that can be applied to our lives and to our illnesses and surgeries. We have to believe in ourselves—even when the odds are way against us. We have to persevere—even when other people don't think we can.

I believe all of us, deep down, have greater physical strength, greater emotional endurance, and greater creativity and intellect than we can even imagine. Unfortunately, we don't discover this potential until we are severely tested.

Coming back against the odds is getting a second chance. I truly believe God gives us a second chance with ostomy surgery. It's what we do with it that counts!

More Challenges

As I put the finishing touches on this book, my life has undergone several other major changes.

Following our marriage in February, 1990, Mary and I endured three miscarriages and a stillborn child at twenty-five weeks before we were finally able to have a daughter. Unfortunately, little Kari was born thirteen weeks prematurely, and she weighed in at just over two pounds. She wasn't supposed to survive. When it was apparent she would, the doctors braced us for the worst. She had been badly infected with *E. coli* bacteria at birth, and she had suffered a stroke and a grade four bilateral brain bleed.

For the entire ten weeks Kari was in the neonatal intensive care unit, the possibility of a brain shunt was very imminent, but it was finally averted by continual spinal taps to relieve pressure building up in her brain.

What saw Kari through? Constant prayer by Mary and me and countless others, plus a complete reliance on God and the good medical treatment she received at the same hospital where I had undergone my major operations thirteen years earlier.

Today, Kari is a bright, precious daughter who has a mild case of cerebral palsy in her legs, yet she is a blessing that I can not possibly explain.

I have little doubt that my own hospitalizations equipped me with the experience I needed to help my wife through the ordeal of Kari's premature birth and her subsequent hospitalization.

Unable to have any more children, Mary and I began looking into adoption, and in the spring of 1996, we adopted two young boys from a Russian orphanage. It is a long story of how we were led to this remote place on the other side of the world, but the quick version is that we had already tried unsuccessfully to adopt locally.

On one occasion, the mother changed her mind after we had had the child in our home for eight days! Her sudden change of heart was devastating to us, but God in his amazing way made it clear that He had other plans.

While we were still sorting this out, we had the opportunity to hear Pat Williams, the general manager of the Orlando Magic NBA basketball team, share his testimony of adopting thirteen children internationally after having four kids of his own. Mary was particularly touched by his story, and we began to see God open doors for us to proceed along similar lines.

Those doors opened the opportunity to adopt a four-year-old Russian boy named Valery. Unfortunately, just after completing the paperwork, we found ourselves caught in an adoption moratorium, a time when Russia decided to stop all adoptions so they could standardize the procedure. We agonized over what to do, and the uncertainty was very frustrating.

Seemingly out of the blue, another adoption opportunity came available in San Diego, but, unfortunately, that one again didn't work out, and we were left once more to ponder what God had in store for us. We didn't have to wait long, however, because just two days later we received a call from Russia explaining that the adoption freeze had been lifted and that we were cleared to go over and pick up our little boy immediately.

Naturally, we were elated, and ten days later I was on a plane to Kalliningrad, a coastal town on the Baltic. We decided it was best to have Mary stay home with our daughter while I traveled with my brother-in-law to pick up young Valery.

When I arrived, I discovered that Valery had a younger

brother named Viktor. Viktor was a little over two years old, but he weighed only eighteen pounds. When I was introduced to him in the orphanage, I was appalled at his gaunt frame and listless behavior. There appeared to be something very wrong, and I found my heart breaking. I didn't know what to do.

The Russian authorities, however, made it very clear to me that if I wanted to go through with the adoption of Valery, I would also have to take Viktor.

For two days I prayed, read my Bible, and did everything I could to find out what God wanted me to do. Worst of all, I couldn't even call my wife and discuss the situation.

But God was once again faithful, and He made it very clear to me that I had to trust Him like I had never trusted Him before. With that understanding, I felt I was meant to bring both kids home.

I hope you can understand what an interesting phone call that was when I finally reached Mary to explain to her that I was bringing two boys back!

Within a few short months, Erik (Valery) and Timothy (Viktor) became an integral part of our family. Their English is now excellent, and they are healthy, active Southern California boys.

It is impossible to explain the feelings we have for our three children. Each in our eyes is a special gift from God and a miracle we witness every day. The difficult times we endured with each one are now just memories, used to remind us of why we are so blessed.

CHAPTER 22

A New Chapter in Life

It's been more than three years since Erik and Timmy joined our family from Russia. As it turns out, we didn't have to worry how the family dynamics would change with the addition of two energetic brothers for Kari. Our preschool daughter adapted quickly to her new siblings, and they soon became best friends.

Shortly after our frightened little boys arrived in America, we discovered that routines helped them feel secure and safe, so we began integrating them into our family's way of doing things—eating meals together, taking baths, going to church, and reading bedtime stories.

As we tried to comprehend what our new sons must have gone through, we experienced some heart-wrenching behavior. Since we couldn't speak ten words of Russian, we had to resort to sign language and voice tone in order to communicate. If we said "no" with any kind of authority, however, the boys would become very upset and run out of the room to cower under a desk or bed in absolute terror. In the evening they wouldn't let us rock them to sleep even if they were exhausted. In the orphanage they had learned not to rely on caregivers, who were too often not there. The boys, especially Timmy, calmed themselves by vigorously rocking their tired bodies to sleep.

Erik and Timmy had an almost unimaginable fear of dogs and would scream hysterically at the sight of even the smallest pooch. We learned later that, as infants lined up in their cribs in the orphanage, large dogs would be allowed to wander around and sniff and lick the kids through the crib bars. With no ability to get away and no one around to remove these "monsters," they developed a phobia for dogs.

From what Mary and I had read about orphaned children, we knew that food would likely be an issue. It was. The first week we discovered that the boys were hoarding leftovers and storing them in secret places. We'd find rolls stuffed in their pockets and cookies tucked under their pillows or stashed in the back of their clothes drawers. It was clear these kids had been severely deprived, and, most likely, harshly treated. That knowledge broke our hearts.

At times, however, hidden food seemed the least of their past scars. In the first six months, we experienced dozens of tantrums and witnessed angry episodes that seemed to come from nowhere. I would often come home from work and find Mary in tears after a particularly stressful day with the boys. It was during those difficult moments that we reminded ourselves that Erik and Timmy were gifts from God. We believed that with lots of love, consistent discipline, and time to feel secure, their emotional scars would heal.

Yet it was almost a year before we felt Erik and Timmy finally turned the corner and began to accept the love and security we offered them. To this day, however, we still discover new and peculiar idiosyncrasies, and we realize that we will never be able to completely repair all that they experienced in their early years. They are wonderful kids, though, and we feel so fortunate to have them in our family.

Still Yearning

As our household finally became more settled, Mary began expressing a desire for adopting a fourth child. Growing up as one of six daughters in the tiny rural community of Green Isle, Minnesota, Mary had always longed for a large family. But with all of the issues we were facing with our three preschoolers, I was hesitant to add more to the mix.

One evening when I was not home, Mary happened to catch a segment on a TV newsmagazine show about a new treatment for women who had had multiple miscarriages or who had experienced difficulty carrying a pregnancy to term.

Mary, who had endured the painful loss of three unborn children through miscarriage and a stillborn little girl at twenty-four weeks, watched attentively. Piqued by the segment but not wanting to alarm me, Mary quietly made an appointment to see her OB-GYN and learn more about this new treatment.

After a complete physical, the doctor explained, "Before we can even consider any new therapy, we have to wait until your next period begins." It was while charting her cycle that Mary discovered that she was already pregnant.

"How did that happen?!" I joked in disbelief. The shocking news excited us, but it raised major concerns since Mary had not yet started any new therapy.

Knowing what we were up against, we worked closely with our doctors, who determined that in her sixteenth week she would have a cerclage—a procedure in which the doctor stitches up the opening to her cervix. Following that minor operation, Mary was put on complete bed rest: no cooking, no housecleaning, no exercising of any kind, no playing with the kids, no getting up for *anything* except to go to the bathroom.

Initially Mary resisted, not because she didn't believe the doctor, but because she didn't want to burden others. Fortunately, we had arranged for a young Austrian au pair to join our family even before we discovered Mary was relegated to the couch. Maria arrived in the fall of 1997 just as Mary was forced off her feet. She proved invaluable, and the timing couldn't have been better.

But our new helper couldn't do it all. Word of Mary's condition quickly spread to our friends, who immediately set up a schedule to help take the kids at different times and arrange for hot meals to be delivered five days a week. They must've known our family would never survive on my cooking!

While we marveled at the way our friends pitched in so unselfishly, Mary found it humbling to accept kindness that she felt she could never repay. When weighed against the possibility of losing the precious child growing inside her, however, she swallowed her pride and resigned herself to watching the world pass by from our living room couch.

Five months of anxious bed rest passed before Mary reached a time when the doctors felt the child could be born without complications. During her thirty-sixth week, after a long and emotional pregnancy filled with daily highs and lows, no one was happier than us when the doctor delivered our baby boy by Cesarean section, just four weeks ahead of his due date.

Ryan Joseph Benirschke joined our family on February 12, 1998. With a five-year-old, four-year-old, three-year-old, and now an infant under one roof, life turned hectic and stressful in a hurry. A full night's sleep became a distant memory, but we were ecstatic about our new family.

Some Added Insurance

As our household regained some measure of normalcy, I realized that because of all the new additions to our family, I needed more life insurance. With four children so young, I wanted to be sure Mary was adequately provided for in the event of—to use insurance jargon—my "untimely demise."

Before insurance companies issue a policy, they require a medical exam that includes an analysis of blood, urine, and an EKG, plus a thorough review of your health history. I had gone through this several times before and was very familiar with the process. In fact, I had been working in the insurance industry for over ten years.

When the medical examiner dropped by my office one summer morning to perform his tests and get the necessary samples, I didn't give it much thought. In my mind, I was in excellent health for someone in his early forties, and my previous battle with ulcerative colitis was a distant memory.

A month later, it was no surprise to me that one of the insurance companies that I had applied to declared me a "preferred risk," and offered me a policy at the best rates for my age. A week later, however, I was somewhat taken aback when another carrier came back with a "no offer, pending further examination of blood." When I inquired why, I was told that my liver enzymes were slightly elevated.

I had seen this kind of discrepancy with clients over the years, and in fact, I had had slightly abnormal enzyme readings myself in the past. I still wasn't alarmed because doctors had always explained them away due to my history with ulcerative colitis. To make sure I had the coverage I needed, however, I went ahead and insured myself with the first carrier.

Still feeling no sense of urgency, but because I was forty-three years old and hadn't had a comprehensive physical since my playing days, I decided to make an appointment with my doctor, Mark Bracker.

As I walked into his office, he didn't appear too surprised to see me.

"Rolf, how's the family?" he asked, as he shook my hand. "Let me guess. You're here to make sure you don't have any more kids, aren't you?" he said with a chuckle. Dr. Bracker had heard about our Russian boys and the birth of little Ryan. "We do our vasectomies on Fridays. Should I schedule you?"

"No," I grinned. "I'm here for a physical and to try to understand why my AST and ALT liver enzymes are out of the normal range." I explained about the results of my most recent blood work and asked what we should do about it.

A look of concern came over his face as he offered me a seat. "First, we have to have some more blood drawn," he replied. "I'm going to order some specific liver tests for the lab tech to run. But before we do, let's have a look at you."

After my examination, Dr. Bracker handed me a lab slip. "Have that blood drawn today," he said. "It will be seven to ten days before we get the results. I'll call you when I learn something."

"Fine," I said. I left the office, at least glad that I was going to find out what this was all about.

Right to the Point

It was eight days before I heard from Dr. Bracker. "Rolf, I have the results from your tests. I'd like to see you in my office."

"When do you want me to come in?" I asked, a little concerned with the tone I heard in his voice.

"How about today?" he said. "I have an opening at four o'clock."

He's in a hurry, I thought. "No problem, that will work," I said.

Unlike the previous visit, there was no easygoing smile on his face when we met in his office. Dr. Bracker didn't waste any time getting right to the point.

"Rolf, how have you been feeling?"

"Great," I said.

"Tired?"

I smiled ruefully. "Remember, Doc, with four kids under the age of six, my wife and I are exhausted all the time."

"How's your weight?"

"I've lost a few pounds, but I'm up several times during the night and not able to sleep like I normally do. Besides, I can't seem to find the time to work out regularly anymore."

"Any abdominal pain?"

"No."

"Rolf, when you had your first surgeries back in 1979, do you remember if you needed any blood transfusions?"

"Did I need blood?" I rolled my eyes. "I practically don't have any of my own left! Before it was all over, they pumped me with seventy-eight units."

Dr. Bracker glanced at his chart, then looked up as he slowly adjusted his glasses. "Rolf, it appears you are infected with the hepatitis C virus."

It was a good thing I was sitting down. I had read something about hepatitis C and the growing number of people suddenly discovering they had the virus, but that was as far as my knowledge went.

"What does this mean?" I asked hesitantly, not sure if I was going to like what I was about to hear.

"Hepatitis C is a virus that gets into the bloodstream and then attacks the liver. It was formally identified in 1989, and a year later a hep C antibody test was developed. Prior to that, physicians knew there was something out there. They were calling it non-A, non-B hepatitis because it attacked the liver and acted like hepatitis. A more specific screen was developed in 1992, and that is when most blood banks and testing facilities began using it. Today, our blood supply is very safe, but before the implementation of that test, many people who received blood became infected with the virus unknowingly."

"Are you saying that anyone who had a transfusion prior to 1992 is at risk?" I asked incredulously.

"Yes, but there are other ways to contract hepatitis C. The virus can be transmitted whenever there is blood-to-blood contact. It doesn't have to be a transfusion. In fact, people who share contaminated needles while doing intravenous drugs are the ones who most often pass hep C. Health-care workers must be on guard against accidental needle sticks. It is even believed that tattoo parlors and body-piercing places can spread the virus through unclean needles and tainted dyes," said Dr. Bracker. "There is also a concern about sexual transmission, although the chances appear to be quite low."

I sat in the office, stunned at this development. How could something like this happen *twenty years* after the infection had occurred? Wasn't the blood I had received supposed to have saved my life, not infect me with a strange new virus? Wasn't I cured? *This just isn't fair*, I thought to myself.

As if reading my mind, the doctor gently brought me back to reality. "Rolf, let's try to keep this in perspective. The fact is that it's a small miracle you don't have AIDS. Remember, we weren't testing for the HIV virus back in the late 1970s either."

"Yes, I suppose so," I sighed, still trying to comprehend what this all meant.

As we wrapped up our visit, I couldn't help but think that I was about to travel once again down the path less taken. But I knew from my previous experience with ulcerative colitis that before I let my imagination run away to the worst possible scenario, I needed to learn more about what I was up against. This time, however, it wasn't just my life that would be impacted. I had a wife and four special children depending on me.

CHAPTER 23

Breaking the News

I thanked Dr. Bracker for his time and headed home, overwhelmed with what I had just learned. Once in my car, I punched in my father's phone number.

"Hi, Dad," I began. "Listen, I just left Dr. Bracker's office. You're not going to believe this, but it looks like I have hepatitis C."

"Oh, no, Rolf," replied my father in a concerned voice.

"Dad, what the doctor told me has me scared to death. Do you know much about the hepatitis C virus?" I asked, my voice starting to shake. "I need more information before I tell Mary."

"Actually, I do," he answered, measuring his response carefully. "We just had a briefing for all the medical personnel at the hospital. Apparently, there are now vaccines against hepatitis A and B, and more treatment options are available for those viruses. Unfortunately, hepatitis C is a different story altogether. The good news is that new and improving treatment methods are being developed as we speak, but the bad news is that the current therapies are only about 40 percent effective."

"And I heard that those same therapies also have difficult side effects. What else do you know?" I asked.

"Hepatitis C attacks the liver, initially causing inflammation, then fibrosis, and if left untreated, can eventually lead to cirrhosis and even liver cancer. Hepatitis C is a huge problem that is just now emerging as the next big health epidemic. It has been called 'the silent killer' and is very serious."

"But Dad, I had no idea I was a carrier. I've been feeling great. Could I really have been infected for almost *two* decades?"

"Apparently so, Rolf. The difficulty with the virus is that it generally doesn't show any symptoms for a long period of time. It's a good thing you don't drink much because alcohol is very hard on the liver and can accelerate the damage."

I thanked Dad and began thinking how I would break the news to Mary. I decided that before I could, I needed to do some more research on my own.

Later that night, after Mary had gone to bed, I got on my computer and began searching the Internet. I visited a handful of helpful Web sites, including the Hepatitis Foundation International, the American Liver Foundation, and the Hep C Connection.

The liver, I learned, is the largest and most complex organ humans have and plays a vital role in many processes that keep us alive. It performs numerous complicated tasks that are essential to the proper functioning of the entire body. The liver is on the job twenty-four hours a day, performing a wide range of duties. Some of these involve regulating organ functions and metabolism, and detoxifying the blood.

Since I had had my large colon removed nearly twenty years earlier, I found my liver was an even more important organ for my digestive system. The liver stores sugar and vitamins and makes bile acids necessary for digestion. It also serves as a filtering station, removing wastes and toxins from the bloodstream.

251

I discovered that Dad had been right: hepatitis C is a serious form of liver disease, affecting more than four million Americans and tens of millions worldwide. Approximately 30,000 people become infected each year, and the disease claims the lives of around 10,000 persons annually—a number expected to triple in the next decade.

Hepatitis C is also already the leading cause of liver transplants, and although 4,000 people get new livers each year, 12,000 other folks are waiting to receive one. Many die before a liver can be found.

As I learned more about this lurking killer, I realized that there had to be hundreds of thousands of people like myself who are totally unaware that they are carrying the hepatitis C virus in their bodies. How many had experimented with drugs in their younger days, even just one time, and become infected? How many had unknowingly received blood transfusions tainted with the hepatitis C virus prior to 1992? I could only imagine.

Whereas inflammatory bowel disease and ostomy surgery are not pleasant subjects to discuss, I discovered that hep C has its own difficulties. Studies indicate that almost 80 percent of the people with hepatitis C became infected after participating in some high risk activity such as illicit drug use, tattooing, body piercing, or having multiple sexual partners when they were younger—and not wiser. For someone to volunteer to be tested for hepatitis C, it might mean having to explain their past behavior to a spouse, boss, or friend.

And then there are people like me who were the recipients of contaminated blood during a surgery. It turns out that there are a lot of women who unknowingly received a small amount of blood during a Cesarean section. It is only after getting diagnosed with Hep C and reexamining their medical records that they learn the fateful truth of how they must have become infected.

On the other hand, my research informed me that many others with hepatitis C can never pinpoint exactly how or when they got the virus. They never participated in "at risk" behaviors or received a transfusion. The Centers for Disease Control estimates that approximately 10 percent of the infected population falls into this "uncertain" category, their infection origin remaining a mystery.

The vast majority of people discover they have the virus quite by accident—usually through a routine physical examination. Elevated liver enzymes in the blood are generally the first indicators, although symptoms like fatigue, poor appetite, weight loss, jaundice, appearance of dark urine, fever, and vomiting may also be early signs. I had not experienced any of these symptoms, except for the fatigue and weight loss that I had attributed to sleepless nights with our newborn son, Ryan.

After spending four hours staring at the computer, I finally headed for bed. In the morning Mary rolled over, still half asleep. "Nice of you to return to bed," she said. "Was I kicking you last night?"

"No, Mary. Listen, I have some bad news," I said, having a hard time looking her in the eyes.

She sat up quickly, now wide-awake. "What is it?"

"I was up late last night on the computer learning as much as I could about a new health problem."

"What health problem?" I could see the panic rising in her face.

"My health problem. You see, my physical last week confirmed that I am infected with the hepatitis C virus. Apparently, I have been carrying it for almost twenty years. Because you and I share nail clippers, a toothbrush every now and then, and even a razor, there is a chance you could also be infected. I'm so sorry." Tears began to well up in my eyes.

"Oh, Rolf," Mary snuggled over and squeezed me. "You've been through so much. We're going to be all right."

"I feel so unclean." I sputtered, trying unsuccessfully to control a deep, body-shaking sob. I knew our world had just been altered. I just didn't know by how much.

Plans for the Future

It took both of us a few days to fully grasp how our lives were going to change living with hepatitis C. As the reality of our situation became clearer, we organized a family meeting with parents, brothers and sisters, and a few close friends. We wanted to explain what had happened, but also to express our optimism and excitement to see what God had in store for us. I knew from the past that the Lord had always given us only what we could handle, and we clung to that belief now.

The first order of business was learning how far the disease had progressed in my body. Dad and Dr. Bracker suggested that I see Dr. Tarek Hassanein, a hepatologist on the forefront of hepatitis C research at the University of California San Diego (UCSD) campus.

"Rolf, before a treatment can be prescribed, we need to draw some more blood, do an ultrasound, and take a liver biopsy," Dr. Hassanein explained.

Great, more blood work, I thought. And just thinking about having a long needle inserted into my side to extract some liver tissue was a frightening prospect.

"Is this going to hurt?" I asked hesitantly, imagining the worst.

"Actually, the liver biopsy has become fairly routine," he replied. "It is very quick and with the new drugs available, you won't remember anything."

Dr. Hassanein was right. With the exception of a little trouble putting an IV line into my arm, the procedure was not difficult. After liver cells were removed and sent to the lab, the severity of the disease was graded. The result: I had beginning stages of fibrosis but I had not progressed to cirrhosis. This was good news since the liver can sometimes regenerate itself if it has not become too damaged.

"Is there a treatment program?" I asked cautiously.

"Well, there are options, Rolf," Dr. Hassanein answered. "The first treatments that were developed were only about 10-20 percent effective in keeping the virus in what we call a 'sustained response.' Lately, however, we are seeing all kinds of studies being done that have bumped the successful treatment rate to about 40 percent. A lot depends, however, on which mutation of the virus you have, what your viral load is, and how quickly we can get your enzymes back to normal."

"Viral load?" I asked quizzically.

The physician was an expert on hepatitis C, and he must have explained this a thousand times in his practice.

"Viral load is the amount of virus in your blood. We measure in copies per milliliter. If you have a load of less than two million, you are considered to have a light load. If you have more than five million copies, then you have a high viral load. Studies seem to indicate that with a lighter load, we have a greater chance of pushing the virus to an undetectable level. It turns out you have a light viral load, only about 500,000 copies per milliliter."

"Well, finally some good news," I said.

"Oh, there's one more thing," he cautioned. "Any alcohol will injure your liver that much quicker, making it even harder for the organ to replace the damaged cells. You need to stop drinking completely—no beer, no wine, no margaritas. No liquor of any kind."

The Next Step

It turns out that Dr. Hassanein was intensely involved with several new promising studies. He knew which therapies were having good results, and I felt comfortable under his care.

Based upon the biopsy results, and the fact that I had a low viral load, I was a good candidate for treatment. Since I was relatively young and my liver was still in good shape, Dr. Hassanein wanted to get me on an experimental program right away.

"Now there will be some side effects," he warned. "You'll be taking a bunch of pills and injecting yourself with interferon every day for a year."

"Injecting myself?!" I wasn't sure if I heard right. For someone who hated needles, I couldn't imagine actually pushing one into my arm, leg, or abdomen, as he explained I would need to do.

"Don't worry. We'll teach you how," he said encouragingly.

Interferon, I learned, was given at different dosages and in varying frequencies, and often prescribed in combination with an antiviral drug called ribavirin. The side effects were quite onerous, as I discovered when I started my treatment program.

I'm not going to sugarcoat this. The first few weeks were horrible. After each injection, I developed terrible shaking chills, fever, drenching sweats, and a fatigue that drained all of my energy. For someone who doesn't like needles or pills, I was now compelled to live with both every day for one year.

I was told to drink as much water as I could and try and maintain my weight. This became almost impossible, as even my favorite foods were unappealing and tasted metallic. I finally resorted to protein shakes blended with fruit and ice cream as a way of taking in calories.

Fatigue overwhelmed me. For the first few months of treatment, I found it difficult to work with any effectiveness. On many days, I left the office after lunch and went home to nap for several hours before dinner.

In addition to being tired all of the time and losing weight, I also experienced extreme sensitivity to light, blotchy skin problems, and hair loss. Friends noticed that I looked thin and worn out. Although my doctor encouraged me to keep up my exercise regimen, all I could really do was take gentle walks around the neighborhood.

I wasn't much help around the house for four or five months either until my body began to get used to the medications. The new drug trial that I was participating in required a particularly high dose of interferon. As a result, my blood needed to be examined every few weeks. I felt like a pin cushion with all the needles I was being poked with, but I was willing to proceed because Dr. Hassanein assured me that it was going to give me the best possible chance of getting rid of the virus.

During my lowest moments, however, I fought waves of depression. The thought of hanging in there for a whole year was daunting, especially since there was no guarantee of success. Was it all going to be in vain?

I didn't know.

I recalled what I had learned from my previous illness and from reading about POW survivors in World War II and Vietnam. They managed to persevere through horrible circumstances by breaking time down into bite-sized increments, by discovering a tenacious inner strength they didn't know they possessed, and by relying on a faith that may have been latent—but blossomed—during their trials.

I also sought encouragement from others who had successfully overcome their battle with hepatitis C. I began communicating with optimistic Thelma Thiel, the founder of Hepatitis Foundation International, and hearing firsthand from other patients.

Above the Fold

Several months into my treatment program, I decided to call Tom Cushman, a columnist with the *San Diego Union-Tribune* that I had known over the years and whom I respected greatly. My desire was to tell Tom—and readers of San Diego's largest newspaper—that there may be many people like myself in our own community who are also infected with hepatitis C but they don't know it. My previous experience with ulcerative colitis had taught me that because of my visibility as a football player, I had an opportunity to raise the awareness of a disease and perhaps help people talk more openly about a difficult subject.

Tom listened as I described the events of the last few months and then wrote a compelling and informative story that was played above the fold on page one of the front section of the paper.

"Benirschke's hope is that by personalizing the disease with a name familiar in San Diego, some in the at-risk category will be encouraged to undergo testing that may detect hepatitis C," Cushman wrote.

I pointed out that the road to the doctor's office is always paved with good intentions, but hepatitis C is too serious a disease to take lightly. I noted that I was forced again to appreciate the value of life and how precious family and friends are. Since I now have a wife and four children, the fight to stay alive was no longer just about me—it was about all of us.

I firmly believe that with all of the research being done and the promising new therapies on the horizon, those of us with hepatitis C have great reason for optimism. We have too many people on our side—doing everything they can to unravel the mystery of this virus—to feel sorry for ourselves and give up.

My year of interferon treatment ended in the fall of 1999, and as of this writing, my liver enzymes remain normal, and I still have no detectable virus in my blood. This is, of course, great news, made better by learning that Mary has not become infected. I do realize, however, that there is no guarantee that the virus has been completely removed from my liver. Future tests will tell me whether the disease will relapse or if I will continue to have "undetectable virus" in my blood.

Despite this uncertainty, I feel upbeat about my future. If there is anything I have learned from my years of living with ulcerative colitis, it's that we must continue to hang in there and appreciate the precious gift of life.

We are extremely fortunate to live in an era when treatment is possible and new therapies are being developed all the time. Although I don't know what lies in store for me, I do know that I will keep fighting for as long as it takes.

Besides, I believe that God does have a plan for our lives. Even though His ways are often a mystery, I am comforted to know He has not failed me yet. All we have to do is keep up the good fight.

(Author's Note: I've included two interviews I conducted which I think will be of value to the reader.)

An Interview with Marvin Bush

It was 1986 when Marvin Bush, the youngest son of Vice President George Bush, suddenly required surgery for ulcerative colitis. Not only was his life saved, but he was able to witness his father becoming the 41st President of the United States.

Rolf: Unlike some people with IBD, your symptoms of ulcerative colitis seemed to develop rather quickly.

Marvin: Yes, it was strange. I was twenty-seven years old, and up to that point, I had been very healthy, leading what I considered to be an ideal life. But then this thing came out of nowhere.

Rolf: What was your first clue something was wrong?

Marvin: My symptoms were blood in my stools, cramps that got increasingly more painful, and spiking fevers. I'd wake up in the middle of the night, and my sheets would be soaking wet. Typically, the fevers would be accompanied by the cramps. It got to a point where my family and I knew something major was wrong. I had had bloody stools, fevers, and cramps before, but I had never had a situation where all three of them existed at the same time.

Rolf: Did you see a doctor right away?

Marvin: I did. I went to see my general practitioner, who is a wonderful doctor, for a preliminary examination. He found some cyst-like growths around my anus, and he removed one of them. That helped for a period of time, but, as I was to learn later, those were just side effects of the real problem.

Rolf: Denial—especially to a healthy person—is something we all go through. I read somewhere where you actually saw on television a doctor's report on President Reagan and all of his struggles with colon cancer.

Marvin: Yeah. I'll never forget that as long as I live. The year was 1985, and I was up in Kennebunkport, Maine, spending a weekend with my parents. My dad said, "Come on inside, there's a report on the President." Believe me, we were all concerned, especially since my father was next in line for the presidency. You may remember, Rolf, that the President's doctors told the world every small detail about the colon cancer.

Rolf: I do, especially seeing the whole digestive tract drawn up right on the screen!

Marvin: Right. What was kind of shocking was how the doctors started clicking off all of the symptoms of colon cancer.

Rolf: Did you hear your symptoms?

Marvin: I heard all of them. I really almost got nauseous, knowing that I hadn't followed up very completely with my general practitioner. A wave of guilt came over me because on one hand, my parents were expressing a tremendous amount of concern for the President, while on the other hand, Mom—and she didn't get to be the popular figure that she is today by being an idiot—figured out very quickly that her son was struggling with similar symptoms. I remember her looking over at me, nodding her head, and saying we should go see a doctor.

Rolf: What did you do then?

Marvin: I went to see a GI specialist. For some reason, my case was like so many others in which the diagnosis confused the doctors. They basically wanted to eliminate the possibilities one by one. But they were forthright with me and suggested that I could very well have ulcerative colitis.

Rolf: So you had to go through all of those horrible tests, including the upper and lower GI, the barium swallows, and the colonoscopies?

Marvin: I sure did. But the anticipation of the exams was far worse than the exams themselves. It was humiliating. When you are lying on your side and somebody sticks an object into your rectum, and there's a nurse walking in and out of the room. It can be very, very humbling. You learn to put your dignity aside.

Rolf: I remember. The worst was when the nurse walked in on me when I was in such an uncompromising position and commented, "So, this is what a pro football player really looks like." Anyway, did your doctors make a clear diagnosis of ulcerative colitis?

Marvin: It wasn't crystal clear, so the doctors started me off with medication. The first drug I remember taking was Sulfasalazine, which is a sulfa-based drug that was supposed to taper the frequency of my bowel movements. It turns out, however, that I was allergic to that drug. I remember sitting home one night with my wife, Margaret, when all of a sudden she noticed my face turning bright red. I started itching, and when I looked in a mirror, my face was disfigured. Then my throat started closing up. I was rushed to the hospital, where they put me on an IV to counteract the Sulfasalazine. That was a scary time.

I think the Purple Heart should go to Margaret. It seems like the people who are closest to you are the ones who suffer the most. In my case, Margaret caught the brunt of it. I am not a violent or volatile person, but I would lose my temper very quickly when I wasn't feeling well. As for my illness, I didn't want to know the truth. I finally asked the doctor if he thought I had cancer. I was so concerned about that image of President Reagan waving from his hospital room. I was relieved when my doctor said no.

Rolf: What happened after you got that good news?

Marvin: I tried to carry on with life. But I was frequently running off to bathrooms. If I had a fifteen-minute meeting, I would go to the bathroom beforehand and hope the meeting wouldn't last longer than fifteen minutes. If it did, I often had to excuse myself again. It was awful.

Rolf: Were you talking to anyone about it?

Marvin: Besides Margaret and my immediate family, just a few friends. But they never really knew how serious the problem was.

Rolf: Let's move the clock forward to when your health worsened.

Marvin: I'll never forget that day, either. Margaret was in Richmond, Virginia, visiting her mother and father, and I took the opportunity to go over to the Vice President's residence in Washington. I was watching a video with Mom, but I had to go to the bathroom at least six times, causing her to hit the pause button each time. Mom is a patient person, but this was ridiculous. Then she heard me retching in the bathroom. I had lost about 10 pounds at that point—not a lot of weight, but I was having a hard time holding down food. Finally, Mom and Dad sat down with me. "We're worried about you," they said. We looked at each other, and we both knew. We gathered some things together, and then we went over to Georgetown Hospital in Washington.

Rolf: Did the doctors examine you that night and determine that you needed surgery?

Marvin: No. And, again, I am mixing up days, because I have tried my best to forget that period. I was lying in bed and had a continual plethora of exams going on daily, but by that time I was out of the decision-making loop.

Rolf: Really?

Marvin: I was in the loop as it related to receiving information, but as the situation got increasingly serious, I could read the doctors' concern. I was bleeding internally. I was also losing a lot of blood and weight. I could not keep any food down. They finally started feeding me intravenously, but it was a losing battle.

Rolf: At that point, did anyone talk to you about the possibility of an ostomy?

Marvin: Two days before my surgery, one of the doctors came in and outlined what the ultimate conclusion could be. He said, "Look. Two things can happen. We can get the disease under control, but frankly, we are beginning to lose confidence in that option. Or, we could do ostomy surgery."

Rolf: Did you know what an ostomy was?

Marvin: No. I hadn't done any research or talked to anybody about it, but I said, "Whatever relieves the pain, I am interested in." I was worn out at that stage. As you know, you don't get a lot of shut-eye in hospitals, especially in a teaching hospital, where people keep parading through the rooms to study you. Talk about degrading. Don't you love those curtain dividers? They swing those things open and twelve people your age—I was twenty-seven at that time—were looking over me.

One of the worst experiences was when I had an NG tube running up through my nose and down my throat. For some reason, one of the interns had not turned the suction up high enough, so food was going in and out. Bile was going in through my nose and back down. At that point, six or seven people came in on their rounds, and vomit was dribbling all over my face. I couldn't control it, and I was too tired to yell. It was one of the most degrading moments.

Rolf: So they didn't prepare you for the surgery, other than to say this might be an option?

Marvin: One day, I remember a foggy image of looking through the window and seeing that famous white hair of my mother. "Whoa, what is she doing here?" I asked. "Why is she back?" Then Mom came in with the doctor and Margaret, and the doctor began to explain to me about the surgery. He said, "We think there is a perforation in your intestine because there is just so much bleeding. It's critical that we do this surgery immediately."

Rolf: Did they mark your abdomen where the ostomy would be located?

Marvin: I don't remember much, except them pointing to my stomach and saying I was going to have something protruding from there and that they were taking my colon out. At that point, I was in so much pain and in such a haze that I wasn't concerned with the specifics of the surgery. All I wanted was to be relieved of the agony.

Rolf: So they do the surgery and you wake up with a major incision and an appliance attached to your side. What was that like?

Marvin: Although my doctor had tried to describe to me what ostomy surgery was two days before, I can tell you that I didn't even begin to understand what was going to happen. My first concern when I woke up was the pain in my stomach, and you know what that's like. I was very weak, and I had lost thirty-five to forty pounds, and was down to around 150 pounds.

Rolf: A lot had to be going through your mind. What were your emotions like?

Marvin: I don't like taking even over-the-counter drugs, but I can tell you, I was begging for some pain killers. I took Demerol and morphine for a period of time to ease the incisional pain but had one particularly horrible experience with the morphine. I had been given a dose of morphine through my IV, when all of a sudden the cross over my door started flying around the room, and balloons seemed to be swirling everywhere. I remember being very hot and sweating profusely and all of a sudden jumping out of bed to cool off. It was at that point that I began ripping IV lines out of my arm, which was no small task, since normally I was in so much pain that I couldn't move at all. Boy, did I get the attention of the horrified nurses.

Rolf: It's interesting you say all that because I had an almost identical experience, probably also due to a bad reaction to morphine. Scary. So, that left you in the hospital about how long? Ten days? Two weeks?

Marvin: I was in there about ten days, but toward the end, they began to focus on what this ostomy was going to mean to me for the rest of my life.

Rolf: Did you have a good ET nurse?

Marvin: At that point, I was working with a wonderful nurse named Irene—a bossy, demanding nurse who made me walk but to whom I owe a lot.

Rolf: Blow those blow tubes! Ventilate those lungs!

Marvin: Blow tubes—I had forgotten about those things. But Irene would force me to get up and struggle down the hall. I'll tell you, those trips were very good for me, because as I went down the hall, I saw people who were much off than I was. People who were experiencing double-bypass surgery and more and with no relatives or friends to support them. I was blessed to have Margaret and my parents, who were with me every step of the way. Before checking out of the hospital, I spent a couple of sessions with Irene, going over how the appliance worked. I was concerned about smell. I was concerned that when I walked on the street it would fall off. I was concerned when to drain and change it.

Rolf: Do you remember the first time you changed your appliance without her help?

Marvin: Yes, I do, because Margaret did it. It was embarrassing and degrading. I was nervous and scared, and I was still recovering from surgery. My suture line was still sore, obviously, and I didn't understand how the appliance worked yet or how my body was going to function. Remember, your body is also having to make adjustments just as you're sorting everything out mentally. It's a wonderful process, but your bowels are much more volatile at the outset. That's something I wish someone had prepared me for, because that was tough to cope with.

Rolf: Perhaps that's why I got a certain phone call. I'll never forget the occasion. I was in my office, when my secretary, Debra Marshall, buzzed me. She explained that, "The Vice President is on the telephone." I remember answering, "The vice president of what?" And her saying, "Well, he just said the Vice President." When I picked the phone up it was your father!

Marvin: Boy, was he concerned. He's a sports nut, so he knew about your ostomy and all that you had gone through in getting back to play in the NFL. He figured that you would be a good person for me and my family to talk to. The timing was just right, and I don't want to say this to embarrass you, but your call was one of the most important I've ever received in my life.

But equally important to me, Rolf, was a visit from a friend of my surgeon. One day this down-home guy from Virginia, who lives just outside of Washington, comes walking into my hospital room and starts talking to me. I'm thinking, *Who let this yahoo in and what the heck is he doing here anyway?* I tried to be polite and we shot the breeze for some time. All the while I'm thinking, *Why is this guy talking to me?* As if he was reading my mind, he says, "Marvin, I have an ostomy." My immediate reaction was "No way, you look too healthy!"

Then he did something incredible. He said, "One of the most important things for you to do is figure out what brand of appliance you're going to wear." You wear what's out there on the market, I thought. The next thing I know, this guy says, "Let me show you something." Oh my gosh! Shut the door! I didn't want the nurses to see this guy in my room pulling his pants down! Before I knew it he was lowering his underwear and showing me his ostomy. "This is what it looks like," he said. "It's no big deal." He had been wearing his appliance for five years, I believe. And, now that I've worn mine for ten years, I can easily see the perspective he was coming from.

At that point, I began asking him more specific questions: "Will it fall off when you take a shower?" "Can I wear it in the swimming pool or the ocean?" "Will people stare at me because they can see it?" "Does it smell?" "What about the noises that I am making?" He answered each one patiently, and then I began to ask even more personal questions. "What about intimacy with my wife?" He said it wouldn't affect that relationship at all. "Besides," he said, "you're not going to believe how much better you're going to be feeling now that you are rid of the disease.

Rolf: Are there any things you are careful about?

Marvin: Well, I'm careful with some of the foods I eat, but I eat spicy kung pao chicken so I push the envelope a little! My view is that you just have to be a little cautious and try things slowly. Your body will tell you what you are able to do. For instance, I am very careful when I eat popcorn because I had a bad experience. I had a blockage once, and had to go to the hospital and have them relieve it. That was not a pleasant situation.

Rolf: What about changing your appliance? Do you have a routine?

Marvin: What I typically do is wear the pouch four to five days, but before I change it, I try to plan ahead. I say to myself, okay, if I am going to go out and exercise strenuously, then I need to check around the edges of the flange and see how soft it is, particularly on the lower part of the flange. If it gets too soft down there that's where I find the propensity for leaking. If I am going to do something strenuous I find it's better to be proactive and change it a day sooner rather than wait a day and have it start leaking.

We've all had leaks but I've found I generally have only an accident about once every two years.

Rolf: There are a bunch of different appliances out there. How did you find the right one that fits you?

Marvin: What I did was wear three different types over a period of time. It was pretty easy to tell which one of them wasn't going to work the minute I put it on. Much of it is trial and error and talking to other ostomates and ET's; people who have had experience with what is available.

Rolf: Do you ever have a problem with gurgling sounds?

Marvin: Yes, but only once in a while now. At first it was much worse. Somehow it always seems to happen to me when I get in a crowded elevator. But, the sound isn't really offensive, just embarrassing. Margaret was wonderful with me when I'd ask, "Does anybody notice that noise?" She would always say no and ask me what I was talking about.

An Interview with Al Geiberger

In 1977, playing at the Colonial Country Club in Memphis, Tennessee, Al Geiberger became the first golfer to break 60 in a PGA professional event. Only one other golfer has done it since then– Chip Beck, who shot 59 at Las Vegas' Sunrise Golf Club in 1991. Yet Al is still known as "Mr. 59" after all these years, and he remains a popular fixture on the PGA Senior Tour with Jack Nicklaus and Lee Trevino.

But Al nearly didn't make it to the senior golf tour. After years of struggling with ulcerative colitis, he almost died in 1980 before being rushed into emergency surgery.

I sat down with Al not long ago and asked him to share his story:

Rolf: Al, what did you think when you heard you were going to have an ileostomy?

Al: When I got the news, I thought, "Well, there goes a good golf career." But I knew my choices were to be either six feet under or to stick around, so I chose the latter. Little did I know I would fully recover and that wearing an appliance would be no problem whatsoever.

Rolf: Let's go back to when you first learned about your illness. What were the symptoms?

Al: My problems started way back in 1965 or 1966, when I started noticing blood in my stool. At the time, doctors diagnosed it as ulcerative colitis. They told me I was going to have to live with it, and they tried to manage the disease with drugs such as Azulfidine and Prednisone.

For years, my colitis would come and go. When I had bouts of diarrhea, I was forced to take Lomotil to slow down my bowels. I still had flare-ups, though, and when those happened during a golf tournament, I had to live with them.

Rolf: Did your doctors ever talk about surgery?

Al: They felt that my colitis wasn't bad enough, and since it appeared to be isolated in one area, surgery wasn't discussed much. But each year I was careful to have a lower GI and a complete battery of tests. In 1979, I wasn't feeling very well, so I went in for a barium swallow. The radiologist just whistled as he watched the barium go down. He pointed out a large mass of polyps on the right side of my colon, noting that they were the cause of my problem.

In a very short time, the pain became unbearable, and the doctors finally decided to remove the polyps. While they were in there, they took a good look around my digestive tract. Afterward, they told me, "There isn't much healthy colon left, so we're going to have to take it out." That news depressed me because I figured when that happened, my golfing days were over.

I had a few commitments I hoped to keep, so I traveled to Vail, Colorado, to play in Gerald Ford's tournament. It wasn't a regular tour event, but I always enjoyed playing in the President's pro-am.

While in Vail, I was struck with a severe bout of abdominal pain and hospitalized in Denver, where I needed an emergency surgery to have part of my colon removed. I was extremely depressed at the time, and I felt very sorry for myself. I was scheduled to fly home to Santa Barbara, where my doctors were planning to take out the rest of my colon and leave me with an ileostomy.

In the Denver hospital, an ET nurse walked into my room while I was watching a football game. She noticed the Chargers were on television, and a wry smile came over her face. "You know, you're going to have the same surgery that the Chargers' kicker, Rolf Benirschke, had a year ago. As you can see, he's back kicking for San Diego, and just last week he kicked a bunch of field goals to beat my Broncos!"

After I heard that, I said to myself, "Hey, if Rolf can come back in one year and play football, I should be able to play a non-contact sport like golf. I mean, come on!"

Hearing your story really lifted my confidence. Before, I thought my whole life was going to change and I wouldn't be able to do anything. I thought my sex life was going to be bad, that I couldn't go out socially, and traveling would be out. But everything turned out to be the opposite of what I expected, and that's been a pleasant surprise.

Rolf: **That ET nurse taught you quite a lesson. How valuable were your ET nurses?**

Al: Well, I had several. Not only did they bolster my spirits, but they gave me practical help when it came time to learn about my stoma and how my appliance would work. I had a million questions, and they had a million answers.

I clearly remember the first time an ET nurse showed me how to use the appliance. All the while, I was thinking, "You mean I have to do this the rest of my life?"

Not long afterward, I had my first blowout and made a big mess on my bed at home. When I called my ET nurse, she said, "Don't worry about it, accidents happen."

Rolf: **Did you develop a routine about when to change your appliance?**

Al: Yes, I did. I change it every five to seven days in the morning, first thing after getting up. I'll jump in the shower, take off my old appliance, wash around the stoma with soap, get out and dry off, and then attach my new appliance. It just takes me a minute, but I have learned to make sure I do it before eating breakfast.

When I am out on the tour, the appliance might not last quite as long, so I check it carefully every morning. I also change it earlier than necessary if I'm about to depart on a long trip.

But blowouts will happen. I've been on the golf course and had accidents. In those situations, I've learned not to panic. I find a bathroom and put some Kleenex in there and wait until I get back to the hotel.

Usually I've had a blowout because I've done something I shouldn't have--like drinking several glasses of fresh orange juice. I remember one tournament fresh OJ was set out for the players, and I couldn't resist, but I should have. There must be too much acid in orange juice, or something, because it really irritated my skin. Boy, did I learn from that mistake.

Rolf: **You still travel quite a bit, and you're often in Europe and Japan. Any problems with flying?**

Al: No, I can't think of any. Obviously, I've learned that I should change my appliance before any intercontinental flights. Also, I make sure I hand-carry extra appliances on board—I don't check them. I've also found that if I ever run out of appliances in other countries, I can easily find the brand I use in local pharmacies.

Rolf: What about your clothes? When you're playing golf, you're always on television and out there all alone in front of the gallery. Do you worry about people knowing?

Al: In the beginning, I was very self-conscious and concerned that my appliance might show. After a while, I realized that it was obvious it wasn't visible. I've had fellow players come up and ask, "Are you wearing that bag today? I can't tell."

"Of course," I'd reply, "I have to wear it every day all day."

Some thought I wore my appliance in the back—near my rear end, I guess. My appliance doesn't show—even with tight clothes. Now that pleated pants are in, nobody can see it.

Rolf: How have people reacted to you when you've explained your situation?

Al: In the beginning, it was hard for me. I decided I wasn't going to talk about it at all. Well, after talking to you, Rolf, I realized that it was okay to talk about it, and in fact, I discovered that I could help a lot of people. I've learned that most folks take their cues from me. If I'm relaxed and comfortable with my appliance, then they will feel comfortable talking about it. Being relaxed and confident, I've found, puts other people at ease.

Once I got back on the PGA tour, reporters asked me to do interviews about my ileostomy. Most of them had no clue what the procedure entailed. I didn't mind explaining the whole thing to them, and I took my time outlining my story.

When those articles appeared in local newspapers, the response I would receive from the galleries was always very supportive. Invariably, someone would come up and say, "Gee, I loved your article. I have an ostomy, too. Thanks for talking about it."

Rolf: Al, you've gone through a lot in your life. Has staring death in the face and going through a difficult ileostomy surgery changed you in any way?

Al: It certainly has. Anybody who comes close to dying learns what's important in life and what isn't. It's great to be able to play golf again, but when I have a bad round or a bad week, it doesn't bother me like it used to.

The biggest thing is that I've had three children since my ileostomy. I guess that's proof my sex life didn't end with an appliance.

Rolf: Do you ever have a problem with odor?

Al: I had a lot of concern about odor in the beginning. Those fears went away very quickly, though, when I learned about the types of appliances available today and how they minimize the chance of a leak.

Rolf: People often wonder if you had to change your diet.

Al: I've found I can eat everything I did prior to my surgery. I am a little careful, however, about things that might cause a blockage. I was warned by my ETs about mushrooms, stringy vegetables like celery, too much popcorn, and fruits like oranges. Most of the stuff I can eat without a problem. It's just that if I eat too much of it, I could have some trouble.

I think the main thing for everyone to remember is that the surgery can save your life. All the fears we have about whether we can resume the activities before we were sick rarely come true. The surgery and the appliances give us a second chance. We can lead full, productive lives and enjoy happy, healthy relationships.

Looking back now, I wonder why I felt so sorry for myself. I also wonder why I put off the surgery. It wasn't easy, but the ileostomy gave me my life back.

To those wondering whether they should have ostomy surgery, I say, "It's the illness that handicaps your life, but there is no handicap with this surgery whatsoever."

Living With an Ostomy

When first considering ostomy surgery, many people are concerned that the operation will dramatically alter their lives. Though any surgery should be considered carefully, an ostomy can be the key that opens the door to opportunities locked away by illness. For people who have ulcerative colitis, this operation offers a cure. The following are questions that are most commonly asked by people who are considering ostomy surgery.

What is an ostomy?
There are various types of ostomy surgery, depending on the nature of the illness. A common option for ulcerative colitis is the creation of an ileostomy. The entire colon and, in some cases, the rectum are removed in a one- or two-step procedure. The surgeon creates an opening in the abdominal wall, through which the ileum is rerouted to the outside, creating a stoma. To collect stool as it exits the ileum, a disposable pouch is attached to the skin around the stoma with medical adhesive. Since a permanent ostomy is not a cure for Crohn's disease, it is performed only when the disease cannot be controlled medically. Some conditions (e.g., a bowel perforation or abscess) may require a temporary ostomy.

How much time must I allow for daily care?
The maintenance of an ostomy requires only minor modifications in your routine. Daily care consists of emptying the pouch when it becomes one-third to one-half full. You can do this in any bathroom, private or public. This process requires no additional equipment and takes little more time than you previously required to "go to the bathroom." In fact, it may be less time-consuming, especially if diarrhea plagued you before surgery.

Ostomy pouches, like your rectum, have a finite capacity and will overflow or leak if they become too full.

275

Most people report that they need to empty the pouch four to six times a day. You should note the occasions when the stoma is more active (e.g., after meals), and set aside time to empty your pouch. To avoid interrupting sleep, it is helpful to drain the pouch at bedtime, but you may want to empty it again should a full bladder awaken you.

What kinds of pouching systems are available?

Ostomy "appliances" are designed to meet individual needs. There are one- and two-piece systems, pouches with built-in skin barriers, drainable and closed-end pouches, styles offering various depth of convexity, pouches with built-in gas relief valves and filters, and combinations of these features. Years ago, certain types of pouches were designated for specific surgeries (e.g., an ileostomy required a drainable pouching system). Though more options are available today, some ostomies are more difficult to manage than others and require recommendations by health-care professionals.

How can I find the system that is best for me?

You may want to consult an enterostomal therapy nurse (ETN), a registered nurse who specializes in ostomy care. The ETN will recommend a pouching system and will teach you how to care for the stoma. After your discharge from the hospital, she is available for follow-up care. In time, your pouching needs may change, as normal post-operative stomal swelling diminishes or your weight changes. As your self-reliance grows, you can work with your ETN to select a new system.

How do I care for the skin around the stoma?

Proper attention to the skin around an ileostomy can eliminate painful bouts of raw or reddened skin. Known as "stomal effluent," the stool from an ileostomy usually is liquid and contains enzymes and other digestive acids native to the small intestine. These materials break down the proteins in food, making them easier to absorb. The enzymes, however, cannot distinguish between the proteins they attack and your skin. Thus, if the stomal effluent remains in contact with the skin for too long, painful irritation can result.

People who have ileostomies should never patch a leaking pouch with tape. Change the entire system, and be sure to clean the skin first. Burning or itching under the pouch indicates that some stomal effluent has leaked onto the skin. Pectin based or hydrocolloid skin barriers always should be used for ileostomy management. They may be used in conjunction with a skin barrier paste. Avoid harsh soaps when cleaning this area. The opening in the pouching system should be accurately sized to prevent the possibility of stool leakage.

Will I require a special diet?

If a particular food bothered you before surgery, it probably will continue to do so. For example, if you suffered from lactose intolerance before surgery, dairy products still may cause diarrhea, bloating, and gas. Some people find, however, that they are able to eat foods that they could not tolerate before.

You may need to avoid high residue or "stringy" foods, such as popcorn and peanuts, because they can cause blockages in the bowel. Don't worry if seeds from cucumbers, tomatoes, or fruits appear whole in your pouch. Even an intact intestinal system will not digest these foods.

If you are unsure about a particular food, try a small portion. If you have no problems, you might try a larger portion next time. Remember, also, that taking time to chew food thoroughly will improve digestion.

People who have ileostomies need to maintain a fluid intake of eight to ten glasses a day or more. To replace potassium and sodium lost in ileostomy effluent, drink such fluids as tea and tomato or fruit juices, in addition to water. "Sports drinks," such as Gatorade and 10K, are also excellent for replacing vital electrolytes.

Will the stool in my pouch cause odor?

With proper care, odor need not be a concern. Indeed, you probably have met someone with an ostomy and were unaware of his condition. (Up to 1 million people in North America have ostomies!)

To combat odor, avoid foods that cause gas. You may also use products specifically designed to control pouch odor:

- *Pouch deodorizers.* These commercially available products, usually liquids, are placed inside the pouch each time it is emptied. The most effective agents attack the odor-causing bacteria, rather than simply mask odor.
- *Internal agents,* such as chlorophyll tablets or bismuth subgallate. These over-the-counter products are taken orally several times a day, or with meals.
- *Room deodorizers.* One spray of a concentrated ostomy deodorizer can freshen the air after you empty your pouch.

Can I have a normal sexual relationship?

It's natural to be concerned that an ostomy may alter your ability to function sexually, to feel desirable, and to be the recipient of another's love. But many people find that their sex life improves after ostomy surgery.

Your ability to feel attractive and "sexy" comes from feeling good about yourself. When you are ill, your sex drive may decrease. Perceiving ostomy surgery as a release from illness can help you return to healthy sexual functioning.

In general, an ostomy's impact on your sex life is related to your *mind,* not your body. Occasionally, however, surgical removal of the rectum can affect a male's ability to have an erection. But this is the exception, not the rule. When careful excision of the rectum is performed, most males retain their ability to have and to maintain an erection.

Discussing your concerns about sexuality with your surgeon or ETN, both before and after surgery, will help you through the initial adjustment period.

Will ostomy surgery affect my ability to have children?

An ostomy provides no barriers to a woman's ability to become pregnant or to have a healthy baby. The only inconvenience may be changes in stomal contour and size during pregnancy, due to increases in abdominal girth.

These changes are easily managed by accommodating the pouching system to the fluctuations of the stoma size and shape. A vaginal birth is possible, unless your obstetrician recommends a caesarean section. It's important that your obstetrician consult your surgeon during your pregnancy.

Will an ostomy restrict my physical activity?

Activities, such as jogging, skiing, aerobic exercise, swimming, and even rollerblading, are not contraindicated because of an ostomy. But you will have to avoid vigorous contact sports and heavy lifting. For example, playing football can injure the intestinal tissue from which the stoma is created. Lifting anything heavier than twenty-five pounds can increase intra-abdominal pressure, which can lead to further complications, such as parastomal hernia. This does not mean, however, that you cannot pick up your baby! If work demands heavy lifting or some other strenuous activity, discuss this situation with your surgeon and your employer. Indeed, if you're in doubt about any activity, consult your physician.

Remember, ostomy surgery can give you a new lease on life. Enjoy it!

Gwen B. Turnbull, R.N., B. Sed, C.E.T.N.

INFLAMMATORY BOWEL DISEASE FACTS

The Ten Most Common Myths About Crohn's Disease and Ulcerative Colitis

MYTH 1: Crohn's disease and ulcerative colitis are caused by stress.

There is no evidence that Crohn's disease and ulcerative colitis are caused by stress. But, with any chronic illness, symptoms may worsen during a particularly stressful period in a person's life.

MYTH 2: Certain personality types are more prone to develop ulcerative colitis or Crohn's disease.

IBD sufferers were once perceived as people who were emotional or nervous. However, a study conducted by Johns Hopkins University and Medical School concluded that the personality profile of people with IBD does not differ significantly from that of healthy persons.

MYTH 3: Crohn's disease and ulcerative colitis affect primarily older adults.

Anyone can get IBD, but young adults between the ages of 20 and 40 are most susceptible. (Ten percent, or 200,000, of those afflicted are youngsters under the age of 18.) It is estimated that only 5 to 15 percent of IBD patients develop the disease later in life.

MYTH 4: Symptoms can be controlled through diet.

There is no evidence that diet causes IBD. Most people can tolerate a normal diet. In some cases, however, dietary restrictions must be imposed. Some IBD sufferers find that the lactose in milk causes cramps, pain, gas and diarrhea. Others find a low-fiber diet (avoiding such foods as fruit, vegetables, nuts, bran and whole grains) helps control symptoms.

MYTH 5: Crohn's disease and ulcerative colitis are "Jewish diseases."

It's true that individuals of Jewish ancestry are two to three times more likely to develop IBD. But researchers know that IBD does not discriminate. Crohn's disease and ulcerative colitis affect persons from every ethnic and racial group, men and women equally.

MYTH 6: African-Americans are not susceptible to IBD.
IBD has always been considered more common in whites. However, recent studies show a rising trend among black women.

MYTH 7: Individuals with ulcerative colitis eventually will develop colon cancer.
Under 5 percent of ulcerative colitis patients develop colon cancer. These usually are persons who have had the disease for ten years or more. As a preventative measure, gastroenterologists recommend that patients have a colonoscopy every two years. This exam allows the physician to spot cancer or precancerous changes within the colon.

MYTH 8: Women with IBD have difficulty becoming pregnant.
Women with IBD whose symptoms are under control as easily as women in the general population. Women with active Crohn's disease, however, may have difficulty becoming pregnant until their symptoms are brought under control.

MYTH 9: Many IBD sufferers end up on disability.
While disability may be the only solution in particularly severe cases, most people are able to work and lead productive lives. Indeed, people with IBD are employed in all areas of business and government, at every level.

MYTH 10: People with Crohn's disease and ulcerative colitis cannot live active lives.
Doctors encourage persons with IBD to follow a normal routine. Most people live fulfilling, active lives: they work, raise families, have healthy sex lives, and exercise regularly.

Facts About Inflammatory Bowel Disease

• Crohn's disease and ulcerative colitis (collectively known as inflammatory bowel disease, or IBD, because their symptoms and complications are similar) are chronic digestive disorders of the small and large intestines.

• It is estimated that two million Americans suffer from IBD, with 30,000 new cases diagnosed in the U.S. each year. New cases per day average 82, or 3.5 an hour.

• Anyone can get IBD, but young adults between the ages of 20 and 40 are most susceptible. (Ten percent, or 200,000, of those afflicted are youngsters under the age of 18.)

SYMPTOMS

• Symptoms range from mild to severe and life-threatening and include any or all of the following:

- persistent diarrhea
- abdominal pain or cramps
- blood passing through the rectum
- fever and weight loss
- skin or eye irritations
- delayed growth and retarded sexual maturation in children

• Approximately 20 percent of patients have another family member with IBD, although a specific genetic pattern has not been identified.

• Both the cause of and cure for IBD are unknown.

TREATMENT

• Medications currently available alleviate inflammation and reduce symptoms but do not provide a cure. The principal drugs used to treat both Crohn's disease and ulcerative colitis are sulfasalazine and corticosteroids.

• A number of new medications, derivatives of corticosteroids and sulfasalazine, are currently awaiting FDA approval. Four such drugs, Asacol®, Rowasa®, Dipentum®, and Pentasa®, have been approved since 1988.

• Immunosuppressive agents, such as azathioprine (Imuran®) and 6-murcaptopurine (6-MP), are other medications used to treat IBD, especially in persons who do not respond to more standard treatments.

• IBD is an unpredictable illness - some patients recover after a single attack or are in remission for years; others require frequent hospitalizations and even surgery. Symptoms may vary in nature, frequency, and intensity.

• Without proper treatment, symptoms may worsen considerably and complications may occur.

• Colon cancer may be a serious complication of long-term ulcerative colitis involving the whole colon, even in a patient who is in remission.

SURGERY

• Surgery is sometimes recommended when medication can no longer control the symptoms, when there are intestinal obstructions, or when other complications arise.

• An estimated two-thirds to three-quarters of persons with Crohn's disease will have one or more operations in the course of their lifetime. The surgery for Crohn's disease, however, is not considered a permanent cure, because the disease frequently occurs elsewhere in the gastrointestinal tract. For ulcerative colitis, surgical removal of the entire colon and rectum (colectomy) is a permanent cure. Approximately 25-40 percent of ulcerative colitis patients will require surgery at some point during their illness.

EMOTIONAL FACTORS

• IBD is not a psychosomatic illness - there is no evidence to suggest that emotions play a causative role. IBD flare-ups may occur, however, during times of emotional or physical stress.

DIET

• There is no link between eating certain kinds of foods and IBD, but dietary modifications, especially during severe flare-ups, can help reduce disease symptoms and replace lost nutrients.

EFFECTS ON THE PERSON WITH IBD

• The economic and social burden on patients and their families can be enormous. Children and adults must interrupt school and work for repeated hospital stays, and medical and disability insurance often are unavailable.

HEPATITIS C
FREQUENTLY
ASKED QUESTIONS

What is hepatitis C?

Five different viruses (termed A,B,C,D, and E) cause viral hepatitis. Four other viruses that are believed to cause hepatitis have been identified, but not much is known about them. Hepatitis C virus (HCV) accounts for the great majority of what was referred to as non-A, non-B hepatitis. The hepatitis C virus was identified in 1989, and in 1990 a hepatitis C antibody test (anti-HCV) became available to identify individuals exposed to HCV.

How will I know if I have hepatitis C?

In general, individuals infected with HCV are often identified because they are found to have elevated liver enzymes on a routine blood test or because a hepatitis C antibody is found to be positive at the time of blood donation. In 1992, a more specific test for anti-HCV became available and eliminated some of the false positive reactions that were previously troublesome. In general, elevated liver enzymes and a positive antibody test for HCV (anti-HCV) means that an individual has chronic hepatitis C. The anti-HCV test will remain positive for several years after recovery from acute hepatitis C. A small percentage of patients still may have false positive hepatitis C antibody reactions. In these two cases, liver enzymes are typically normal. A small percentage of patients (less than 10 percent) may recover from acute hepatitis C, but their anti-HCV test will remain positive.

It appears that the formation of antibodies in response to the virus (associated with immunity in other forms of viral infections) does not apply with hepatitis C. Researchers believe this is because the virus changes to new forms of the original virus that caused the body to produce antibodies.

It is estimated that up to 85 percent of the people infected with the hepatitis C virus each year will develop chronic infection. There are more than 4 million Americans chronically infected with HCV.

Can I give the disease to others?

HCV can be transmitted through blood transfusions. However, all blood is now tested for the presence of this virus by the antibody test. It is estimated that the risk of post-transfusion hepatitis C has been reduced from the 8-10 percent frequency of infection several years ago (before 1990) to less than 0.5 percent (after 1990). Other individuals who may come in contact with infected blood, instruments, or needles, such as I.V. drug users, health care workers or laboratory technicians are also at risk of acquiring hepatitis C, as are those who undergo tattooing or body piercing. Currently, there is no vaccine available to immunize individuals against this virus.

The risk for transmitting hepatitis C sexually is unknown. There have been occasional documented cases of people with chronic hepatitis C transmitting the virus to their only, long-term sexual partner. The U.S. Public Health Service says that because of the lack of sufficient information, those with only one, long-term sexual partner need not change their sexual practices. Many physicians who counsel patients with hepatitis C recommend the same thing to those in a monogamous relationship. Spouses or long-term sexual partners of newly diagnosed patients are advised to be tested for hepatitis C. The Centers for Disease Control and Prevention (CDC) say there is a slight increased risk of becoming infected with hepatitis C if you have multiple sex partners. Whether the use of latex condoms is 100 percent effective in preventing someone from infecting their sexual partner or becoming infected is uncertain.

What is the natural history of hepatitis C?

Specific information regarding the natural history of hepatitis C is not yet available. In general, however, chronic hepatitis C appears to be a slowly progressive disease that may gradually advance over 10-40 years. There is some evidence that the disease may progress faster when acquired in middle age or older. In one study, chronic hepatitis confirmed by liver biopsy was identified on the average of ten years following blood transfusions and cirrhosis on an average of 20 years. It also appears that HCV, like the hepatitis B virus, is associated with an increased chance of developing hepatocellular carcinoma, a type of primary liver cancer. Almost all HCV-related liver cancer occurs with cirrhosis (scarring) of the liver. The exact magnitude of this risk is unknown but appears to be a late risk factor occurring on the average of 30 years after the time of infection. This is more prevalent in the Far East than in the U. S.

Is there a treatment for chronic hepatitis C?

The drugs interferon alpha-2b and interferon alpha-2a have been approved for the treatment of chronic hepatitis C. Approximately 35-40 percent of patients treated for six months with interferon will respond, showing normalization of liver tests and reduced inflammation on liver biopsy. However, of those who respond to treatment, approximately 60 percent will suffer a relapse during several months after interferon treatment is discontinued. Thus, only 10-15 percent of patients treated with interferon have a sustained, long-lasting response. Patients can be treated a second time and 85 percent of patients will enter a second remission; however, the duration of treatment and dosage required for long-term remission in this group of patients has yet to be determined. The hope is that improvement or normalization of liver tests and reduced inflammation in the liver will slow or interrupt the development of progressive liver disease. However, the true impact of interferon treatment on the long-term course of chronic hepatitis C and survival is unknown.

Side effects caused by interferon therapy can include "flu-like" symptoms, depression, headache, and decreased appetite. The "flu-like" symptoms can be minimized by taking acetaminophen (e.g. Tylenol). In addition, interferon may depress the bone marrow leading to reduced levels of white blood cells and platelets. Frequent blood tests are needed to monitor white blood cells, platelets and liver enzymes. A liver biopsy is typically done prior to treatment to determine the severity of liver damage and provide confirmation of the underlying disease.

The information contained in this excerpt is provided for information only. This information does not constitute medical advice and it should not be relied upon as such. The American Liver Foundation (ALF) does not engage in the practice of medicine. ALF, under no circumstances, recommends particular treatments for specific individuals, and in all cases recommends that you consult your physician before pursuing any course of treatment.

Copyright © 1997 The American Liver Foundation

What is the relationship between diet and hepatitis C?

Hepatitis C (HCV) is a virus that infects the liver. Up to 85 percent of people exposed to this virus develop chronic liver disease. In general, chronic HCV appears to be a slowly progressive disease that may gradually advance over 10-40 years. While not as yet totally defined, many factors influence the rate of disease progression. Diet may play an important role in this process, as all foods and beverages that we ingest must pass through the liver to be metabolized.

General guidelines for individuals infected with HCV include maintaining a healthy lifestyle, eating a well-balanced, low-fat diet, and avoiding alcohol. A diet high in complex carbohydrates may be helpful in providing calories and maintaining weight. Since HCV infection may lead to loss of appetite, those individuals whose appetite is diminished may find frequent, small meals more easily tolerated. Adequate rest and moderate exercise can also contribute to a feeling of well-being.

Alcohol and hepatitis C

Alcohol is a potent toxin to the liver. Excessive intake can lead to cirrhosis and its complications, including liver cancer. Heavy drinkers are not the only individuals at risk for liver diseases, as damage can occur in even some moderate "social drinkers." The hepatitis C virus has frequently been isolated from patients with alcoholic liver disease. In fact, these patients have been found to have a higher incidence of severe liver damage, cirrhosis, and a decreased lifespan, when compared to individuals without the virus. It is suggested that the combination of alcohol and HCV accelerates the progression of liver disease. The consensus statement concerning management of HCV released in March 1997 from the National Institutes of Health further warned about the dangers of excessive alcohol use, and advised limitation of alcohol to no more than one drink per day. Therefore, patients with HCV would be unwise to drink alcohol in excess, and total avoidance of all alcohol intake is recommended.

Iron and hepatitis C

The liver plays an important role in the metabolism of iron since it is the primary organ in the body that stores this metal. The average American diet contains about 10-20 mg of iron per day. About 10 percent of this iron is absorbed, in keeping with the body's need for 1 to 2 mg. of iron per day. Patients with chronic HCV sometimes have an increase in the iron concentration in the liver. Excess iron can be very damaging to the liver. Studies suggest that high iron levels reduce the response rate of patients with HCV to interferon. Thus, patients with chronic HCV whose serum iron level is elevated, or who have cirrhosis, should avoid taking iron supplements. In addition, these patients should restrict their intake of iron-rich foods, such as red meats, liver, and iron-fortified cereals, and should avoid cooking with iron-coated cookware and utensils.

Fat and hepatitis C

Overweight individuals are often found to have abnormalities related to the liver, ranging from fatty deposits in the liver (steatosis) to fatty deposits accompanied by inflammation (steatohepatitis). In overweight patients with a fatty liver who subsequently lose weight, liver related abnormalities improve. Therefore, patients with chronic HCV are advised to maintain normal weight. For those who are overweight, it is crucial to start a prudent exercise routine and a low-fat, well-balanced, weight-reducing diet. Diabetic patients should follow a sugar-restricted diet. A low-cholesterol diet should be followed in those with hypertriglyceridemia. It is essential that patients consult with their physician before beginning any diet or exercise program.

Protein and hepatitis C

Adequate protein intake is important to build and maintain muscle mass and to assist in healing and repair. Protein intake must be adjusted to one's body weight and medical condition. Approximately 1.0 to 1.5 gm. of protein per kilogram of body weight is recommended in the diet each day for regeneration of liver cells in non-cirrhotic patients.

In a small but significant number of individuals with cirrhosis, a complication known as encephalopathy, or impaired mental status, may occur. Affected individuals may show signs of disorientation and confusion. The exact cause(s) of encephalopathy is not fully understood. While some experts do not believe there is a link between dietary protein and encephalopathy, others believe in substantially reducing or even eliminating animal protein and adhering to a vegetarian diet, in order to help improve mental status. Patients who are at risk for encephalopathy may be advised to eat no more than .6-.8 gm. of animal source protein per kilogram of body weight per day. (Animal source proteins are meat, fish, eggs, poultry, and dairy products. Each provides 7 gm. of actual protein per ounce of food.) There is no limit on vegetable protein consumption. Maintaining adequate protein intake and body weight should be considered a priority if vegetarian protein substitutes are not utilized.

The following table gives recommended grams of animal source protein intake per pound of body weight. (Note: The chart is intended to provide guidelines for patients with hepatitis C. For specific recommendations, consult your physician.)

Weight	Recommended avg. protein intake for regeneration of liver cells in non-cirrhotic patients	Max recommended intake for patients at risk for encephalopathy
100 lbs.	45-68 gm. (6-9 oz. meat or equiv.)	27 gm.
130 lbs.	59-87 gm. (8-12 oz. meat or equiv.)	35 gm.
150 lbs.	68-103 gm. (9.7-14 oz. meat or equiv.)	40 gm.
170 lbs.	77-166 gm. (11-16 oz. meat or equiv.)	46 gm.
200 lbs.	91-136 gm. (13-19 oz. meat or equiv.)	54 gm.

Sodium and hepatitis C

Advanced scarring of the liver (cirrhosis) may lead to an abnormal accumulation of fluid in the abdomen, referred to as ascites. Patients with HCV who have ascites must be on sodium (salt) restricted diets. Every gram of sodium consumed results in the accumulation of 200 ml. of fluid. The lower the salt content of the diet, the better this excessive fluid accumulation is controlled. Sodium intake should be restricted to 1,000 mg. a day or less. This requires careful shopping and reading all food labels. It is often surprising to discover which foods are high in sodium. For example, one ounce of corn flakes contains 350 mg. of sodium; one ounce of grated parmesan cheese, 528 mg. of sodium; one cup of chicken noodle soup, 1,108 mg. of sodium; and one teaspoon of table salt, 2,325 mg. of sodium.

Avoid fast food restaurants because most fast foods are high in sodium. Meats, especially red meats, are high in sodium, so meat consumption may need to be reduced and vegetarian alternatives considered. Patients with chronic HCV without ascites are advised not to overindulge in salt intake, although their restrictions need not be as severe.

Medications are not food, but. . .

Like foods and beverages, medications also pass through the liver to be metabolized. Individuals with chronic liver disease should be careful about taking medications, even those sold over-the-counter. Read package labeling carefully before taking medications, and discuss any questions you may have with your physician and/or pharmacist.

Author: Melissa Palmer, M.D.
Reprinted with permission from the American Liver Foundation

CROHN'S DISEASE, ULCERATIVE COLITIS & OSTOMY RESOURCES

Contact the following organizations for valuable information about inflammatory bowel disease, ostomy care, support groups, educational information, and products.

Crohn's & Colitis Foundation of America, Inc. (CCFA)
National Headquarters
386 Park Avenue South
New York, NY 10016-8804
(800) 932-2423
Web site: www.ccfa.org

United Ostomy Association (UOA)
19772 MacArthur Boulevard, Suite 200
Irvine, CA 92612
(800) 826-0826
Web site: www.uoa.org

Wound, Ostomy and Continence Nurses (WOCN)
National Office
1550 South Coast Highway, Suite 201
Laguna Beach, CA 92651
(888) 224-WOCN
Web site: www.wocn.org

Better Together Club®
ConvaTec
100 Headquarters Park Drive
Skillman, NJ 08558
Web site: www.convatec.com

ConvaTec Professional Services
If you have questions or experience problems with
your stoma or appliance.
P.O. Box 5254
Princeton, NJ 08543
(800) 422-8811
Web site: www.convatec.com

Great Comebacks® Awards Program
P.O. Box 9922
Rancho Santa Fe, CA 92067
(800) 560-9700
Web site: www.greatcomebacks.com

Appendix   HEPATITIS C RESOURCES

Contact the following organizations for valuable information about hepatitis C, support groups, educational information and products.

American Liver Foundation (ALF)
75 Maiden Lane, Suite 203
New York, NY 10038
(800) GO-LIVER (465-4837)
Web site: www.liverfoundation.org

Centers for Disease Control (CDC)
Web site: www.cdc.gov

Hepatitis Foundation International (HFI)
30 Sunrise Terrace
Cedar Grove, NJ 07009-1423
(800) 891-0707 *(Ask about HFI's Patient Advocacy Information Telecommunication System [PATS] telephone support network.)*
Web site: www.hepfi.org

Hep C Connection
1177 Grand St., Suite 200
Denver, CO 80203
(800) 522-4372
Website: www.hepc-connection.org

HIV and Hepatitis.com
P.O. Box 14288
San Francisco, CA 94114
Web site: www.hivandhepatitis.com

Rolf Benirschke is available for speaking engagements. For more information, call (800) 560-9700.

To purchase additional copies of *Alive & Kicking*, please send $15, postage paid, to:

> Rolf Benirschke
> Rolf Benirschke Enterprises, Inc.
> P.O. Box 9922
> Rancho Santa Fe, CA 92067

For credit card purchases, call (800) 560-9700.

Quantity discounts of *Alive & Kicking* are available. Write or call for more information.

Also available is an audiocassette series entitled "You're Not Alone," featuring Rolf's candid discussions with Marvin Bush, Al Geiberger, Suzanne Rosenthal, and Tip O'Neill, all who have overcome ostomy surgery. The cost is $22.95, postage paid, for this two-cassette series.

About the Authors

Rolf Benirschke is a former placekicker for the San Diego Chargers, having played in the National Football League for ten seasons from 1977-1986. He retired with sixteen team records and as the third most-accurate kicker in NFL history. Today, he is in the financial services business with Eastman Benirschke Financial Group, and he is a sought–after inspirational speaker around the country as well.

Rolf remains active in the community and serves as a National Trustee of the Crohn's & Colitis Foundation of America (CCFA) and as a spokesman for ConvaTec, a Bristol-Myers Squibb company. He is also a long-time supporter of the United Ostomy Association, the United Way, and the San Diego Zoo.

Rolf and his wife, Mary, are the proud parents of four children: Erik, Kari, Timmy, and Ryan. They live in the San Diego area.

Mike Yorkey attended La Jolla High School with Rolf, and served as an editor of *Focus on the Family* magazine for eleven years. Most recently, he is the author or co-author of seventeen books. He and his wife, Nicole, reside in Encinitas, California, with their two children, Patrick and Andrea.